中国思想文化术语多语种对外翻译
标准化建设项目成果
CHINESE THINKING AND CULTURE
MULTILINGUAL TERMINOLOGY DATABASE

中华源·河南故事
CHINESE CIVILIZATION
Stories from Henan

文物
CULTURAL HERITAGE

主编 田 凯
EDITOR-IN-CHIEF: TIAN KAI

河南大学出版社
HENAN UNIVERSITY PRESS
·郑州·

图书在版编目（CIP）数据

中华源·河南故事．文物／田凯主编．— 郑州：河南大学出版社，2021.4

ISBN 978-7-5649-3672-3

Ⅰ．①中… Ⅱ．①田… Ⅲ．①地方文化 - 河南 - 通俗读物②文物 - 河南 - 通俗读物 Ⅳ．① G127.61-49 ② K872.61-49

中国版本图书馆 CIP 数据核字（2019）第 073995 号

责任编辑	马　博
责任校对	屈琳玉
封面设计	翟淼淼
出版发行	河南大学出版社
	地址：郑州市郑东新区商务外环中华大厦2401号　邮编：450046
	电话：0371-86059701（营销部）
	0371-86059750（高等教育与职业教育分公司）
	网址：hupress.henu.edu.cn
排　版	河南大学出版社设计排版部
印　刷	河南博雅彩印有限公司
版　次	2021年4月第1版　　印　次　2021年4月第1次印刷
开　本	710 mm×1010 mm　1/16　印　张　18.5
字　数	295千　　　　　　　　定　价　85.00元

版权所有，侵权必究

本书如有印装质量问题，请与河南大学出版社营销部联系调换。

"中华源·河南故事"系列丛书编委会

顾　　问　黄友义　杨　平　范大祺
名誉主任　穆为民　何金平　刘炯天
主　　任　付　静
副 主 任　陈　岩　陈志伟　刁玉华　方启雄　介晓磊
　　　　　孔留安　李冰冰　李向前　李　镇　梁留科
　　　　　刘金锋　牛卫国　屈鹏飞　史永庆　田　凯
　　　　　万正峰　王建修　王清义　王自文　许二平
　　　　　杨建伟　杨玮斌　张改平　张俊峰　张明超
　　　　　张松文　赵卫东

主　　编　付　静
副 主 编　李冰冰
编　　委　陈　玮　丁　锐　高　阳　徐恒振　郑延保

中华源·河南故事·文物

主　　编　田　凯
副 主 编　郑小玲　陈彦堂　钱建成（英文）
中文撰稿　陈彦堂
英文译者　钱建成　王志伟　张军平　李文竞
英文审校　〔英〕Ronald Torrance
摄　　影　牛爱红　陈彦堂　祝　贺　陈申如

The Editorial Committee
Chinese Civilization
Stories from Henan

Consultants	Huang Youyi Yang Ping Fan Daqi
Honorary Directors	Mu Weimin He Jinping Liu Jiongtian
Director	Fu Jing
Deputy Directors	Chen Yan Chen Zhiwei Diao Yuhua Fang Qixiong
	Jie Xiaolei Kong Liu'an Li Bingbing Li Xiangqian
	Li Zhen Liang Liuke Liu Jinfeng Niu Weiguo
	Qu Pengfei Shi Yongqing Tian Kai Wan Zhengfeng
	Wang Jianxiu Wang Qingyi Wang Ziwen Xu Erping
	Yang Jianwei Yang Weibin Zhang Gaiping
	Zhang Junfeng Zhang Mingchao Zhang Songwen
	Zhao Weidong
Chief Editor	Fu Jing
Deputy Chief Editor	Li Bingbing
Editors	Chen Wei Ding Rui Gao Yang Xu Hengzhen
	Zheng Yanbao

Chinese Civilization
Stories from Henan
Cultural Heritage

Editor-in-Chief	Tian Kai
Associate Editors-in-Chief	Zheng Xiaoling Chen Yantang
	Qian Jiancheng (English Text)
Writer	Chen Yantang
Translators	Qian Jiancheng Wang Zhiwei Zhang Junping
	Li Wenjing
Translation Proofreaders	Ronald Torrance (U.K.)
Photographers	Niu Aihong Chen Yantang Zhu He Chen Shenru

总　序

中国是世界四大文明古国之一，也是世界上唯一的古代文明传统未曾中断的国家。河南省地处中国中东部，是中华文明和中华民族的重要发祥地，在中国五千年的文明史上，河南作为国家政治、经济、文化的中心就长达三千多年。从某种意义上讲，一部河南史就是半部中国史。这里是中华人文始祖黄帝的故乡，是古丝绸之路的东方起点，是少林功夫和陈氏太极的发源地，这里创建了中国历史上最早的都城，镌刻了中国最古老的文字，诞生了中国最初的商业文明。

伴随着新时代的荣光，河南经济社会发展迅速，人民生活水平显著提升，这是河南人民自力更生、艰苦奋斗的历史结果，也是对外开放带来的益处。河南经济社会的发展、人民生活方式的改变都植根于深层次的文化积淀。为了让世界更多地了解河南，让河南更好地走向世界，2018年以来，河南省人民政府外事办公室认真研析了这片古老土地上的历史文化资源和时代风貌，组织各领域权威专家学者，编译了"中华源·河南故事"中外文系列丛书，选取黄河文化、河洛文化、老子、庄子、黄帝、少林功夫、太极拳、中医、汉字、丝绸之路、古都、农业、大运河、文物、陶瓷、青铜器、手工艺、书法、杂技、豫菜、豫剧、脱贫攻坚、空中丝绸之路、航空城、南水北调、中国粮谷、红旗渠、焦裕禄等多个主题，力图以故事的方式向世界展现一个立体、全面、真实的河南。

当今世界，人类文明无论是在物质还是在精神方面都取得了巨大进步，特别是物质的极大丰富，这在古代世界是完全不能想象的。同时，当代人类也面临着许多突出的难题，比如，贫富差距持续扩大，物欲追求奢华无度，个人主义恶性膨胀，社会诚信不断消减，伦理道德每况愈下，人与自然关系日趋紧张，等等。要解决这些难题，不仅需要运用人类今天的智慧和力量，而且需要运用人类历史上积累和储存的智慧和力量。河南历史文化底蕴深厚、包容性强，在今天仍极具现实意义。中原文化蕴含的思想智慧有助于修身养性，推动人类社会进步发展，焦裕禄精神、红旗渠精神所体现的为民爱民、艰苦奋斗的价值取向是构建人类命运共同体的力量源泉。我们期待与读者们一起从河南故事中汲取更多的智慧和力量，共同创造更加美好的未来。

Series Foreword

China is one of the four ancient civilizations in the world, and is also the only country in the world where the ancient civilization has not been interrupted. Located in east-central China, Henan Province is an important cradle for the Chinese nation and Chinese civilization. In the course of the five thousand years of Chinese history, for more than three thousand years it served as the political, economic and cultural center of the country and therefore, as generally accepted, represents half of the history of China. Henan is the native place of Yellow Emperor, the cradle of Chinese culture, the starting point of the ancient Silk Road in the east, and the birthplace of Shaolin Kungfu and Chen-style Taijiquan—typical examples of the world-renowned Chinese martial arts. It was here that the earliest capital city in China was founded, the oldest Chinese characters engraved, and the earliest commerce took shape.

In the new era, Henan has witnessed rapid growth in its economy and remarkable improvement of people's living conditions owing to the national reform and opening-up policy and unremitting endeavors of the people. Modern economic achievements and social development as well as the changes of way of life could be traced back to its traditional values and cultural heritages. To enable people from other countries to understand Henan, and let the Province integrate more efficiently into the world development, the Foreign Affairs Office of the People's Government of Henan Province has organized teams of authoritative experts and scholars in relevant fields to compile this *Chinese Civilization: Stories from Henan* in Chinese and foreign languages since 2018 by crystallizing the excellence of traditions and outstanding features of modern development. The book series include *The Yellow River Culture*, *Heluo Culture*, *Laozi*, *Zhuangzi*, *The Yellow Emperor*, *Shaolin Kungfu*, *Taijiquan*, *Traditional Chinese Medicine*,

Chinese Characters, *The Silk Road*, *Ancient Chinese Capitals*, *Feeding the People—Agriculture*, *The Grand Canal*, *Cultural Heritage*, *Ceramic*, *Bronze*, *Handicraft Art*, *Calligraphy*, *Acrobatics*, *Henan Cuisine*, *Henan Opera*, *Poverty Alleviation*, *Silk Road in the Air*, *Zhengzhou—An Aviation City*, *South-to-North Water Diversion*, *China Grain Valley*, *Man-Made River—Hongqiqu Canal*, *A Model Official—Jiao Yulu*, etc., presenting a panoramic picture of the Province.

In today's world, human civilization has made great progress in both material accumulation and ethical advancement, and the great abundance of materials today, especially, is beyond the imagination of the ancient people. At the same time, however, modern people are also confronted with a lot of problems, such as the widening gap between the rich and the poor, the indulgence in pursuit of luxury and extravagance, the undesirable extension of individualism, the decline of social integrity, and the increasingly tense relationship between man and nature. To solve the problems, we need to draw on the wisdom and powers developed today as well as those accumulated in the past. Henan is endowed with rich historical and cultural heritages characterized by its inclusiveness, and such heritages remain significant today. The intelligence and wisdom in Henan culture are conducive to self-cultivation and to the promotion of social development. The spirit of serving the people and relentless struggle, as embodied in Jiao Yulu and Man-Made River—Hongqiqu Canal provides source of strength for building a community with a shared future for mankind. It is our hope that wisdom and strength from Henan stories could lead us to a shared brilliant future.

绪　言

河南地处中原，是孕育并滋养华夏文明的沃土和温床。一部中原文明史就是华夏文明史的缩影。河南古代文化底蕴极其丰厚，行走在中原大地，碎瓦残砖俯拾皆是，"一个瓦片就是一段故事、一块残砖就代表着一段辉煌"的说法，并非虚妄之言。

在数千年的历史进程中，有许多王朝和政权定都于河南。在每个文化发展阶段，河南都是核心区域，在政治、经济、文化、科技等方面经常处于领先地位。汉唐时期更成为中外文化交流的重要枢纽。因此，古代河南对中华文明的形成与发展做出了无可替代的贡献，这在中国是罕有其匹的。

宋代杰出的政治家、文学家、史学家司马光"若问古今兴废事，请君只看洛阳城"的诗句，实际可视为对河南在中华文明体系中重要地位的客观中肯的评价。那些留存在中原大地以及典藏在各个博物馆的各类文物，则是中原古代文明乃至整个华夏文明的实物印证。

距今数万年的旧石器时代晚期的人类遗存，星罗棋布的新石器时代的灿烂文化，商周时期高度发达的文明体系，以及永载史册的汉唐盛世，还有《清明上河图》所描绘的北宋东京汴梁城这个世界大都会的繁荣喧嚣，极少有地域像河南这样拥有如此丰厚的文物文化资源，且见证了一个文明体系从发生、发展到鼎盛、中衰的全过程。这一绵延不断的文化链条，是全中国乃至全人类共同的文化遗产和精神财富。

截至2018年，河南全省拥有不可移动文物65,519处，居全国第二位。其中世界文化遗产5处，全国重点文物保护单位358处，省级文物保护单位1,231处。同时，河南又拥有国家考古遗址公园13处，国家级历史文化名城8个，中国"八大古都"河南有4座。全省共有博物馆、纪念馆340家，可移动文物478万件。由此可见，河南文物具有数量多、分布广、品类全、价值高的特点。这一笔丰厚的文化遗产，既是华夏祖先对后人的无私馈赠，也是无数生生不息、勤勉智慧的河南人奉献给全人类的文化财富。

Preface

Henan, located in the Central Plains of China, is a fertile field and center for breeding and nourishing the Chinese civilization. The history of the civilization of the Central Plains is undoubtedly the epitome of the history of the Chinese civilization. You will find remnants of broken bricks and tiles anywhere you go in the Central Plains. Therefore, it is not exaggerating to claim that "A broken tile is a story and a broken brick represents a period of glory".

Over the course of Chinese history, many dynasties and regimes established their capitals in Henan. In the development of each culture, Henan never failed to be the core region, often with a leading position in politics, economy, culture, science and technology. During the Han and Tang dynasties, Henan became an important hub for cultural exchanges between China and foreign countries. Therefore, the ancient Henan made irreplaceable contribution to the formation and development of the Chinese civilization—a rare case in China.

Sima Guang, an outstanding politician, litterateur and historian in the Song Dynasty, said, "If you want to ask questions about the rise and fall of ancient and modern times, please just look at Luoyang", which can be regarded as an objective and pertinent evaluation of Henan's important position in the Chinese civilization system. All kinds of cultural relics preserved in the Central Plains and stored in various museums are the physical evidence of the ancient civilization of the Central Plains and even of the whole Chinese civilization.

No other place than Henan has such rich cultural relics as the human remains of the late paleolithic period tens of thousands of years ago—the splendid neolithic cultures scattered all round, the highly developed civilization system in the Shang and Zhou dynasties, the flourishing ages of the Han and Tang dynasties that have been recorded in history forever, the prosperity and bustle of the world metropolis Bianliang of the Northern Song Dynasty described in

Landscape in the Qingming Festival along the Bian River, and has witnessed the whole process of a civilization system, from its emergence and development to its prosperity and moderate decline. This continuous cultural chain is the cultural heritage and spiritual wealth of the whole China and even the whole mankind.

As of 2018, Henan has 65,519 immovable cultural relics, ranking the second in the country. Among them, there are five world cultural heritage sites, 358 key cultural relics under national protection, and 1,231 under provincial protection. Meanwhile, Henan has 13 national archaeological parks, 8 national famous historical and cultural cities, and 4 of the 8 ancient capitals of China, 340 museums and memorials, and 4.78 million movable cultural relics. Accordingly, Henan cultural relics are characterized by large quantity, wide distribution, complete category and high value. This rich cultural heritage is not only the generous gift of the Chinese ancestors given to their future generations, but also the cultural wealth contributed to the whole mankind by generations of people in Henan with diligence and wisdom.

目 录　　Contents

第一章　文明曙光：史前时期的中原文化图谱　001
　　一、从茹毛饮血到刀耕火种　002
　　二、从定居农耕到文明曙光　008

Chapter I　The Twilight of Civilization: Prehistoric Culture on the Central Plains　001
　　I. From the Age of Eating Animals Raw to Slash-and-Burn Cultivation　003
　　II. From Sedentary Farming to the Dawn of Civilization　009

第二章　文明肇始：华夏文明的核心　027
　　一、从大禹治水到二里头王都　028
　　二、从郑州商城到安阳殷墟　040
　　三、从西周到东周：周王室东迁与春秋战国时代开启　046

Chapter II　The Beginning of Civilization: The Center of Chinese Civilization　027
　　I. From Yu Taming Flood to Erlitou Capital City　029
　　II. From Shangcheng in Zhengzhou to Yin Ruins in Anyang　041
　　III. From the Western Zhou Dynasty to the Eastern Zhou Dynasty: Eastward Movement of the Zhou Dynasty and the Beginning of the Spring and Autumn Period and the Warring States Period　047

第三章　有容乃大：中原文明的汉唐雄风　073
　　一、汉唐时期的中原　074
　　二、融汇东西：丝绸之路的东方起点　080
　　三、贯通南北：隋唐大运河的中枢　112

Chapter III Diversity and Wideness: Central Plains Civilizations in the Han and
            Tang Dynasties   073
    I. Central Plains Civilizations in the Han and Tang Dynasties   075
    II. Linking the West with the East: The Eastern Starting Point of the Silk Road 081
    III. Linking the South and North: The Center of the Sui and
         Tang Grand Canal   113

第四章 东京梦华：中世纪的国际都会   127
    一、张择端的《清明上河图》   130
    二、孟元老与《东京梦华录》   134
    三、北宋皇陵：一个王朝的夕阳   138

Chapter IV A Dream of Splendor in the Eastern Capital: A Metropolis of the Middle Ages 127
    I. *Landscape in the Qingming Festival along the Bian River* by Zhang
       Zeduan   131
    II. *A Dream of Splendor in the Eastern Capital* by Meng Yuanlao   135
    III. The Mausoleums of the Northern Song Dynasty: The Sunset of
         a Dynasty   139

第五章 巧夺天工：河南古陶瓷的技术和艺术成就   147
    一、瓷器摇篮：古朴浑厚的河南夏商周原始瓷器   148
    二、盛世华章：富丽华美的中原汉唐陶瓷   152
    三、大雅大俗：宋元时期生机盎然的民窑与典雅深邃的官窑   158

Chapter V Exquisite Workmanship: The Technical and Artistic Achievements of
           Ancient Pottery and Porcelain in Henan Province   147

I. The Cradle: Simple and Vigorous Protoporcelain of Xia, Shang and Zhou Dynasties in Henan Province　　149

II. Prosperous Times: Magnificent and Colorful Pottery and Porcelain of the Central Plains in the Han and Tang Dynasties　　153

III. Aristocratic and Popular: The Elegant Official Kiln and the Vibrant Folk Kiln During the Song and Yuan Dynasties　　159

第六章　火的精魂：灿烂的中原古代冶金　　167

Chapter VI　The Spirit of Fire: The Splendid Ancient Casting Technology of the Central Plains　　167

第七章　河南的世界文化遗产　　177
　　一、龙门石窟　　178
　　二、安阳殷墟　　194
　　三、登封"天地之中"历史建筑群　　204
　　四、丝绸之路（河南段）　　242
　　五、大运河（河南段）　　262

Chapter VII　World Cultural Heritage in Henan　　177
　　I. The Longmen Grottoes　　179
　　II. The Yin Ruins in Anyang City　　195
　　III. Historic Monuments of Dengfeng at "the Centre of Heaven and Earth"　　205
　　IV. The Silk Road (Henan Section)　　243
　　V. The Grand Canal (Henan Section)　　263

第一章
文明曙光：史前时期的中原文化图谱

Chapter I

The Twilight of Civilization: Prehistoric Culture

on the Central Plains

一、从茹毛饮血到刀耕火种

1. "许昌人":惊世发现与中国现代人的起源

2008年,河南中部许昌市灵井镇西侧的一个小村子,突然成为国际古人类研究者关注的热点,河南省考古机构举行新闻发布会,正式宣布在这里发掘出土了距今10万—8万年、被命名为"许昌人"的古人类头骨化石。同时出土的,还有很多石器和牛、马、鹿、犀等动物的骨骼化石,总量约3万件。鉴于发掘成果在古人类起源领域的重要性,此项发掘被评为当年度的全国十大考古新发现之首。

"许昌人"的重要性在于填补了中国境内古人类进化过程中的重要缺环,对人类起源这一重大学术课题的研究提供了新资料,尤其对东亚地区古人类的起源具有重要学术意义。国际学术界关于现代人类起源有两种说法:一是"非洲起源说",即人类是从非洲起源后向全世界扩散的,全人类拥有一个共同的祖先。中国的北京周口店人等在距今约20万年前消失,中国现代人都是来自非洲的人类的后代。另一说是"多地

"许昌人"头盖骨化石
Skull Fossil of the Xuchang Man

I. From the Age of Eating Animals Raw to Slash-and-Burn Cultivation

1. The Xuchang Man: An Amazing Discovery and the Origin of the Modern Chinese

In 2008, a small village in the west of the Lingjing Town of Xuchang City in central Henan Province suddenly became a hot spot for international ancient human researchers. The Henan Provincial Archaeological Institute held a press conference and officially announced that it had unearthed the fossils of the early human crania dated back to 100,000 to 80,000 years ago, which was named "the Xuchang Man". Unearthed at the same time were many stone artifacts and bone fossils of cattle, horses, deer, rhinoceros and other animals, totaling about 30,000 pieces. In view of its importance in ancient human origin exploration, the excavation was selected as the Number One on the country's Top Ten archaeological discoveries of that year.

The discovery of "the Xuchang Man" was of great importance because it filled the gap in the human evolution in China, and provided new information for the world academia on the human origin, especially in East Asia. Regarding the origins of mankind, there were two popular views in the international academic community. One was about the African origin, holding that human beings

"许昌人"的工具：打制石器
Tools of the Xuchang Man: Chipped Stone Tools

区进化说",并由此衍生出"中国古人类连续进化学说"。中国现代人是本区域内起源并逐步进化而来的,其重要依据是中国境内发现了200万年前的巫山人、115万年前的蓝田人、50万年前的北京人、20万—10万年间的辽宁金牛山人、4万—1万年间的北京山顶洞人等,几乎是一个完整的进化体系。但是,这个体系却存在着关键缺失:没有10万—5万年前的人类化石。而这一时期正是"非洲起源说"推断非洲智人走向世界取代各地早期智人的关键时段。此次发现距今10万—8万年的"许昌人"头盖骨,正处在这个非常关键的时间段。据此,古人类学家们又开始重新思考现代人尤其是中国现代人的起源问题。

"许昌人"的发现,不仅是中国考古学和古人类学领域的一次重大发现,而且对研究东亚古人类演化和中国现代人起源具有重大学术价值。

spread from their African origins to the whole world, and all human beings had a common ancestor. It was also believed that the Zhoukoudian Man in Beijing disappeared about 200,000 years ago, and the modern Chinese were descendants of human beings in Africa. The other was the belief in the multi-regional evolution, holding that mankind evolved from different origins, and as a derivative view, the ancient Chinese would continue in successive evolution. To support the latter, much evidence was provided, including the Wushan Man 2, 000,000 years ago, the Lantian Man 1, 150, 000 years ago, the Peking Man 500, 000 years ago, the Jinniushan Man in Liaoning Province 200, 000 to 100,000 years ago, and the Peking Cavemen 40, 000 to 10,000 years ago. The second belief that the modern Chinese evolved in its locality was perfect, except for the fatal gap or absence of human fossil evidence 100,000 to 50,000 years ago. This was precisely the key period for the African Homo sapiens to go around the world and to replace the local Homo sapiens. Therefore, the discovery of the crania of the Xuchang Man 100,000 to 80,000 years ago happened to match well the very critical period of time. It was for this reason that paleoanthropologists began to rethink the origin of modern people, especially that of the modern Chinese.

The discovery of the Xuchang Man is not only of great significance in the field of the Chinese archaeology and paleoanthropology, but also of great academic value for the study of the human evolution in East Asia, in particular, the origin of modern Chinese people.

2. 李家沟：古代中原人生活方式转变的关键过渡期

如果说"许昌人"的发现为我们呈现了古代中原人如何起源的远古图画，那么李家沟遗址的发掘，则给我们描绘了古代中原人如何从"茹毛饮血"的渔猎游牧生活开始向定居种植生活转变的关键时期的鲜活场景。

李家沟遗址位于河南省新密市，处于从旧石器时代向新石器时代过渡的阶段，距今10,500—8,600年（约前8500—前6600年）。遗址中出土有数量可观的细石器等。这些远古工具显示，该遗址居民拥有十分精湛的石器加工技术，且所用原料多是不见于本地的优质燧石，应该是远距离采集运输所得，表明该遗址的居民生活具有一定的流动性，可能与周围的古老文化存在着一定程度的交流。

更为重要的是，李家沟遗址具有成熟的制陶技术。北区仅10平方米的发掘区内发现100多片陶片，已发现的陶片均为夹砂粗陶，部分陶片的质地较坚硬，显示其烧成火候较高。这是河南境内已知的年代最早的陶器，也是中原地区从旧石器时代向新石器时代过渡、由种植渔猎向定居农耕过渡的重要标志。

李家沟遗址出土陶片
Pottery Pieces Unearthed at the Lijiagou Site

2. Lijiagou: Key Transition of the Life Styles on the Central Plains

The discovery of the Xuchang Man presents an evolutionary picture of the ancient people on the Central Plains while the excavation at the Lijiagou site shows us a vivid picture of how the ancient people on the Central Plains began to transform from eating animal meat raw in their fishing and nomadic life to sedentary farming.

The Lijiagou site, located in Xinmi of Henan Province, shows the transition from the Paleolithic Age to the Neolithic Age 10, 500 to 8, 600 years ago (about 8500-6600 B. C.). A considerable number of microlithic tools were unearthed from the site, showing that its residents had very sophisticated stone processing techniques. Moreover, most of the raw materials used were high-quality firestones not found in the local area, indicating the mobile life of the residents and the certain exchange and communication with other ancient culture in the vicinity.

More importantly, the Lijiagou site shows that people at that time had already grasped the technology of making ceramics. More than 100 pieces of pottery were found in the excavation area of only 10 square meters in the North District. These pieces are all sand-filled stoneware. Some of them have a very hard texture, indicating their mastery of high fire temperature control. This is the earliest pottery known in Henan Province, serving as an important symbol of the transition from the Paleolithic Age to the Neolithic Age, and the transition from fishing to sedentary farming.

二、从定居农耕到文明曙光

1. 从裴李岗到贾湖：中原古代农业文明的兴起

在郑州南部传说中的黄帝故里附近，一个叫裴李岗的普通中原小村，因为一个距今9,000—7,500年（前7000—前5500年）的新石器时代文化遗存的发现，而在当代中国考古史上声名显赫。此后，这一被命名为裴李岗文化的古老遗存在河南中部屡有发现，尤以新郑裴李岗和舞阳贾湖最具代表性，也最为著名。其古朴的陶器、先进的石器和精美的骨器，代表了中原地区在文明前夜的文化发展水平。

遗址中出土的以石磨盘、石磨棒为标志的粮食加工工具，以及经过浮选和鉴定出的水稻种子，表明这一时期的中原人不仅有了成熟的定居生活和旱地粮食作物的种植，而且也有了成熟的水稻种植生产。其粮食脱粒和深加工工艺高度发达，甚至已经产生了早期的酿酒手工业。因此，以贾湖遗址为代表的裴李岗文化遗址的发掘，确立了中原地区在东亚农业文明发生阶段无可替代的角色，奠定了河南在中国农业经济体系中不可撼动的地位。

裴李岗文化的粮食加工工具：石磨盘与石磨棒
Grain Processing Tools: Stone Grinding Disc and Rod in the Peiligang Culture

II. From Sedentary Farming to the Dawn of Civilization

1. From Peiligang to Jiahu: The Rise of Ancient Agricultural Civilization on the Central Plains

In the hometown of the legendary Yellow Emperor in the south of Zhengzhou, a small village called Peiligang is famous in the history of contemporary Chinese archaeology because of the discovery of a Neolithic cultural relic of 9,000-7,500 years ago (7000-5500 B.C.). Since then, the so-called Peiligang culture has become well known, represented in particular by Peiligang in Xinzheng and Jiahu in Wuyang. The quaint pottery, advanced stone tools and exquisite bone objects represented the cultural development level on the Central Plains on the eve of civilization.

The grain processing tools, with the stone grinding discs and rods to be the most representative, and the rice seeds excavated in the sites, indicated the mature settlement, sedentary farming, and mature rice planting and production on the dry land. The sites were also famous for their grain threshing, deep processing technologies, and even the winemaking industry. Therefore, the Peiligang culture, represented by the Jiahu site, has established the irreplaceable role of the Central Plains in the agricultural civilization in East Asia, earning Henan Province a firm and solid position in China's agricultural economic system.

贾湖遗址的重要意义，不仅仅局限于远古先民在种植农业方面取得的物质成就，同时展现出了9,000—7,500年前中原大地上的宗教仪式和艺术创作。在这个遗址中，出土有成套的乌龟甲壳，背、腹甲扣合放置，龟腹内装有石子。据研究，这是用来占卜的道具，现今一些少数民族依然使用的占卜方式与此几乎一样。而腹甲上使用尖锐的道具刻画出来的一个符号，与数千年后安阳殷墟甲骨文的"目"字几乎一样，不仅佐证了这是一件用于占卜的道具，更提示了汉字的起源至少可以追溯到裴李岗文化时期。

　　尤其不可思议的是，舞阳贾湖遗址出土的以鹤的翅骨加工而成的笛子，在历经数千年的尘封后，依然能够吹奏出动人的旋律，这是人类音乐史上弥足珍贵的一个重大发现。其中一件保存完好的骨笛，长22.2厘米，共有7个音孔，在第6与第7孔之间还有辅助发声的小音孔。这件精心磨制、精确计算、精湛加工的吹奏乐器，至今能够演奏中国传统的五音和现代乐理的七音，而且富有韵律和变化。这件弥足珍贵的文物，是目前所知中国最古老的吹奏管乐器之一，也是中原大地上的最为珍贵的远古乐器之一。

裴李岗文化的宗教用具：贾湖遗址出土的龟甲
Religious Tools of the Peiligang Culture: the Turtle Shell Unearthed from the Jiahu Site

裴李岗文化的艺术品：贾湖遗址出土的骨笛
The Artwork of the Peiligang Culture: The Bone Flute Unearthed from the Jiahu Site

The significance of the Jiahu site is not only the material achievements of the ancient ancestors in planting agriculture, but also the religious rituals and artistic creations on the Central Plains over 9,000 years ago. In the Jiahu site, a complete carapace and web of the turtle was unearthed, with pieces of stones placed in its abdominal cavity. According to researchers, these are believed to be divination props, which are still used by some ethnic minorities today. The symbol engraved on the turtle's web with a sharp prop is almost the same as the Chinese character for the eye on the oracle bones in the Yin ruins in Anyang thousands of years later. Therefore, it is not only the evidence for divination, but also a sign indicating that the origin of Chinese characters can be traced back at least to the period of the Peiligang culture.

What is especially incredible is that the flute made from the wing bone of the crane at the Jiahu site in Wuyang is still able to play a moving melody after thousands of dust-laden years. This is a discovery of extreme significance to the music history of the world. One of the well-preserved bone flutes, 22.2 cm long, has 7 sound holes, one of them being smaller to assist the sounding next to the 6th hole. This carefully polished, accurately calculated, and exquisitely crafted wind instrument can still be used not only to play the traditional Chinese five-tone and modern seven-tone music, but also to express the musical melodies and changes. This precious cultural relic is one of the oldest wind instruments ever known in China, and is also one of the most precious ancient instruments on the land of the Central Plains.

2. 仰韶文化：在中原竖立起来的中国考古学里程碑

1921年，一个深目高鼻、戴着眼镜的欧洲人突然出现在河南西部黄河岸边的一个名叫仰韶的小村子里。他抛开手杖，满脸的兴奋和惊讶，在田间地头和黄土断崖上不停地捡取一个个被当地人称为碎瓦碴的彩陶片。他时而凝视彩陶片上的花纹，时而眉头紧锁，闭目思考这美丽的纹饰与中亚两河流域彩陶的异同。他意识到，一个石破天惊的考古大发现诞生了。

这个欧洲人就是瑞典地质学家安特生（Johan Gunnar Andersson）。他本来是被当时的中国北洋政府聘请为农商部地质调查所顾问，为中国政府寻找矿源的。但考古学素养和学识以及对中国古代文化的热情，使他对中原地区的文物格外敏感。因此当他在黄河南岸的田野中发现被人视为弃物的彩陶片时，立刻意识到这是一种古老的文化遗存。此后，安特生又陆续在甘肃、青海等地发现了类似的彩陶。然后，他对这一系

中国考古学的圣地：河南渑池仰韶村遗址
The Holy Land of Chinese Archaeology: Ruins of Yangshao Village, Mianchi, Henan

2. The Yangshao Culture: A Chinese Archaeological Milestone on the Central Plains

In 1921, a man from Europe with deep eyes, a big nose, and a pair of glasses suddenly appeared in a small village called Yangshao on the bank of the Yellow River in western Henan Province. He put away his cane, out of excitement and surprise, and kept picking up broken pieces of colored pottery on the fields and on the loess cliffs. He sometimes stared at the patterns on the painted pottery pieces, his brows knit, his eyes closed, lost in deep thoughts about the similarities and differences between this beautiful ornament and the painted pottery in the two-river basin in Central Asia. It struck him that a shocking discovery in archaeology was born and would rock the world.

This man is the Swedish geologist Johan Gunnar Andersson. He was originally hired by the Beiyang government of China as a consultant to the Geological Survey of the Ministry of Agriculture and Commerce to find the mine source. However, his archaeological literacy and knowledge and enthusiasm for ancient Chinese culture made him particularly sensitive to the cultural relics

仰韶文化的发现者、瑞典学者安特生
Swedish Scholar Johan Gunnar Andersson, Discoverer of the Yangshao Culture

瑞典远东博物馆
The Museum of Far Eastern Antiquities

列的考古发现进行了深入研究，并出版了《中华远古之文化》的研究专著。尽管这部著作里安特生关于中国古代文化起源的论断充满争议，但这是西方学者第一部基于考古调查和发掘的关于中华文明起源的著作，很快成为欧美学者了解和认知古代中国的必读书。

　　安特生在河南仰韶村遗址的发现与发掘影响深远。他的考古发掘与研究成果标志着中国史前考古学及中国近代考古学的诞生，揭开了中国田野考古史的第一页。仰韶文化成为中国考古史上第一个被正式命名的远古文化体系，为后来发现并被命名的其他新石器时代文化奠定了规范化基础。因此，仰韶文化的发现与确立，在中国考古学史上是划时代的里程碑。仰韶村遗址成为中外史学界、考古界向往的"文化圣地"，仰韶文化的发现也理所当然地入选"中国20世纪100项考古大发现"并永载史册。

　　此后，在安特生研究成果的基础上，经过中外考古学家几代人的努力，仰韶文化成为中国考古学体系中最著名的考古学文化之一，也是研究最为深入、成果最为丰硕的史前文化体系之一。在安特生之后的半个

on the Central Plains. Therefore, when he discovered the painted pottery pieces abandoned in the field on the south bank of the Yellow River, he immediately realized that it was an ancient archaeological cultural relic. Since then, Andersson successively discovered similar painted pottery in Gansu and Qinghai. He then conducted an in-depth study of the series of archaeological discoveries and published a monograph *An Early Chinese Culture* (1923). Although his work was full of controversy concerning the origin of the ancient Chinese culture, this was the first book by western scholars to discuss the origin of Chinese civilization on the basis of archaeological investigations and excavations. The book soon became a cornerstone for European and American scholars to understand and recognize ancient China.

Andersson's discovery and excavation at the Yangshao Village site in Henan Province has far-reaching effects. His archaeological excavations and research marked the birth of the Chinese prehistoric archaeology and modern Chinese archaeology, and created the first page in the history of the Chinese field archaeology. The Yangshao culture became the first ancient cultural system officially named in the Chinese archaeological history, laying a standardized foundation for other Neolithic cultures that were later discovered and named. Therefore, the discovery and establishment of the Yangshao culture is an epoch-making milestone in the history of Chinese archaeology. The Yangshao Village site has become a "sacred cultural place" for scholars of history and archaeology at home and abroad. The discovery of the Yangshao culture was also undoubtedly selected for the 100 major discoveries of Chinese archaeology in the twentieth century.

Since then, on the basis of Andersson's research, the Yangshao culture has, with the joint efforts of several generations of Chinese and foreign archaeologists, become the most famous archaeological culture in the Chinese archaeological system, and it is also the most in-depth and most fruitful prehistoric cultural system. In more than half a century after Andersson's discovery, Chinese and foreign archaeologists have made unremitting explorations of the same type of archaeological culture, and named the same or similar cultural relics in northern China as the Yangshao culture. This prehistoric culture, which was named after the first discovery at the Yangshao Village of Mianchi County in Henan Province

仰韶文化：郑州大河村遗址出土的彩陶双联壶
The Painted Pottery of the Yangshao Culture Unearthed at Dahe Village

多世纪里，中外考古学家对这类考古学文化进行了不懈的探寻，把具有相同或相近特征的中国北部地区的文化遗存统统命名为仰韶文化。这个以最先发现于河南渑池仰韶村而命名、以彩陶为标志符号的史前文化，持续时间大约在前5000—前3000年，长达2,000年左右。其分布范围，东起豫东平原，西至甘肃、青海，北到河套内蒙古长城一线，南抵江汉平原，涉及陕西、河南、山西、甘肃、河北、内蒙古、湖北、青海、宁夏9个省区，涵盖了北中国的大部，而中心区域在关中、豫西和晋南。目前，可以确认的包含仰韶文化内涵的古代遗址，数量已经超过5,000处。仰韶文化在中国考古中的重要性由此可见一斑。

　　正是由于仰韶文化分布范围广、持续时间长，其文化面貌在彩陶这个统一标志之下，呈现出不同的时间特征和区域特征，因此被区分出来不同的考古学类型。比较著名的如黄河上游甘青地区的马家窑类型，黄河中游陕西关中地区的半坡类型和河南三门峡地区的庙底沟类型、郑州地区的大河村类型等。这些不同区域的仰韶文化，不仅出土了热情奔放、色泽艳丽的彩陶，而且发现了规模宏大、规划严谨的城址和聚落，城址内更有保存完好、功能齐备的房屋建筑、公共墓地和宗教场所，向世人展示了距今7,000—5,000年前中原大地鲜活的生产、生活场景。

and marked by painted pottery, ranged from about 5000 B. C. to 3000 B. C., and lasted about 2,000 years. The Yangshao culture encompasses a large geographic area, ranging from Eastern Henan in the east, across to Gansu and Qinghai in the west, from the Great Wall of Hetao and Inner Mongolia in the north, across to the Yangtze and Han rivers in the south. It covers nine provinces or autonomous regions, including Shaanxi, Henan, Shanxi, Gansu, Hebei, Inner Mongolia, Hubei, Qinghai and Ningxia. It centers on Middle Shaanxi, Western Henan, and Southern Shanxi, and expands to most parts in North China. The number of ancient sites of the Yangshao culture that can be confirmed at present is more than 5,000, indicating its evident importance in Chinese archaeology.

It is precisely for its wide distribution in scope and its long duration in time that the Yangshao culture has taken on different temporal and regional characteristics under the unified symbol of painted pottery, thus giving rise to different archaeological types. Famous types include the Majiayao type in Gansu, the Banpo type in Shaanxi, the Miaodigou type in Sanmenxia of Henan, and the Dahe Village in Zhengzhou of Henan. Labeled under the Yangshao culture, these different types are represented not only by the unearthed enthusiastic and colorful pottery, but also by large-scale and well-planned city sites and settlements in which the well-preserved and functional housing buildings, public cemeteries and religious sites have been discovered, presenting the modern world a vivid picture of ancient life on the Central Plains 7,000 to 5,000 years ago.

仰韶文化：郑州大河村遗址联间排房
The Attached House of the Yangshao Culture in Dahe Village

仰韶文化：汝州阎村遗址出土的彩陶鹳鱼石斧图缸
The Painted Pottery of the Yangshao Culture Unearthed at Yan Village, Ruzhou

仰韶文化已经发展出比较成熟的农业生产和生活，农业生产仍以种植粟类作物为主。如陕西西安半坡遗址一座房子内的罐、瓮中都盛放着粟，另一座房子的小窖穴中也发现了粟壳遗存。临潼的姜寨遗址还发现了另一种耐旱作物——黍。靠近长江北岸的河南淅川下王岗遗址，发现了稻谷痕迹。在洛阳孙旗屯、郑州林山寨、淅川下集等遗址，也都发现了粮食遗迹。上述情况表明，仰韶文化的农业生产比较发达，粮食作物品种不仅有旱地作物，还有水田作物。同时，人们还掌握了蔬菜种植技术，半坡遗址的一座房子内，一个陶罐里装满了已经炭化的白菜或芥菜之类的菜籽。

仰韶文化处于原始的锄耕农业阶段，采用刀耕火种的方法和土地轮休的耕作方式，使用尖木棒等木质工具及石铲、石锄等挖掘土地。收割农作物则用两侧有缺口的长方形石刀和陶刀。加工粮食使用石磨盘、石磨棒、木杵、石杵等。在汝州大张、郑州大河村等遗址，还出土有大型、通体磨光的长条形石铲或有肩石铲。

The Yangshao culture has developed relatively mature agricultural production, dominated by planting millet crops. For example, the pots and urns in a house in Banpo, Xi'an, were filled with millet, and the remains of the shells are also found in the small caves of another house. The broomcorn millet (Panicum miliaceum), grain of another drought-tolerant crop was found in the Jiangzhai site in Lintong, Shaanxi. The traces of rice were found at the Xiawanggang site in the north bank of the Yangtze River, Xichuan County, Henan. Grain relics were also found in Henan such as the Sunqi site of Luoyang, the Linshanzhai site of Zhengzhou, and the Xiaji site of Xichuan. Discoveries indicate that the agricultural production of the Yangshao culture was relatively developed, and the varieties of food crops included not only dryland crops, but also paddy crops. At the same time, people have mastered the vegetable planting technology. In a house at the Banpo site, for example, a pottery jar was filled with carbonized seeds like rapeseeds or mustard seeds.

The Yangshao culture was in the primitive stage of hoe farming, using the method of slash-and-burn cultivation and the fallow system in farming. Tools for farming included the wooden tools such as pointed sticks, stone shovels and stone axes, and so on. Harvesting tools were rectangular stone knives, and ceramic knives with gaps on both sides. Grain processing tools included stone grinding discs, stone grinding rods, wooden and stone shovels. At the Dazhang Village site of Linru and the Dahe Village site of Zhengzhou, kinds of large, full-length polished stone shovels were also unearthed.

仰韶文化：郑州大河村遗址出土的彩陶片
The Painted Pottery Pieces of the Yangshao Culture, Unearthed at Dahe Village

仰韶文化制陶业发达，较好地掌握了选用陶土、造型、装饰等工序。其彩陶器造型优美，表面用红彩或黑彩画出绚丽多彩的几何形图案和动物形花纹，其中人面形纹、鱼纹、鹿纹、蛙纹与鸟纹等形象逼真生动。不少彩陶器为精美的艺术珍品，如水鸟啄鱼纹船形壶、人面鱼纹彩陶盆、鱼蛙纹彩陶盆、鹳衔鱼纹彩陶缸等。陶塑艺术品也很精彩，有附饰在陶器上的各种动物塑像，如隼形饰、羊头器钮、鸟形盖把、人面头像、壁虎及鹰等，皆栩栩如生。

在一些彩陶器物上，还发现有50多种刻画符号，可能具有原始文字的性质，为汉字的起源提供了更为丰富的材料。在濮阳西水坡所发现的用蚌壳摆塑的龙虎图案，是中国迄今所知最完整的史前时代龙虎形象。以蚌塑的龙和虎作为随葬品，墓主人的身份应该非常高，有人认为，这应该是中国古代传说中的五帝之一的颛顼；也有人认为，这是当时掌握着沟通天地权利的大巫师，其身旁的龙和虎分别象征着天上的星宿。

仰韶文化：濮阳西水坡遗址出土的蚌塑龙虎图
The Shell Dragon and Tiger of the Yangshao Culture, Unearthed from the Xishuipo Site, Puyang

仰韶文化：灵宝西坡遗址出土的生产工具——玉铲

A Tool of the Yangshao Culture: The Jade Shovel Unearthed from the Xipo Site, Lingbao County

The ceramics industry of the Yangshao culture was well developed, and there was a good mastery of the procedures of selecting clay, modeling and decoration. The painted pottery was beautiful in shape, with its surface painted with colorful geometric patterns, and animal-shaped patterns in red or black. Of all the patterns, images of the human face, fish, deer, frog and bird were vivid. Many items of colored pottery remain today as exquisite art treasures, such as the boat-shaped ewer with a waterfowl eating a fish, the pottery pot with a human face, and the painted pottery pot with a fish and a frog. The ceramic figures were also splendid, because of the various true-to-life images such as the eagle-shape ornaments, sheep-headed buttons, bird-shaped lids, human face images, and the geckos-eagle images and so on.

On some of the painted pottery objects, there were more than 50 kinds of engraved symbols which might bear the nature of original characters, which may provide more abundant materials for the origin of Chinese characters. At the Xishuipo site of Puyang, the dragon and tiger pattern formed by the clam shells was discovered, and this was the most complete image of the dragon and tiger in ancient China. If the dragon and tiger images in the form of shells are used as funerary objects, it is believed that the tomb owner must be a person of distinguished position. Some people think that this should be Zhuanxu, one of the five emperors in ancient Chinese legends. Others believe that this is the great wizard who, accompanied by the dragon and the tiger, was in charge of communicating with the heaven at that time.

3. 文明前夜：郑州西山古城

1993—1995年，为培养中国田野考古发掘的骨干队伍，国家文物局在郑州市北郊黄河南岸一个名叫西山村的古遗址上，先后举办了三期考古领队培训班。从这个培训班毕业的学员，将取得国家文物局颁发的田野考古领队证书，意味着从此可以独自主持一个考古发掘项目了。

学员来自全国各地考古研究所，分别毕业于全国各个院校。他们本来是为了自己的领队执照而来的，但未曾想，他们艰苦卓绝的考古发掘，揭开了中原考古乃至中国考古学的新篇章：西山遗址发掘出了一座属于仰韶文化时期的大型城市！

这座城池的年代为前3300—前2800年，属于仰韶文化晚期，这是迄今中原地区最早、建筑技术最为先进的史前城址。城市的平面大致呈圆形，最大径180米，面积约34,500平方米。城垣使用分段夯筑技术，这在中国古代建筑发展史上是一件具有里程碑意义的大事，它开启了后代大规模城垣建筑规制的先河，其建筑方法、形制结构无疑对中国古代城址的建筑产生了深远的影响，显示了巨大的进步和创造力。西山城址的发现不仅仅对于探讨中国早期城市的起源，而且对于华夏早期文明的起

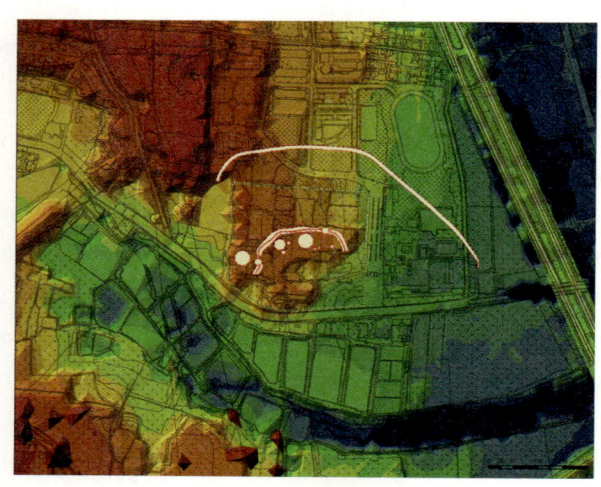

西山古城平面图
The Xishan Ancient City Plane

3. The Eve of Civilization: Xishan Ancient City in Zhengzhou

In order to cultivate the team of the Chinese field archaeologists, the National Administration of Cultural Heritage held three training courses from 1993 to 1995 for archaeological team leaders on the ancient site of the Xishan Village on the south bank of the Yellow River in the northern suburbs of Zhengzhou. The graduates from these training programs would receive a certificate issued by the National Administration of Cultural Heritage, which would assure them to host an archaeological excavation project as the leader of the field archaeologists.

The participants who had been educated in different colleges or universities came from archaeological research organizations across the country. They had all intended to come for the team leader license, but what was surprising was that they happened to open a new chapter in the history of the archaeological excavations in Henan Province, or even in China. At the Xishan site, they happened to discover a large buried city belonging to the Yangshao culture.

The city was built from 3300 B. C. to 2800 B. C., of the late Yangshao period. It is the earliest prehistoric city site with the most advanced construction technology on the Central Plains. The city's plane is roughly circular with a maximum diameter of 180 meters and an area of about 34,500 square meters. The use of segmental construction technology in the city is a milestone in the history of ancient Chinese architecture. It started the precedent for the construction of large-scale urban buildings in later generations. Its architectural methods and structures, which are considered to be progressive and innovative, had great and far-reaching influence on the later construction of buildings in ancient Chinese cities. The discovery of the Xishan site is of great significance not only for the study on the origin of early cities in ancient China, but also for the study of the origin and formation of early Chinese civilization and the historical role of the Central Plains.

源和形成以及中原地区在其中所起的历史作用等课题的研究,都具有非常重要的意义。

西山遗址所处的时代,与传说中的黄帝时期基本吻合,而且在地域上与被认为是黄帝故里的新郑市相距不远。有的学者认为,结合古代文献中"黄帝筑城"的记载和传说,分析西山遗址的文化性质、聚落形态、社会组织、丧葬习俗、生态环境、与周边文化关系等,可以认为,西山古城有可能就是传说中的黄帝之城。

无论如何,西山遗址已经显示出在仰韶文化时期,中原地区已经存在规模可观的城市。而构建这样的城市,必须要有一个强有力的政权组织。这一时期发现的围壕、中心聚落、精美随葬品等,也昭示着社会组织结构存在着层阶的差异。因此,以西山古城为代表的考古学文化,已经开始产生政治强权和阶级分化,以沟通天地为主要形式的宗教和艺术形式都出现了不同于以往的表现。因此,这一时期,应该已经开始跨入文明社会的门槛。这一时期的居民,正在准备迎接文明社会的曙光。

西山遗址出土的陶器
Pottery Unearthed from the Xishan Site

The era of the Xishan ruins is basically consistent with the legendary Yellow Emperor period and, geographically, is not far from Xinzheng, hometown of the Yellow Emperor. Some scholars believed that Xishan city could be the legendary city of the Yellow Emperor, if we put together the records and legends of "The City the Yellow Emperor Built" in ancient literature, and analyze the cultural nature, settlement form, social organization, funeral customs, ecological environment, and the surrounding cultural relations of the Xishan site.

In any case, the Xishan site has already shown that considerably large cities have already appeared on the Central Plains in the period of the Yangshao culture. To build such cities, there must be a strong political organization. The cofferdams, central settlements, and exquisite funerary objects discovered during this period also indicate that there are differences in the hierarchy of social organizations. Therefore, according to the archaeological discoveries about the ancient city, the Xishan site has shown the existence of political power and class hierarchies. The religious and artistic forms that focused on linking the heaven and the earth are different from those in the past. Therefore, this period has already begun to enter the threshold of civilized society, and the residents of this period have begun to enjoy the twilight of a new civilization.

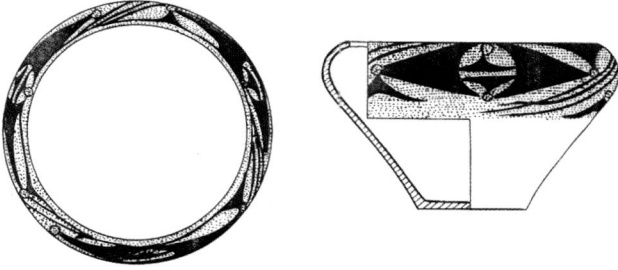

西山遗址出土的陶器线描剖视图
Pottery Unearthed from the Xishan Site

第二章

文明肇始：华夏文明的核心

Chapter II

The Beginning of Civilization: The Center of Chinese Civilization

一、从大禹治水到二里头王都

1. 人类共同记忆的洪荒时代：大禹治水的传说与王城岗城址的考古发现

分别居住在欧亚大陆东西两端的早期人类，尽管后来各自创造出不同的文化体系，但是却都保留有关于大洪水的记忆和传说。这个共同记忆，也成为后世学者探寻东西方文明起源的重要切入点。

在古代中国，关于大洪水的记忆具体表现为大禹治水的传说。在遥远的洪荒时代，东方大地上洪水肆虐，人民流离失所。这一时期，中原地区已经建立起有效的政治组织，实行"选贤与能"的禅让制。于是，担任部族首领的舜选择大禹作为接班人，并命大禹接替其父亲鲧去治理洪水。大禹抛弃了鲧堵塞河流决口的治理思路，把全国的河流作为一个整体、一个统一的系统进行规划，然后进行疏导，最终导流入海。为了实现自己的宏图大略，大禹踏遍了全国主要山河，也因此对全国的主要山水形胜和物产风俗了如指掌。据此，他把全国划分为九州，从而实行有效的治理。

在治水过程中累积起来的崇高威望使得大禹顺利通过了舜帝的考察和部族的选举，他把都城建立在嵩山脚下的阳城，成为新的统治者，也就是中国古史传说时代禅让制的最后一位君主。他的儿子启在他死后，以强大的军事和政治实力废除了禅让制而建立起君主世袭制，并将自己的王国命名为"夏"。这是中国历史上第一个国家政权，中国历史从此进入了文明阶段。

大禹治水、禹都阳城与启建立夏王朝的传说，数千年以来在中国代代相传，并且被中国最伟大的历史学家司马迁写入了他的伟大著作《史记》中。司马迁不仅把传说和他之前的文献资料进行了整理和分析，而且还亲自踏遍山水，考察辨析大禹治水的种种遗迹。他确信，大禹父子

I. From Yu Taming Flood to Erlitou Capital City

1. The Prehistorical Era in the Common Memory of Mankind: The Legend of Yu Taming Flood and the Archaeological Discovery at Wangchenggang Site.

The early human beings living on the eastern and western ends of the Eurasian continent retained the memory and legend of the Great Flood, although they later created different cultural systems. This common memory also became an important point for scholars to explore the origin of the Eastern and the Western civilization.

In ancient China, the memory of the Great Flood is based on the legend of Yu Taming Flood. In the remote pre-historical era, floods ran wild on the Eastern land, and people became homeless. In this period, an effective political system was established in the Central Plains, which implemented the abdication system of talent promotion. Shun, a tribal leader, chose Yu (also known respectfully as Great Yu or Yu the Great) as his successor, and ordered him to control the floods in place of his father Gun. Yu carried out a unified and systematic water-control planning for all the rivers in the country, channeling water into the sea rather than clogging the river gaps. In order to realize his ambitious plan, Yu travelled all the main mountains and rivers of the country to learn of its landscape, products and customs, and divided the whole country into nine states for effective governance.

The lofty prestige accumulated in the course of controlling floods enabled Yu to win King Shun's trust and the tribal election. He built the capital in Yangcheng at the foot of Mount Songshan and became the new ruler—the last monarch of the legendary abdication system in ancient China. After his death, his son, Qi, abolished the abdication system through mighty military and political power and established hereditary monarchy instead. He named his kingdom Xia—the first state administration in Chinese history, which symbolizes the beginning of the Chinese civilization.

The legends of Yu Taming Flood, Capital Yangcheng, and Qi's founding of the Xia Dynasty have been handed down from generation to generation in China for thousands of years, and have been written by Sima Qian, China's greatest historian, in his great work—*The Records of the Historian.* Sima Qian

所建立的夏就是华夏文明中的第一个统一王朝。中原地区不仅是文明的肇始,也是华夏文明的核心。

河南位于禹贡九州中的豫州,中部巍然耸立的嵩山被确定为五岳中的中岳。就在中岳嵩山脚下,坐落着一对大型石质礼仪建筑——启母阙,这是汉代人为了缅怀大禹以及纪念大禹的妻子涂山氏为大禹生下了启而建造的,可以视作是汉代为大禹和启建造的纪念碑,已经被联合国教科文组织列入世界文化遗产名录。这一对石阙建于汉安帝延光二年(123年),其上刻有长篇铭文,回顾了上古时期惊心动魄的大洪水,追述了大禹治水的丰功伟绩,赞颂了大禹的美德。文中还指出,大禹的业绩随着时间的流逝到秦时已逐渐被人遗忘。汉王朝建立之后,秉承上天旨意,建庙祭祀大禹父子,建阙刻文纪功,使之流传于后世子孙。

雄才大略的汉武帝在嵩山建立启母庙,汉安帝又在此建立启母阙。说明至少在两汉时期,官方和民间都认可环嵩山一带是传说中的夏王朝

中岳嵩山
Mount Songshan (the central mountain)

not only collected and analyzed the legends and the preceding documents but also personally travelled through the mountains and rivers to inspect the traces of Yu Taming Flood. He was convinced that the Xia Dynasty, founded by Yu and his son, was the first unified dynasty in Chinese civilization, and that the Central Plains area was not only the beginning but also the center of the Chinese civilization.

Henan is located in Yuzhou, one of the nine states established by Yu. Mount Songshan, which stands majestically in the middle of Yuzhou, was regarded as the central mountain (of the five sacred mountains in China), at the foot of which erects a pair of large stone buildings for sacrificial service—Qimu (literally, Qi's mother) Que (a part of a gate), built in the Han Dynasty in memory of Yu and his wife, Tushan, who gave birth to Qi. This pair of stone buildings, which has been included on the World Heritage List by the UNESCO, was erected in the second year of the Yanguang reign of Emperor An of the Han Dynasty (123 A.D), with a long inscription recalling the thrilling Great Flood in the ancient time (before the Xia Dynasty), recounting the great achievements of Yu in combating the floods, and extolling the virtues of Yu. The inscription also points out that Yu's achievements had been gradually forgotten in the Qin Dynasty with the passage of time. After the founding of the Han Dynasty, a temple was built in accordance with the heaven's will to offer sacrifices to Yu and his son, and their achievements were engraved in the monument so that they could pass down to future generations.

The construction of the Qimu Temple by talented and ambitious Emperor Wu of the Han Dynasty and the Qimu Que by Emperor An of the Han Dynasty at least shows that the area around Mount Songshan was officially and civilly recognized to be where the legendary Xia Dynasty was located, which suggests that the middle of Henan Province is the early center of the Chinese civilization.

的建国之地，也意味着中华文明的早期核心就在河南的中部。两千余年来，这种观念相沿不改。随着现代考古学从西方进入中国，考古学家们拿起手铲，进入田野，在一层层叠压累积的地层中，寻找神话传说和历史文献中的夏王朝，追溯中华文明的起源地。

天道酬勤。从20世纪70年代至今，考古学家们在嵩山周围发现了众多的古代遗址，并在距离启母阙不远的登封告成镇一个名叫王城岗的遗址中，发掘出了大小两座古城，大城的面积超过30万平方米。古城的建造年代在前2100年前后，与历史记载中的夏王朝建立的年代基本吻合。而王城岗遗址出土的夯土建筑基址、奠基坑、青铜器残片等重要文物表明，这里曾经建有大型宫殿建筑，曾经有宗教祭祀活动，曾经有金属冶炼技术。所有这一切，引导着考古学家们去思考去辨析当时的社会结构和社会属性，有相当一批学者认为，这里就是大禹父子建立的夏王朝的发生地，也就是文献中记载的禹都阳城。

This view has been held for more than two thousand years. As modern archaeology entered China from the West, archeologists began to look for the Xia Dynasty documented in fairy tales and historical literature from layers of earth with hand shovels, tracing the origin of the Chinese civilization.

From the 1970s, archeologists have found many ancient sites around Mount Songshan and two ancient cities (the bigger one covering 300,000 square meters) at Wangchenggang Site in Gaocheng, Dengfeng, not far away from the Qimu Que. The two cities were built around 2100 B.C., basically consistent with the time when the Xia Dynasty was established. The important relics such as rammed foundations, cornerstone pits, and broken bronze vessels unearthed from Wangchenggang Site are evidences that there existed large palaces, religious sacrifices and metal smelting technology, which lead archeologists to speculate and analyze the social structure and attributes of that time. There are quite a number of scholars who believe the place to be where Yu and his son built the Xia Dynasty, i.e, the so-called Yudu Yangcheng (Yangcheng, the capital city of Yu's Dynasty) recorded in the literature.

2. 从传说到实证：二里头王都与夏文化的探索

传说和文献记载中，夏代的都城是不停迁徙的。迁徙的原因，既有政治性的，也有资源利用方面的。比如夏代到了太康继位为王的时候，被来自东方的夷人推翻了，这就是所谓的太康失国、后羿代夏，持续了七八十年，直到少康中兴复国。这期间国都就被迫迁徙了。

如果说夏代最早的都城在王城岗的阳城，那么晚期或者最晚的都城在哪里呢？考古学家们一直在苦苦探索。参考《史记》等经典历史文献，立足于从20世纪50年代开始、持续至今的考古发掘，中国考古学家们在洛阳东部的偃师二里头发现了一个巨大的遗址，并且以此为标准确立了二里头文化。遗址现存面积300万平方米，规划缜密，布局严整，被认为是当时中国乃至东亚地区最大的都邑之一，也是中国最早的王国都城遗址之一。

经过严谨细致的考古调查和发掘，以及几代人不懈的研究和探索，考古界确认二里头文化的分布范围主要在河南西部和山西南部，以及河北南部和陕西东部，基本与传说和文献中的夏王朝活动区域相吻合。二里头文化的年代，基本介于前1800年至前1600年，与少康中兴以后的夏文化年代吻合。从出土文物考察，二里头文化出土有精美的绿松石牌

二里头遗址出土的绿松石龙
Turquoise Dragon Unearthed from Erlitou Ruins

2. From Legend to Truth: Exploration of Erlitou (capital city) and Xia Culture

The legends and historical documents state that the capital of the Xia Dynasty was constantly moving because of political reasons or the availability of natural resources. One example was that the capital moved to another place when Houyi, an alien, who ruled the country for 70 to 80 years from the time when he overthrew Taikang (the successor to King Qi) to the time when Shaokang recovered Xia's regime.

If the capital of the early Xia Dynasty was in Yangcheng of Wangchenggang, then where was it in the later or the latest period? This is a question that archaeologists have been trying to answer. Based on the historical documents, such as the *The Records of the Historian* and the archaeological excavations starting in 1950s, Chinese archaeologists discovered a large site at Erlitou, Yanshi, to the east Luoyang. This site, covering 3 million square meters, is well planned and strictly laid out, and is regarded as the largest capital city in China and even in southeast Asia at that time, and China's earliest capital site.

Unremitting archaeological surveys, excavations and studies have confirmed that Erlitou culture was distributed mainly in the west of Henan, south of Shanxi and Hebei, and east of Shaanxi, consistent with the legends and documents

二里头遗址出土的绿松石铜牌饰
Turquoise Bronze Ornament Unearthed from Erlitou Ruins

饰，已有高度发达的铸铜、制造玉石器、制陶和制骨等手工业，最令人瞩目的是已掌握了用复合范铸造青铜礼器的高超技术。不仅如此，考古学家们还发掘出土了规模宏大的宫殿和宗庙，甚至发现了道路和车辙等重要遗迹。

二里头文化所呈现出来的高度发达的社会生活和复杂的社会结构，以及高等级的建筑遗存和青铜、玉石礼器，使研究者们相信，这是一座具有强大政治功能和礼仪功能的王都，应该就是少康中兴之后夏王朝的首都。

城内有复杂的城市道路网络，道路上发现有中国最早的双轮车车辙遗迹。路网把遗址分割出不同的功能区。宫城和大型宫殿建筑群位于遗址的中心区，宫殿区内发现有中国最早的大型"四合院"宫室建筑群和多进院落宫室建筑群。这些宫殿建筑群具有超大体量，建筑在夯筑台基上，土木结构。其方正规整的形制、封闭的庭院式布局以及中轴对称的结构，开后世中国宫室建筑之先河。

制造贵族奢侈品的官营手工业作坊区位于宫殿区近旁的中心区南部，其内已发现有青铜器制造作坊和绿松石器制造作坊。祭祀区域在城

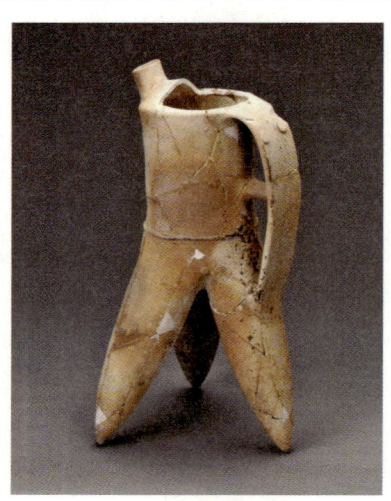

二里头遗址出土的白陶盉
White Ceramic Liquor Vessel Unearthed from Erlitou Ruins

about the Xia Dynasty, and it appeared between 1800 B.C. and 1600 B.C., consistent with the time of Xia culture after Shaokang Resurgence. The relics unearthed from this site include beautiful turquoise accessories, highly developed handicraft industries that cast copper, made jade, pottery and bone vessels, and most remarkably, the advanced technology of making bronze sacrificial vessels. In addition, archaeologists also found large palaces and ancestral shrines, and even traces of roads and ruts.

The highly advanced social life, complex social structure, high-level building remains, bronze and jade vessels demonstrated by Erlitou culture convince researchers that this is a capital city with powerful political and ritual function, and is supposed to be the capital of the Xia Dynasty after Shaokang Resurgence.

There are intricate road networks in the inner city and traces of the earliest bicycle ruts on the roads. The road networks divide the site into different functional sections, with the imperial palace and large palace complex in the center. China's earliest large-scale quadrangle courtyards and multi-entrance courtyards are found in the palace complex section. These large palace structures were built on rammed foundations, with civil structure. The square shape, closed courtyard layout, axis-symmetric structure set up a model for later Chinese palace buildings.

A government-run handcraft workshop producing aristocratic luxuries is located in the south of the central section near the palace complex, where were found a bronze mill and a turquoise mill. The worship section is in the north of the city center, where China's earliest state-level sacrificial site and altar-like round site were found. Numerious and rich categories of China's earliest bronze sacrificial vessels, bronze weapons, jade ritual artifacts, weapons, as well as ceramic, stone, bone, mussel, and lacquer vessels have been unearthed from this site. Of particular historical, artistic and scientific value, are the turquoise bronze ornaments and dragon-shaped vessels, which are closely associated with imperial totem and primitive religions.

All these show the unique magnificence of an Eastern capital city. The discovery of the capital city and its cultural coverage confirm that Chinese history progressed from a multi-state period into one of a vast unified monarchy country, which took place 3,800 years ago, the time of the Xia Dynasty.

市中心区的北部，发现有中国最早的国家级祭祀遗迹和圆形的类似于后世"坛"之类的遗迹。遗址出土了数量众多、类别丰富的中国最早的青铜礼器和青铜兵器群、玉礼器和玉兵器群以及陶、石、骨、蚌、漆器等遗迹遗物。特别是具有极高历史、艺术与科学价值的绿松石龙形器和铜牌饰，与夏后氏图腾和原始宗教关系密切。

上述种种，均显示出东方王都所特有的气魄。二里头大都的出现和其文化波及的范围，证实了中国历史由万邦林立的"多元"邦国时代，进入到众星捧月的"一体"广域王权国家时代。而这个时代恰恰处于距今3,800年左右，也就是中国文献记载的夏王朝纪年内。

西方学术界一般认为，中国历史上的文明阶段应该是从商代开始的。因为不仅发现了商代的城市遗址、宗庙遗址和数量众多的青铜器，而且还发现了商时的文字甲骨文，所以商朝的存在是毋庸置疑的。而有关夏王朝的文字记载，均是夏代之后历代追忆增补的，不是当时的文献资料，因此关于夏王朝的存在是一个疑问。

但是在中国学术界，绝大多数学者对夏王朝的存在是肯定的。这不仅源于数千年以来的历史传统，更源于现代考古学的发现与研究。司马迁在《史记》中记载的商王朝的世系和年表直到19世纪末发现甲骨文后才被证实，从而使商代由传说变成了中西方普遍接受的信史，那么我们有什么理由怀疑同样出自司马迁笔下的夏王朝的世系和年表呢？也许，夏王朝正处在汉字的孕育形成期，文字数量少且不易保存。也许，夏王朝的文字资料在当时被集中保管封存，我们的考古工作迄今还存在盲点。也许，有那么一天，就像甲骨文横空出世一样，我们不经意间意识到了夏朝文字这样一个惊世大发现！

二里头遗址出土的青铜爵
Bronze Goblet Unearthed from Erlitou Ruins

Western scholars generally hold that China's civilization started in the Shang Dynasty, because the discovery of town sites and ancestral shrine sites, bronze vessels as well as oracle bone inscriptions of that dynasty proves its indisputable existence, whereas the written records about the Xia Dynasty are based on subsequent memories rather than on the documents of that time, hence a doubt about its real existence.

The majority of Chinese scholars, however, are convinced of the existence of the Xia Dynasty, drawing not only upon historical tradition of thousands of years but also upon modern archaeological discoveries and research. The genealogical chronology of the Shang Dynasty recorded in Sima Qian's *The Records of the Historian* was not confirmed until the end of 19th century, when oracle bone inscriptions were found, changing the legends of the Shang Dynasty into a true history, widely recognized by both Chinese and Western scholars. Then what reason do we have to doubt the lineage and chronology of the Xia Dynasty also recorded by Sima Qian? Perhaps this is due to the fact that the characters were too few to be preserved in the Xia Dynasty when Chinese characters were just beginning to take shape, or due to the fact that the character materials in the Xia Dynasty were all kept in a place which our archaeology has not been able to reach. It is possible that one day we will incidentally discover Xia's characters, shocking the world as we did with the discovery of the oracle bone inscriptions.

二、从郑州商城到安阳殷墟

《国语·周语上》记载"昔伊、洛竭而夏亡",是说作为黄河支流的伊河、洛河干涸了,处于伊、洛二水交汇处的夏王朝也就灭亡了。而与二里头相距仅六公里的偃师商城以及位于中原腹地的郑州商城的发现,则为夏商王朝的交替找到了考古学的印证。商王朝的开国君主成汤,为反抗夏朝末代君主桀的暴政,从一个屡屡迁徙的方国部族,通过鸣条之战一举灭夏,统一了纷乱的中原,建立了商王朝。

1950年,一位小学教师在郑州二里岗一带发现了绳纹陶片和磨光石器,经鉴定为商代遗物,郑州商城这个3,600年前的商代王都之谜随之揭开。郑州商城的外城面积达13平方公里,内城墙周长近7公里,不少地段至今留存着高达近7米的夯土墙遗迹。3平方公里的内城中集中分

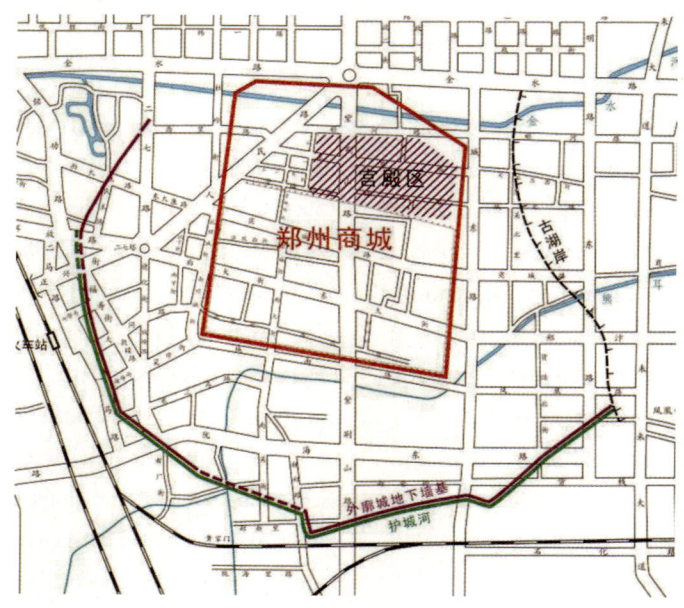

郑州商城遗址
Shangcheng Site in Zhengzhou

II. From Shangcheng in Zhengzhou to the Yin Ruins in Anyang

According to the first book of *Guoyu Zhouyu*, when the Yi River and the Luo River (two tributaries of the Yellow River) dried up, the Xia Dynasty (located at the junction of the two rivers) perished. The discovery of a city of the Shang Dynasty in Yanshi, only six kilometers away from Erlitou, and another city of the Shang Dynasty in Zhengzhou in the hinterland of the Central Plains provides archaeological evidence for the alternation of the Xia and Shang dynasties. Chengtang, who was the leader of a repeatedly migratory tribe named Fang, destroyed the Xia Dynasty through a battle at Mingtiao against the tyranny of the late Xia monarch, unifying the chaotic Central Plains and founding the Shang Dynasty.

In 1950, a primary school teacher discovered veined pottery shards and polished stone tools in Erligang, Zhengzhou, which were identified to be the relics of the Shang Dynasty, unveiling the mystery of Shangcheng in Zhengzhou as the capital of the Shang Dynasty 3,600 years ago. The outer city covers an area of 13 square kilometers, the circumference of the inner wall being nearly 7 kilometers. Remains of rammed walls of up to 7 meters high now can be found in many places. A large number of rammed palace foundations are centrally distributed

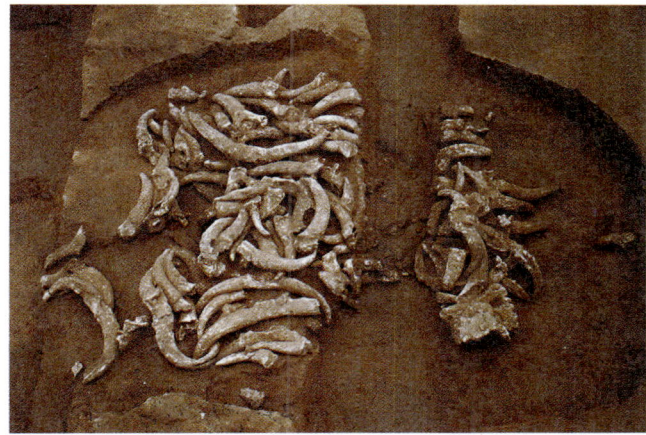

郑州商城祭祀坑
Sacrifice Pit at Shangcheng Site in Zhengzhou

布着大量夯土宫殿建筑基址，手工业作坊、青铜器窖藏、居民点与墓地散布其间。代表着国家社稷权威的大型青铜方鼎、原始瓷尊等数万件文物出土其中。一代代专家学者对郑州商城的性质进行了热烈的争论和研究，一座商代的开国王都——商代开国君王商汤所立的亳都渐次揭开神秘的面纱。

商部族屡次迁徙，辗转于河济间数百载，终于成为君临四方的泱泱大国。自前16世纪初商汤建国，至前11世纪殷纣灭亡，凡17世31王500余年，特别是盘庚迁殷至纣之灭年间，中原一直是殷王朝统治中心。考古发掘表明，商人不仅将青铜文明推向鼎盛，甲骨文的出现也使得中华文明从此史书有载。

世界文化遗产河南安阳殷墟，是殷商王朝后期都城遗址，面积24万平方公里。100年前甲骨文的发现，把人们的目光吸引到了殷墟这块

安阳妇好墓青铜方斝
Bronze Rectangular Jia from Fuhao's Tomb in Anyang

in the inner city of 3 square kilometers, with handicraft workshops, bronze ware cellars, residential areas and cemeteries scattered among them. Tens of thousands of cultural relics such as large bronze quadropods and porcelain liquor vessels, which represent the authority of the state, have been unearthed. Generations of experts and scholars have engaged in heated debate and research on the nature of Shangcheng in Zhengzhou, gradually uncovering the mystery of the place as the capital of the Shang Dynasty built by its first King Shangtang.

The Shang tribe repeatedly migrated in Heji (a place in the east of Henan and the west of Shandong)for hundreds of years, and finally became a great state that controlled many tribes. From the founding of the Shang Dynasty by Shangtang (also known as Chengtang) in the early 1600 B.C. to the demise of the dynasty when Zhou was the king in the 1100 B.C., the Central Plains area was the center of the dynasty, especially during the 273 years from Pangeng relocating the capital in Yin to the death of King Zhou. Archaeological excavation has shown that not

安阳妇好墓青铜鸮尊
Owl-shaped Bronze Zun from Fuhao's Tomb

土地上。1928年开始的殷墟考古，一举使商代的历史成为信史，打开了这座地下商代博物馆的大门。近百年来，考古工作者用他们的双手，拂去尘封的泥土，发掘出殷代的宫殿、王陵、甲骨文、青铜器等重要文物古迹。小屯村一带的宫殿宗庙，是王都的心脏，是殷王生活起居和处理政务的地方，规模宏大，规划严整，已发现的建筑夯土基址有80多处。洹河北岸的武官村北地是殷代王陵，盘庚迁殷以后的帝王死后都埋葬于此，自1934年起，已在王陵区发现13座大型王陵和数以千计的陪葬墓、祭祀坑。另外还发现有城壕沟1,700多米、手工业作坊5处、车马坑30多座，发掘出土甲骨15万片和大批青铜器、玉器、陶器、骨器等珍贵文物。

从郑州到安阳，商王朝完成了华丽的蜕变。一个高度发达的青铜文明，一个具有文字记载、文物实证和传奇故事的文明，在世界的东方建构完成。古老的中原大地，成了这个文明从孕育到茁壮成长的中心舞台。

殷墟出土的象牙杯
Ivory Cup Unearthed from the Yin Ruins

only the Shang people pushed the bronze civilization to its peak, but also that the appearance of oracle bone inscriptions enabled the Chinese civilization to be written down in historical books.

The Yin Ruins in Anyang, Henan Province—a world cultural heritage site—covers an area of 240,000 square kilometers. The discovery of oracle bone inscriptions 100 years ago attracted people's attention to the Yin Ruins. The archaeological work at the place starting in 1928 bears testimony to the existence of the Shang Dynasty, which opened the door of this underground museum of the dynasty. In the past 100 years, archaeologists have excavated important cultural relics such as palaces, mausoleums, oracle bone inscriptions, bronze vessels and historical sites of the Yin Dynasty. The large-scale and well planned palaces and ancestral shrines in XiaotunVillage were the heart of the capital and where the kings lived and worked. More than 80 rammed foundation sites have been found. The royal mausoleum is located in Wuguan Village on the north bank of the Huanhe River, where the kings after Pangeng resettled the capital in Yin were buried. Since 1934, 13 large mausoleum sites, thousands of tombs and worship pits have been found, over 1, 700 meters of moat, 5 handicraft mills, 30 chariot-horse pits, 150, 000 oracle bone inscriptions, and a large number of priceless cultural relics such as bronze, jade, pottery and bone vessels have been unearthed.

From Zhengzhou to Anyang, the Shang Dynasty completed a splendid transformation. A highly developed bronze civilization, with written records, cultural relics and legendary stories, was constructed in the east of the world. The ancient land of the Central Plains has become a central stage for the growth of this civilization.

三、从西周到东周：周王室东迁与春秋战国时代开启

强盛一时的大邑商，在纣王荒淫暴虐中沦落。周武王伐纣后，为控制中原及东方诸部，在今天的洛阳建立了新的大邑。所谓"宅兹中国，自兹乂民"，"中国"之名由此开始。

代商而起的西周王朝推行分封制，就是周王将王畿以外的土地、民众封赏给他的同姓宗亲、异姓先贤后裔和功臣，受封者在封地内建庙立国。西周王朝先后分封一百多个诸侯国。中原居天下之中，地理位置优越，文化传统厚重，所以今河南境内就分布着许多大小不一的封国。河南考古发掘和勘察的两周时期的地上古城遗址多达近150座，占全国同时期古城遗址的四分之一还多。专家作过测算，在河南，几乎每四五十里都有一座古城遗址。

前770年，周平王为避犬戎之乱迁都洛阳，史称"东周"。也正是从这一年开始，进入了历史上的春秋战国时代，洛阳成为天下"共主"周天子的都城，是全国政治和文化的中心。古代哲学家老子曾为周王城国家图书档案典籍馆馆长（守藏室吏、柱下史），孔子曾千里赴洛阳问

应国墓地出土的西周青铜面具
Bronze Mask Unearthed from the Cemetery of the Ying State

III. From the Western Zhou Dynasty to the Eastern Zhou Dynasty: Eastward Movement of the Zhou Dynasty and the Beginning of the Spring and Autumn Period and the Warring States Period

Powerful for a time, the Shang Dynasty declined due to King Zhou's dissolute and tyrannical rule. After overthrowing King Zhou, King Wu built a new city in the present-day Luoyang to control the Central Plains and the eastern tribes. This is what is called "zhai zi zhong guo, zi zi yi min", which means: I occupy the central place and make it my home to control the people here. This is the first time the term "Zhongguo" (China) appeared.

The Western Zhou Dynasty implemented the system of enfeoffment, through which the king gave the land and people outside the capital to his family members, descendants of the wise men of other families, and meritorious officials, who could build temples and states within the land. In this way, the Western Zhou Dynasty was divided into more than one hundred vassal states. The Central Plains was in the center of the dynasty, with superior geographical position and profound culture, which is why the present-day Henan Province at that time had many states of varied sizes. Archaeological excavations and investigations have found that there are nearly 150 above-ground city sites of the Western and

应国墓地出土的西周青铜面具
Bronze Mask Unearthed from the Cemetery of the Ying State

信阳黄国墓地出土的西周青铜器
Bronze Vessel Unearthed from the Cemetery of the Huang State in Xinyang

学于老子，并在中原列国周游，至今洛阳老城还有"孔子入周问礼乐至此"碑传世。

中原地区人口密集，城邑栉比，战乱频仍，处于四方诸侯拓土开疆、图霸天下的中心，许多著名的战役在这里进行，许多改变历史的抉择在这里酝酿。这一时期的中原，也是百家争鸣的中心舞台。儒、墨、道、法、名、阴阳、农、纵横、杂和小说家等所谓"十家九流"的学派，都在中原留下他们游学著书的遗踪。

Eastern Zhou dynasties in Henan Province, making up over a quarter of the total city sites at the same period in China. It is estimated by experts that there is one ancient city site in every 40-50 kilometers in Henan Province.

In 770 B.C., King Ping of the Zhou Dynasty relocated the capital in Luoyang to escape from the Quanrong Rebellion. This year marks the beginning of the Eastern Zhou Dynasty and also the beginning of the Spring and Autumn Period and the Warring States Period. Luoyang became the capital of the dynasty, and thus its political and cultural center. The ancient great philosopher Lao Zi used to be the chief librarian of the National Library of Books, Archives and Classics in the capital city. Confucius once travelled thousands of miles to Luoyang to learn from Laozi and toured all over the Central Plains. Now there is a monument in the old city of Luoyang, which writes: Confucius came to Zhou to study rites and music.

The Central Plains area was a densely populated region with numerous cities and frequent civil wars. It was the center where the lords of the vassal states tried to expand their territories and seek hegemony, and so where many famous battles took place and history-changing decisions were made. The Central Plains area at this period was also a central stage for the contention of hundreds of schools of thought. Schools of the Confucianists, Mohists, Taoists, Legalists, Logicians, Yin and Yang, Agriculturists, Political Strategists, Eclectics and Novelists (so-called "Ten Schools and Nine Streams") left their traces in the Central Plains when they

扶沟出土的楚国金币
Golden Coin of the Chu State Unearthed in Fugou

新兴势力更迭不断，列国文化异彩纷呈。平顶山应国墓地，新郑郑韩故城，南阳、信阳、淮阳等地的楚国贵族墓地，以及江淮诸小国的兴衰遗迹等，大量品类丰富的诸侯国文物，青铜器、玉器、漆器、骨器等金玉交辉，天工匠心，代表了中华民族审美思维和创造才能。其中，应国墓地出土的青铜面具设计独特、情趣天成；淅川下寺出土的楚国青铜礼器至纤至悉，造型奇诡；扶沟出土的楚国马蹄金和郢爰金光闪闪，明亮如新。所有这些，从不同侧面表现了两周时期中原大地上曾经的物质财富和艺术创造，记录了一个充满朝气和活力的时代。

淅川下寺出土的王子午鼎
Wangziwu Tripod Unearthed in Xiasi, Xichuan

were studying and writing books.

The emerging forces were alternating constantly, producing colorful cultures. The noble cemeteries of the Chu State found in Pingdingshan, Xinzheng, Nanyang, Xinyang, and Huaiyang, the ruins that record the rise and fall of the small states in the Changjiang and Huaihe River regions, as well as the rich cultural relics (splendid and ingenious vessels made of bronze, jade, lacquer, and bone) represent the aesthetic thinking and creativity of the Chinese nation. Among them, the bronze masks unearthed in the cemetery of the Ying State were uniquely designed with natural charm; the sacrificial bronze vessels of the Chu State unearthed in Xichuan have strange shapes; the golden coins of the Chu State unearthed in Fugou are bright and glittering. All these showed, from different aspects, the material wealth and artistic creativity in the Central Plains of the Eastern Zhou Dynasty, and recorded a vibrant and dynamic era.

淅川下寺出土的青铜神兽
Bronze Divine Beast Unearthed in Xiasi, Xichuan

1. 虢国考古大发现

西周时期，有些封国也会随着和王室关系的变动等原因而举国迁徙。河南三门峡的虢国墓地，就证实了西周时期虢国从陕西宝鸡东迁到河南的历史故事。

虢国是西周王室的同姓封国，是王室嫡亲。1956年，考古学家们在三门峡上村岭发现了虢国太子墓，确认了虢国墓地的存在。此后的几十年间，陆续发掘了夫人墓、卿士墓在内的18座高等级贵族墓葬，出土了数以万计的精美文物，把原来只存在于文献记载中的虢国以非常具象的形式呈现出来。虢国墓地南北长590米、东西宽550米，占地范围32.45万平方米。墓葬是长方形竖穴土坑墓，有的墓葬底部设有腰坑。葬具为木质棺椁，随葬铜器可分为礼器、工具、车马器等，非常丰富而且精美。

尤其值得关注的是，虢季墓地出土的玉柄铁剑，经鉴定为目前中国发现的最早的人工冶铁制品，在古代冶金史上具有重要地位。两座国君墓、国君夫人墓及贵族夫人墓出土的大量精美玉器令人叹为观止。其独具匠心的设计、精湛的雕刻技艺以及极富韵味的色泽，使之成为中国古代小型雕刻艺术品中最具观赏性的代表作。

虢国墓地出土的玉器
Jade Artifact Unearthed from the Cemetery of the Guo State

1. Archaeological Discovery of the Guo State

In the Western Zhou Dynasty, some vassal states migrated with the change of their relations with the royal family. The excavation of the cemetery of the Guo State in Sanmenxia, Henan Province, gives testimony to the historical story of the Guo State migrating from Baoji, Shaanxi Province to Henan Province in the Western Zhou Dynasty.

The Guo State was a vassal state, with blood relations with the royal family of the Western Zhou Dynasty. In 1956, archaeologists discovered the tomb of a prince, confirming the existence of the state. In the following decades, they successively excavated 18 tombs of high-ranking noblemen, including the tombs of the kings' wives and ministers, and unearthed tens of thousands of exquisite cultural relics, physically presenting the Guo State, which existed only in historical documents, in a concrete form. The cemetery of the Guo State is 590 meters long from north to south and 55 meters wide from east to west, covering 324,500 square meters in total. The tombs are rectangular vertical earth pits, some with waist pits at the bottom, and the coffins are wooden. Funeral objects include rich and exquisite ritual vessels, tools, chariot-horse wares.

In particular, an iron sword with jade handle unearthed from the tomb of Guo Ji was identified as the earliest artificial iron product in China, which occupies an important position in the history of ancient metallurgy. Marvelous jade articles were unearthed from the tombs of two kings, the kings' wives and the noble ladies. The unique design, exquisite carving skills and extremely rich color and luster make them the most ornamental representatives of small carvings in ancient China.

虢国墓地出土的玉器

Jade Artifact Unearthed from the Cemetery of the Guo State

2. 周公营建洛阳与东周王城

周武王之后，其子周成王继位，周公辅政。周公从陕西出发赴河南东征，平定商朝遗族之乱，并营建东都洛阳。因此之故，周公被认为是洛阳城之设计者和创建者。周公在今洛阳金谷园一带所建之城号称"王城"，于洛水之北今白马寺一带所建之城称为"成周"。周平王东迁洛阳，开启东周时代，就是以王城为都城。

周王城作为春秋战国时期东周王室都城遗址，计12世历500余年。城址北依邙山，南临洛河，略呈正方形，重要遗存包括外郭城、宫殿区、仓窖区、手工业作坊区和陵墓区。宫殿群落位于城内西南隅，为两组南北毗邻的大型建筑基址。城外还发现有大型礼制或者馆驿性质的建筑遗迹。仓窖区位于宫殿区东侧，已探出粮窖等80余座，均为口大底小的圆形窖穴，口径约10米，深约10米。手工业作坊区位于城内西北隅，有制陶的窑场，还有制骨、制玉、制作石器的作坊，并发现制造铜器的陶范。东周王陵分为王城、金村、周山3个陵区。王城陵区位于城内中东部，1957年发掘的大型战国墓葬曾出土残留有墨书"天子"字迹的石圭。2002年，在城址东部的王城广场一带，发现"天子驾六"大型车马坑遗存，更印证了王城王陵区的存在。

流落海外的金村文物
Cultural Relics of Jincun Stored Abroad

2. The Construction of Luoyang and the Capital City of the Eastern Zhou Dynasty by Duke of Zhou

After the death of King Wu of the Zhou Dynasty, his son King Cheng ascended the throne, and the Duke of Zhou assisted him in governing the country. The Duke of Zhou made an eastward expedition from Shaanxi to Henan, quelling the rebellion of the descendants of the Shang Dynasty and building an east capital in Luoyang. Therefore, the Duke of Zhou is regarded as the designer and founder of Luoyang. The city that he built in the area around today's Jinguyuan of Luoyang is called "Wangcheng" (capital city), and the city he built in the area around the White Horse Temple is called "Chengzhou". King Ping of the Zhou Dynasty relocated the capital in Wangcheng, opening the era of the Eastern Zhou Dynasty.

Wangcheng used to be the capital of the Eastern Zhou Dynasty in the Spring and Autumn Period and the Warring States Period for more than 500 years, spanning 12 generations. This square city is bounded by the Mang Mountain in the north and the Luohe River in the south. Important remains of the city include the outer city, palaces, warehouses, handicraft workshops and mausoleum area. The palace section is located in the southwest corner of the city and is the site of two large buildings adjacent to each other north and south. Large ritual or inn remains were found outside the city. The warehouse section lies to the east of the palace section. More than 80 round grain cellars have been found, with big mouth and small bottom, about 10 meters in diameter and depth respectively. The handicraft section is located in the northwest corner of the city. There are remains of pottery kilns and workshops for making bone, jade and stone tools. The royal mausoleum is divided into three tomb areas: Wangcheng, Jincun and Zhoushan. The Wangcheng tombs are located in the central and eastern part of the city. A stone spade unearthed from a large Warring-States-Period tomb, excavated in 1957, carries two characters "tian zi" (son of the heaven) in black ink. In the city site, the remains of a large chariot-horse pit "tian zi jia liu" (the emperor's chariot pulled by 6 horses) were found in 2002, which gives testimony to the existence of the royal mausoleum.

经过历年考古发掘,城址内外出土了大量珍贵文物,包括错金银的鼎、敦、壶等铜礼器,错金银狩猎纹铜镜,透雕龙虎大玉璧,以及铜、银质的人物像等,均为罕见艺术珍品。

春秋战国时期,尽管诸侯称霸,王室衰微,但东周王城作为天子之都的重要意义,远非列国都城所能比拟。东周王城在几个世纪的历史时期一直是全国政治、经济、文化、交通的中心,对研究整个东周时期政治、经济、文化和城市发展史,都具有特别重要的意义。

流落海外的金村文物
Cultural Relics of Jincun Stored Abroad

Through archaeological excavations over years, a large number of precious cultural relics have been unearthed inside and outside the city site, including sacrificial bronze articles, such as tripods, grain vessels, and pots coated with gold and silver, copper mirrors with gold-silver hunting patterns, wheel jade (a round and flat piece of jade with a hole in the center) with dragon and tiger patterns, and copper-silver figures, all of which are rare works of art.

In the Spring and Autumn Period, despite the hegemony of vassals and the decline of the royal family, Wangcheng as the capital of the "son of heaven" was far more important than the capitals of other states. It was the center of politics, economy, culture and transportation of the whole kingdom for centuries, and has special value for the study of the political, economic, cultural and urban history of the whole Eastern Zhou Dynasty.

流落海外的金村文物
Cultural Relics of Jincun Stored Abroad

3. 群雄逐鹿：列国征战中原

周平王东迁之后，春秋时代开始，王室的权威不断受到诸侯的挑战，但维护王室的尊严还是整个社会的共识。这个时候，就不断有诸侯高举"尊王攘夷"的旗号，展开征伐战争。殆至战国时代，群雄在中原大地逐鹿，列国滋长问鼎中原的野心，周王室日渐衰微，最终为秦所灭，中原大地归于秦帝国的大一统江山。

东周列国在中原大地的经营与征伐，留下了无数的文物古迹。无论是残垣断壁的古城，荒草萋萋的陵墓，还是美轮美奂的青铜器、玉器和漆木器，无不彰显着这一个朝气蓬勃、骚动不安的时代，彰显着这一个英雄辈出、群星闪耀的时代。

莲鹤方壶
Lotus-crane Vessel

3. Powerful States Fighting in the Central Plains for Supremacy

The Spring and Autumn Period began after King Ping of the Zhou Dynasty relocated the capital in Luoyang. The authority of the royal family was constantly challenged by the vassals, but it was still the consensus of the whole society to maintain the dignity of the royal family. At this time, some vassals launched wars under the banner of "respecting the king and resisting foreign aggression". In the Warring States Period, the powerful states—with their ambition to control the Central Plains growing stronger—fought for supremacy in the Central Plains. The royal family declined gradually and was finally overthrown by the Qin State, which conquered the whole Central Plains.

The states of the Eastern Zhou Dynasty left countless cultural relics in the Central Plains. Whether it is a site of an old city, a mausoleum, or a piece of beautiful bronze, jade, lacquered wooden ware, it is an evidence of a vigorous and unrestful era, full of great heroes.

九鼎
Jiuding (Nine Tripods)

（1）新郑李家楼：莲鹤方壶与河南博物院的诞生

2002年，中国国家文物局发布了《首批禁止出国（境）展览文物目录》，河南新郑出土的莲鹤方壶名列其中。

莲鹤方壶有这样的特殊待遇，除了其本身所具有的艺术魅力和历史价值之外，她的传奇经历也是重要原因。这对珍贵的艺术品于1923年出土于河南省新郑市李家楼郑公大墓，同时出土的还有玉器、陶器等数百件文物，仅铜器就有102件，组合完备、器形规整、制作精美，史称"新郑彝器"。专家们认为，这批文物是郑国王室的祭祀重器，其主人可能是郑国国君。

因为这批重要文物的出土，河南省于1927年成立了河南省博物馆筹委会。1930年，李家楼出土的郑国青铜器文物成了河南省博物馆的首批"镇馆之宝"。因此可以说"先有郑公大墓，后有河南博物馆"。

1937年7月7日，"卢沟桥事变"爆发，日本发动了全面侵华战争，华北各地相继沦陷，河南省政府密令河南博物馆保护博物馆珍品。经河南省政府同意，河南博物馆精心挑选了包括"新郑彝器"在内的部分馆藏文物，分装68箱，共重30吨，紧急运往武汉，暂存在法租界。次年夏

八簋

Bagui (Eight Round Food Vessels)

(1) Lijialou in Xinzheng: Lotus-crane Vessel (Hu) and the Birth of Henan Museum

In 2002, the State Administration of Cultural Heritage of China issued *The Catalogue of the First Batch of Cultural Relics Forbidden to Be Exhibited Abroad*, and the lotus-crane vessels (a pair) unearthed in Xinzheng, Henan Province is on the list.

Its legendary experience, in addition to its own artistic charm and historical value, is what renders it this special treatment. This valuable artwork was unearthed from the mausoleum of the Duke of Zheng, Lijialou, Xinzheng, Henan Province in 1923. At the same time, hundreds of cultural relics, such as vessels and pottery, were also unearthed, including 102 beautiful bronze vessels, perfect in structure and neat in shape, known as "Xinzheng liquor vessels". Experts believe this batch of cultural relics to be important sacrificial vessels of the royal family of the Zheng State and its owner likely to be the king of the state.

Thanks to the discovery of these important cultural relics, the Preparatory Committee of Henan Museum was established in 1927. In 1930, the bronze relics of the Zheng State unearthed from Lijialou became the first batch of "Treasures of the Museum". Therefore, it is justifiable to claim that "The tomb of the Duke of Zheng gives birth to Henan Museum".

郑韩故城

The Old City of the Zheng and Han States

天，武汉突降暴雨，存放文物的库房进水，再加上日军空袭，工作人员只好把更为重要的文物存放进美国花旗银行的金库里，其中就包括莲鹤方壶。

1938年6月，武汉会战拉开序幕，武汉已不再安全。9月，河南省政府决定将暂存在武汉的这批文物运往重庆。终于，满载国之重器的轮船经历险象环生的一幕又一幕，最终抵达重庆。

1945年，抗日战争胜利结束，内战烽烟又起，河南存渝古物一直没有回归的机会。1949年11月，在重庆解放的前两日，国民政府下令把河南博物馆文物全部运往台湾，但是瞬息万变的战局打破了这个计划。最终，只有部分文物被运往台湾，另一部分包括莲鹤方壶在内的文物被留在了重庆。运到台湾的河南文物，被存放于以此为主体而成立的"国立历史博物馆"。河南博物馆南迁的馆藏文物历经传奇般的颠沛流离，从此离散海峡两岸。

1950年，河南省文物保管委员会代表会同中央文化部代表，共赴重庆，接收河南博物馆存渝古物。文化部挑取其中新郑、辉县两地出土的青铜器51件调往北京，后分别为北京故宫博物院和中国历史博物馆收

郑韩故城城墙剖面露出的夯筑痕迹：圆形夯窝
The Round Pits Left on the Rammed Walls of the Old City of the Zheng and Han States

On July 7, 1937, the Lugou Bridge Incident broke out. Japan launched an all-out war of aggression against China. With the consent of the then Henan Provincial Government, Henan Museum selected some of the cultural relics from its collection, including "Xinzheng liquor vessels", packed in 68 boxes, weighing 30 tons in total, and transported them to Wuhan for temporary storage in the city's French concession. The following summer, more important relics among them, including the lotus-crane vessels, were moved to the vault of the United States Citibank, due to the warehouse being flooded by a sudden heavy rain in Wuhan and the Japanese air raids.

In June 1938, the Battle of Wuhan began, and Wuhan was no longer a safe place. In September 1938, the Government decided to transport this batch of cultural relics temporarily stored in Wuhan to Chongqing. The ship carrying the invaluable relics finally arrived in Chongqing after going through a series of hazards.

In 1945, the Anti-Japanese War came to an end, but civil war followed and there was no opportunity for the cultural relics to return to Henan. In November 1949, two days before Chongqing was liberated, the Government of the Republic of China ordered that all the cultural relics of Henan Museum be shipped to Taiwan, but the rapidly changing situation interrupted this plan. In the end, only some of the cultural relics were shipped to Taiwan, while the others, including the lotus-crane vessels, were left behind in Chongqing. The cultural relics transported to Taiwan were stored in the National Museum of History, which was established mainly based on these relics. Since then, the cultural relics of Henan Museum have been isolated on the two sides of the Taiwan Straits, after their legendary vagrancy from place to place.

In 1950, representatives of the Henan Provincial Commission on Cultural Relics, together with representatives of the Ministry of Culture, went to Chongqing to receive these cultural relics. The Ministry of Culture chose 51 bronze articles unearthed in Xinzheng and Huixian and transported them to Beijing for collection by the Palace Museum and China History Museum respectively: including one lotus-crane vessel, which is now stored in the Palace Museum, while the other one was taken back to Henan Museum.

藏。至此，莲鹤方壶中的一件被调往北京，保存在北京故宫博物院，另外一件则被运回河南，入藏河南省博物馆。

莲鹤方壶通高117厘米，重约64公斤。壶口为长方形，长30.5厘米，宽24.9厘米。口上有盖，盖上装饰有盛开的莲瓣两层，中间站立一只仙鹤。壶颈两侧有龙形双耳，腹部装饰着蟠龙纹，四角各铸有一只神兽。圈足下有两只侧身的怪兽，承托壶身重量。其装饰艺术和铸造工艺使之成为东周时期青铜艺术品中的典范。

新郑在春秋时期是郑国的都城，战国时期又成为韩国的都城。高大的城垣依然耸立，记录着这两个东周时期的诸侯国曾经的繁荣与沧桑。历年来，考古学家们在这里发掘出土了郑国公室祭祀祖先和神灵所使用的青铜礼器，包括九鼎八簋和铜编钟，还有韩国王室埋葬国王的巨大陵墓和陪葬的车马坑，以及韩国及其以后用于军事防御和交通运输的城门设施等。这一系列的重要考古发现，把位于中原腹地的分别属于春秋和战国时期的两个诸侯国所具有的文化内涵形象地展示了出来。

（2）楚韵遗音：长台关编钟与《东方红》乐曲上太空

长台关位于信阳市北20余公里处。这里有一处南北向绵延的土岗，淮河顺土岗东侧蜿蜒北流。土岗的两侧，分别是太子城遗址和城阳城遗址。前者据传是西周大夫申伯为太子宜臼所筑，故名。后者则是战国时期楚国的重要军事要塞城阳城的旧址，据文献记载，楚曾自郢都北迁至城阳，并以此为短暂国都。两个古城均依岗傍水而建，高大的城垣依然巍巍矗立，与城圈内俯拾皆是的陶片和偶尔能捡到的蚁鼻铜钱一起，无言地诉说着曾经的繁荣与奢华。

1956年的春耕时节，河南省信阳长台关乡小刘庄村的村民们在打一口水井时偶然发现了古墓。消息不胫而走，随后赶来的考古专家们对墓葬进行了仔细发掘。这是两座战国时期的大型楚墓，是当时河南省所发掘的墓葬中，形制最大、藏品数量最多的楚国古墓葬。

发掘出土的众多陪葬品中，有一套青铜铸造的编钟，共有13枚。这

The lotus-crane vessel is 117 centimeters high and weighs 64.25 kilograms. Its mouth is rectangular, 30.5 centimeters long and 24.9 centimeters wide. The lid is decorated with two layers of blossoming lotuses, with a crane standing in the middle. The neck of the vessel has dragon-shape ears on both sides, and the belly is decorated with curled-up dragon patterns. There is a divine beast at each of the four corners. Beneath the ring foot are two monsters on their sides, supporting the weight of the vessel. Its decorative art and casting technique make it a model of bronze ware in the Eastern Zhou Dynasty.

Xinzheng was the capital of the Zheng State during the Spring and Autumn Period, and the capital of the Han State during the Warring Sates Period. The high walls still stand, recording the prosperity and vicissitudes of the two vassal states in the Eastern Zhou Dynasty. Over the years, archaeologists have unearthed sacrificial bronze vessels used for worshiping ancestors and deities, including Jiuding Bagui (nine tripods and eight round food vessels) and bronze chime bells, and excavated huge royal mausoleums, funeral chariot-horse pits, as well as city gates and other facilities used for military defense and transportation in the Han State. This series of archaeological discoveries vividly demonstrate the cultures of the two vassal states, located in the hinterland of the Central Plains, in the Spring and Autumn Period and the Warring States Period.

(2) Chime of the Chu State: Changtaiguan Chime Bell and *Dongfanghong* Music in Space

Changtaiguan is located 20 kilometers north of Xinyang, Henan. There is a hillock running from north to south, along the east of which flows the Huaihe River northwards. On both sides of the hillock are the Taizi city site and Chengyang city site. The former was allegedly built by Marquis Shenbo of the Western Zhou Dynasty for the crown prince, Yi Jiu, thus the name Taizi (crown prince) city. The latter is the site of Chengyang city—an important military fortress of the Chu State. According to documentary records, this place was the capital of the Chu State for a short time when its capital moved northward from Yingdu to Chengyang. Both the two ancient cities were built beside the hillock and the river. Their high walls (now still standing), together with the ceramic pieces that can be picked up anywhere in the sites and the ant-nose coins that can be occasionally found voicelessly tell the past prosperity and luxury of the city.

长台关七号楚墓
Chu Tomb in Changtaiguan

套编钟造型古朴,纹饰精致,从大到小,排列井然有序。出土之后,经过中央音乐学院的测音,大家惊喜地发现,这套2,000多年前的乐器依然可以演奏,而且能够演奏现代音乐!

于是,音乐家们就小心翼翼又十分精准地尝试着直接使用这套楚国贵族的编钟,演奏了一曲《东方红》,并灌制了唱片。这是当时中国家喻户晓的最有时代特色的一首音乐。1970年,中国第一颗人造地球卫星"东方红一号"飞向太空的时候,把使用这套最具有中华民族特色的乐器演奏的乐曲送上了浩渺的太空。

长台关楚墓引起社会各界极大关注的同时,自然也招引来大量不法之徒的觊觎,这里成了各地盗墓者的云集之地。到了2002年,当大家都沉浸在国庆假期的时候,长台关大墓被盗掘,必须进行抢救性发掘!

这座编号为M7的大墓平面呈"甲"字形,由长方形斜坡墓道和长方形墓室构成。墓室长13.5米,宽12.35米,最下部用方木砌成长9.2米、宽7.95米的棺室,使用木材总量接近100立方米。棺室内又被分隔

In the plowing season of the spring of 1956, some villagers of Xiaoliu Village, Changtaiguan Township, Xinyang, Henan happened to find ancient tombs when they were drilling a well. The news spread quickly, and archaeologists came immediately. A careful excavation identified the two large tombs to be ones of the Chu State: the largest in terms of size and funeral collection among all the Chu tombs then excavated in Henan Province.

Among the numerous funeral objects unearthed was a set of 13 bronze chime bells. They are simple in shape, exquisite in decoration, and arranged in the order of size. After being tested by the Central Conservatory of Music, it was found that this musical instrument made over 2000 years ago could still play modern music.

Then, the musicians tried cautiously and accurately to play on this instrument a piece of *Dongfanghong*, which was the most popular music in China at that time, and put it on record. In 1970, China's first man-made satellite *Dongfanghong* was launched into space, and along with it was the music played on the national-style instrument.

Chuangtaiguan tombs attracted great attention of the whole society, and naturally the covetous eyes of criminals. Even for a time, they became a gathering

长台关七号楚墓出土的扁壶套装
Flat Vessel Set Unearthed from No. 7 Chu Tomb in Changtaiguan

长台关七号楚墓出土的漆木豆
Musical Instrument Unearthed from No. 7 Chu Tomb in Changtaiguan

成主室、前室、左侧室、右侧室、左后室、中后室、右后室共七个互不相通的单元。各室的周壁均使用加工精良的方木,以结构复杂的榫卯扣合。这种复杂精致的木构墓葬,显然非常人所葬。

很不幸,不仅确认了两处50厘米见方的盗洞,而且发现盗洞可以通达好几个墓室。据此已可断定,该墓的主室、左侧室、中后室已被严重盗扰。在两个盗洞中先后清理出了盗墓者遗弃的铁皮水桶一个、电锯使用的小润滑油壶、编织袋等杂物若干(均已移交给当地的公安部门)。这些情况,足见当地近年来盗墓风潮之盛和此墓被盗程度之严重。

很幸运的是,在将椁室的木盖板全部吊装揭取之后,发现除被盗的棺室外,其余五个墓室中堆放着数百件各类文物,而且相当一部分保存完好!

出土文物包括青铜器、陶器和漆木器,分层放置,多达700余件。漆器尤以彩绘漆木案最为精美。其长方形的表面上通髹红漆,以此为底色,绘出黑色的规整的团花式漩涡纹样,图案富丽,色泽光艳。案的四角用铜构件加固,案下方有四个带环的青铜蹄状足。青铜器以铜酒器最

place of tomb robbers. On the National Day holiday of 2002, one tomb was robbed and thus needed a rescue excavation.

The tomb, numbered M7, is shaped like the character of "甲" and consists of a rectangular ramp and a rectangular chamber. The burial chamber is 13.5 meters long and 12.35 meters wide. At the bottom is a coffin chamber of 9.20 meters long and 7.95 meters wide, built with nearly 100 cubicmeters of square wood. The chamber is divided into seven unconnected units: main chamber, front chamber, left chamber, right chamber, left-rear chamber, middle-rear chamber, and right-rear chamber. The wall of each chamber used well processed wood, with complex mortise-tenon joint structures. This intricate and delicate wooden burial is obviously not for an ordinary person.

Unfortunately, two 50cm by 50cm burrows were found leading to several chambers. Thus, it could be assumed that the main chamber, the left chamber and the middle-rear chamber have been seriously disturbed. An iron bucket, a woven bag with a small pot of lubricating oil for chainsaws and other debris left by the robbers (all have been handed over to the local public security department) were found in the two burrows. This situation reflected how seriously tomb robbery was going on at that time when this tomb was robbed.

Fortunately, after lifting and removing the wooden cover of the outer chamber, it was found that, apart from the coffin room and the middle-rear room which had been robbed, there were hundreds of various cultural relics stacked in the other five chambers, quite a number of which were well preserved.

The unearthed cultural relics include up to 700 pieces of bronze vessels, pottery vessels and wood lacquers, all placed in layers. In particular, the painted lacquer case is exquisite, its rectangular surface coated with red paint, which was used as background against black regular round and swirling flower patterns— rich, splendid and lustrous. The four corners of the case were strengthened with copper parts, and below were four bronze hoof-shaped feet with rings. Copper liquor vessels were especially peculiar among the bronze vessels. One group is placed in a flat box with silver patterns, including a total of 28 flat plates, edge-folded plates and round boxes. The plates fit in well with the box, and most of them are rustless and shinning when unearthed. Another group in the copper box contains 40 pieces of copper plates, copper basins and ear cups, which are placed

长台关七号楚墓出土的彩绘漆木俎
Painted Lacquer Case Unearthed from No. 7 Chu Tomb in Changtaiguan

为奇特。一组盛放在一个有错银图案的扁壶内,共有平口盘、折沿盘、圆盒28件(套),盘与盒大小套合,摆放规则,且大部分未生锈,出土时依然金光灿烂。另一组是在铜盒内盛放铜盘、铜匜与耳杯,大小相错叠置,数量达40余件,同样保存完好。扁壶从腹部开合的奇特造型、内盛酒具的盛装方式,以及盛放酒具的圆盒的特殊构造,在中原地区均为首次发现。

长台关七号楚墓的抢救发掘,出土了一大批具有较高艺术价值和科学价值的珍贵文物,丰富了河南楚文化研究的内容,在某些方面还填补了考古学上的空白,是楚文化考古的一项重大发现。

in layers with alternate size, and are well preserved. The flat jar, with its peculiar shape of opening and closing from the abdomen, the way of holding liquor utensils, and the special structure of the round box for holding liquor utensils, was discovered for the first time in the Central Plains.

The rescue excavation of the No.7 Chu tomb in Changtaiguan unearthed a large number of precious cultural relics with great artistic and scientific values, which enriched the research on the Chu culture in Henan Province and in some ways filled a gap in archaeology, thus a significant discovery in the archaeology of the Chu culture.

长台关七号楚墓出土彩绘木俑
Painted Wooden Figures Unearthed from No. 7 Chu Tomb in Changtaiguan

第三章

有容乃大：中原文明的汉唐雄风

Chapter III

Diversity and Wideness: Central Plains

Civilizations in the Han and Tang Dynasties

一、汉唐时期的中原

作为中国历史上第一个一统天下的王朝，秦帝国在中原一带留下了众多的物证，现今灵宝市的函谷关遗址，就是秦国关内关外的分界线。汉取秦鼎，铸就了中原地区的又一次辉煌。凿山为陵、令人叹为观止的西汉梁王陵群，黄河岸边邙山陵上高坟大冢的东汉帝陵，遍及全省的汉代城池，不可胜数的家族墓地，见证并记录了这一辉煌的历程。而洛阳烧沟汉墓建立起来的汉墓分期标准，更成为中国考古学的研究范本。南阳、洛阳、郑州一带的汉代画像砖、画像石墓葬和壁画墓葬，使我们得以感悟汉代博大雄浑的艺术气势，得以走进汉代人上探苍穹浩渺、下察神鬼幽冥的内心世界。汉魏洛阳故城南郊发掘出的东汉皇家天文馆——灵台遗址，反映了东汉时期高度发达的天文学成就，并把张衡这位才华横溢的文学家、天文学家的形象变得更为具体生动。

魏晋北朝时期的中原，既是战火频仍之地，也是不同文化因素交融的温床。汉魏洛阳故城、龙门北魏造像等遗存，反映了这个交流融合的

芒砀山梁王墓出土四神壁画
Four-god Frescoe from King Liang Mausoleums on Mt. Mangdang

I. Central Plains Civilizations in the Han and Tang Dynasties

The Qin Dynasty, the first unified empire in the Chinese history, left many material evidences in the Central Plains. Today, Hangu Pass Site in Lingbao City is the dividing line of Qin, inside which is Guannei and outside Guanwai. The Han Dynasty is another monument in the Central Plains after the Qin Dynasty. This brilliant historic period is witnessed and recorded by majesty mausoleums of King Liang of the Western Han Dynasty built on mountains, and those of the Eastern Han Dynasty all over Mang Mountain Mausoleums on the bank of the Yellow River, the cities of the Han Dynasty all over the Central Plains, and the countless family cemeteries. The classification standards for the tombs of Han in Shaogou Village of Luoyang set a model for Chinese archaeology to study. Portrait bricks, portrait stone tombs and fresco tombs of Han in Nanyang, Luoyang and Zhengzhou show the art and majesty of Han, and the inner hearts of Han citizens in exploring the world. Lingtai Site, the Eastern Han Dynasty royal planetarium excavated in the southern suburbs of Luoyang, reflects the highly developed astronomical achievements of the Eastern Han Dynasty and makes the image of Zhang Heng, a talented writer and astronomer, more concrete and vivid.

The Central Plains in the Wei, West Jin, East Jin, Northern dynasties was not only the place of wars, but also a center of cultures which can be represented by the ancient cities of the Han and Wei dynasties and Longmen Statue of the Northern Wei in Luoyang and other sites. The sculptures unearthed from Yongning Temple are so shocking and amazing that the visitors could appreciate the charm of ethereal metaphysics and Buddhist art.

The Tang Dynasty is another monument in Chinese history, while Luoyang—as the capital—is an indelible memory of this monument, and the Luoyang city site in Sui and Tang the permanent carrier of this memory. The ancient city buildings in both Japan and Korea follow the design concept of Luoyang City in this period. The unparalleled quality and prosperity of Tang can be appreciated by Tang tri-colored pottery kiln site in Huangye Village of Gongyi City, the eastern part of Luoyang and the tri-colored pottery unearthed from

洛阳邙山东汉帝陵
Eastern Han Emperors' Mausoleums on Mt. Mang, Luoyang

过程。而北魏永宁寺塔基出土的震慑观者心灵的雕塑作品，使我们领略了空灵玄学和佛教艺术的无尽魅力。

　　大唐盛世是中国历史上的另一座丰碑，东都洛阳是这座丰碑上不可磨灭的记忆，隋唐洛阳城遗址则是这段记忆的永久载体。日本和朝鲜半岛的古代城市建设，均能看到隋唐洛阳城设计理念的印记。而位于洛阳东部的巩义黄冶唐三彩窑址以及洛阳唐代贵族墓葬出土的唐三彩，以富丽华美的艺术形式，展现了有唐一代无与伦比的气度和繁荣。举世闻名的隋唐大运河，其核心地段就在河南境内，洛阳城则是其中的重要枢

汉代画像石
Portrait Stone of the Han Dynasty

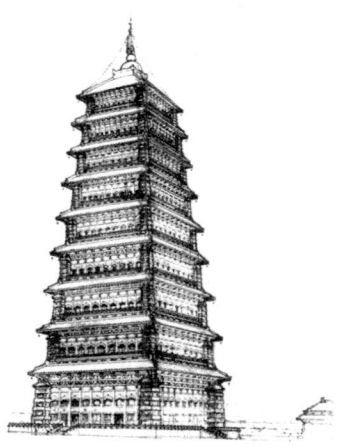

洛阳北魏永宁寺塔复原图
Restored Picture of Yongning Tower of the Northern Wei, Luoyang

the aristocrats' tombs of Tang in Luoyang. The core section of the world-famous Grand Canal in Sui and Tang lies in Henan with Luoyang City the important hub. The large-scale canal wharf ruins recently discovered and the Tang shipwreck unearthed reflect the richness and prosperity of this canal. The Golden Sheet for Elimination of Disaster and Crime which was buried by Wu Zetian unearthed from Songshan Mountain together with Locana buddha in Longmen Grottoes shows the heart and image of Wu Zetian, the only female emperor in Chinese history. Royal secrets and the struggles inside the Tang palace are buried in Tang Gongling mausoleum in Yanshi City. The gold coins and other cultural relics of the Eastern Roman Empire unearthed in Luoyang reflect the grand cultural exchanges between the East an the West in Luoyang, the capital city.

During the Sui and Tang dynasties, Luoyang was the center of foreign exchanges for China. Luoyang is the starting place for Chinese diplomatic envoys and business groups as well as the destination for the messengers, merchants, monks from the West such as Byzantine Empire, Persian Empire, Arab Empire, as well as the Korean Peninsula and the Japanese archipelagos. Luoyang is taken as the coordinate and starting point to measure and describe orientation and distance of various regions beyond the Central Plains according to the archives at that period.

纽。近年来探测出的规模巨大的运河码头遗址以及运河故道发掘出土的唐代沉船，从一些侧面描绘出运河两岸曾经的富庶和喧嚣。嵩山之巅出土的中国历史上唯一一位女皇武则天的除罪金简，与龙门石窟卢舍那大佛一起，向人们展示了一代女杰的内心世界和外在形象。偃师唐恭陵则蕴藏着唐代皇室的种种隐秘和宫闱斗争，极富传奇色彩。洛阳一带发掘出土的东罗马帝国的金币及其他文物，反映了当时洛阳作为东方大都会中外文化交流的盛况。

隋唐时期，洛阳还是中国对外交往的中枢。中国派往国外的使节以及商团都是从洛阳出发的，而来自西方的东罗马帝国、波斯、大食等国家以及朝鲜半岛和日本列岛的使者、商人和僧侣，其目的地也是洛阳。在当时的文献档案中，对中国以外各个地区方位和距离的描写与记录，也是以洛阳为坐标和起点的。

秦汉与隋唐是中国历史发展进程中的两个高峰。从前221年秦始皇统一中国到907年唐帝国灭亡，在这1,000多年间中国社会经历了从分裂到统一、再分裂再统一的轮回，实现了中原民族与周边游牧民族的深度交流与融合，统一的汉民族经历了从形成到茁壮成长的完整过程。在这一个漫长的轮回过程中，中原地区始终为中国的核心区域，因此形成了"得中原者得天下"的社会共识。

作为汉唐盛世的见证，考古发掘出土的文物，形象具体地展现出了这1,000余年间中国社会多彩多姿、多元包容的形态。这些汉唐时期的艺术品，不仅承载了当时社会的审美趣味，也记录着古老的中原大地曾经的勃勃生机和遭受的战火兵刃。

最能体现汉唐雄风的文物古迹，是今天仍然留存在中原大地上的两条线性世界文化遗产：一条是融汇东西的丝绸之路，一条是沟通南北的大运河。

Chapter III Diversity and Wideness: Central Plains Civilizations in the Han and Tang Dynasties

永宁寺出土的陶塑
Pottery Figure Unearthed in Yongning Temple

The Qin and Han dynasties and the Sui and Tang dynasties are the peak periods in Chinese history. From the unification of six states by the First-Emperor of Qin to the perdition of Tang, there is a circle of division and unification, which has promoted the deep communication and fusion between the Central Plains and the nomads as well as the form and development of the unified Han nation. In this circle the Central Plains took the core place, so there is a common sense that the ruler of the Central Plains dominants China.

Cultural relics unearthed by the archaeological excavations as evidence of the great Han and Tang represent the multi-dimensional and multi-inclusive Chinese society in the past 1,000 years. These works of art in this period not only carried the aesthetic taste of the society, but also recorded both the vitality and the wars of the ancient Central Plains.

The cultural relics and sites distinguished in Han and Tang are two linear world cultural heritages still in the Central Plains today: the Silk Road linking the East with the West, and the Grand Canal linking the north with the south.

二、融汇东西：丝绸之路的东方起点

1. 丝绸之路概念的变迁与中原地位的确立

1877年，德国著名的地理、地质科学家和探险家费迪南·冯·李希霍芬（1833—1905年）开始出版他在中国进行地理、地质考察的专著。这部名为《中国》的专著，历时35年才出版完毕。在此书中，李希霍芬发明了"丝绸之路"一词，首次把汉代中国和中亚南部、西部以及印度之间的丝绸贸易为主的交通路线，称作"丝绸之路"，后来进一步指称古代横贯亚洲大陆并沟通地中海沿岸的交通线路。此后，这个名称开始在学术界广为使用并沿用至今。

李希霍芬之后，德国历史学家赫尔曼根据新发现的文物考古资料，进一步把丝绸之路向西延伸到地中海西岸和小亚细亚，确定了丝绸之路的基本内涵，即它是中国古代经由中亚通往南亚、西亚以及欧洲、北非

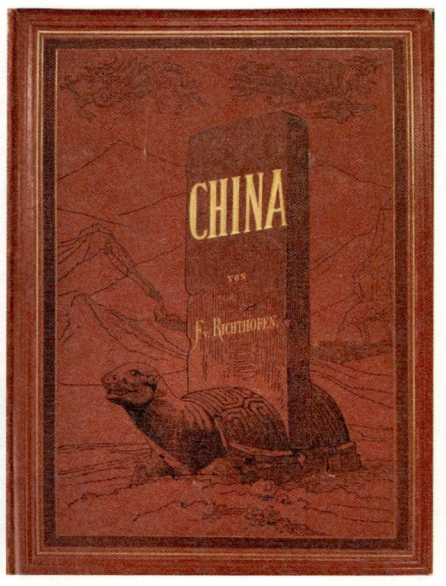

德国地理、地质科学家和探险家费迪南·冯·李希霍芬及他的专著：《中国》
German Geologist and Explorer Ferdinand von Richthofen and His Treatise *China*

II. Linking the West with the East: The Eastern Starting Point of the Silk Road

1. The Changes of the Concept of the Silk Road and the Establishment of the Status of the Central Plains

In 1877, Ferdinand von Richthofen (1833–1905), the famous German geographer, geoscientist and explorer, began publishing his monograph on geographic and geological surveys in China. After 35 years the monograph *China* was completely published. In this book, Richthofen coined the term "Silk Road" to name the silk trade routes linking the ancient societies of China in the Han Dynasty, Central Asia, Western Asia and India. Hereinafter "Silk Road" further referred to transport routes across the Asian continent and reaching the Mediterranean coast. Since then this term has been in use.

According to newly discovered cultural relics and archaeological materials, A. Herrmann, a German historian, extended the Silk Road westward to the western coast of the Mediterranean Sea and Minor Asia, which describes its basic definition that it is the land route from ancient China through Central Asia to Southern Asia, Western Asia, Europe and North Africa.

In August 2006, the World Heritage Centre of United Nations Educational, Scientific and Cultural Organization defined in *Turpan Preliminary Action Plan for the Silk Road as the World Heritage in Trans-country Application* the Silk Road as follows: Silk Road is an interconnected web of trade and cultural communication routes linking the ancient societies of Asia and Europe. It holds a long history, abundant culture, and outstanding value in the world. It starts from 2 B.C. when Zhang Qian started to the Western Regions in the Han to 18 A.D., the middle period of the Qing Dynasty. Starting in Chang'an (now Xi'an) on the Loess Plateau (Luoyang in Northern Han), the Silk Road passed westwards through the Hosi Corridor across Dunhuang, then in Xinjiang separately divided into the northern branch, the central and the southern, finally through Ili and Kashgar in Xinjiang reached Central Asia.

The fact that Richthofen extended the Silk Road in both time and space

的陆上贸易交往通道。

2006年8月,联合国教科文组织世界遗产中心在《丝绸之路跨国联合申遗吐鲁番初步行动计划》中,专门对"丝绸之路"进行了这样的定义与定性:丝绸之路作为横跨亚欧大陆的商旅之路和文化交流之路,具有悠久的历史,丰富的文化内涵,拥有显著的全球突出的普遍价值。丝绸之路中国段沙漠路线始于中国汉代的张骞出使西域(前2世纪),止于清朝中期(18世纪),主要线路分作三道,从长安(今西安)或洛阳出发,向西经河西走廊、敦煌,在新疆界内分为北、中、南路,最终分别从新疆的阿力麻里(今伊犁)和喀什噶尔(今喀什)通向中亚。

这样,无论是在时间还是空间上,基本认可了学者们对李希霍芬丝绸之路概念内涵的拓展,并进一步把东段的时空概念明确化,李希霍芬和赫尔曼定义的"西汉时期的长安"这个丝绸之路的东方起点,被延展为"汉唐时期的两京"。也就是说,西汉之后,随着政治和经济中心的转移,洛阳一度成为中西文化交流的中心,丝绸之路也因此向东方延伸了。

自汉武帝派张骞出使西域、凿通中西交通以后,连接中国与西域的丝绸之路正式开通,西汉首都长安因此成为初期丝绸之路的东方起点。西汉王朝覆亡后,汉光武帝刘秀定都洛阳,在西汉时期时有兴废的丝绸之路随着新兴政权的巩固和国力的恢复又开始重现生机。而至汉明帝时期,班超出使西域,东汉政府随后在西域设置西域都护府等行政管理机构,国都洛阳随之成为中国大一统封建国家的政治、经济和文化中心,因此也成为东西方文化交流、商业贸易、对外联系、内外交通等方面的中心。丝绸之路的东方起点,自然而然地从西汉国都长安转移到了东汉都城洛阳。

自此以降,曹魏、西晋、北魏、后唐等政权先后定都洛阳,隋唐时期也把洛阳作为东都,因此在这1,000余年的时间里,洛阳俨然成为中原王朝与西域诸国商业和文化交流的决策中枢与实施起点。丝绸之路也

and the eastern section clarified had been accepted. The viewpoint proposed by Richthofen and Herrmann that Chang'an in the Western Han Dynasty was the eastern starting point of the Silk Road had been transformed into that both Chang'an and Luoyang in the Han and Tang dynasties were the eastern starting point of the Silk Road. That is to say, with the transfer of political and economical center, Luoyang was considered the center for interchange between the East and the West, so the Silk Road extended towards the East.

Since Emperor Wu of the Western Han Dynasty ordered Zhangqian to the Western Regions and farfetched the Central Plains to the West, the Silk Road linking China and the Western Regions had formerly been built, and Chang'an as the capital of Western Han was its eastern starting point . After the fall of Western Han, Liu Xiu, Emperor Guangwu of Eastern Han built the capital in Luoyang, so the Silk Road regained its vitality after glories and abandonments in Western Han. Until Emperor Ming's reign period, Ban Chao visited the Western Regions where the Central Government set up administrative institutions such as General Protection Prefecture Institution. Luoyang the capital became the political, economic and cultural center of Chinese unified feudal kingdom at that period. It also became the center of cultural exchanges, commercial trades, links and transportations between the East and the West. The eastern starting point of the Silk Road was transferred from Chang'an the capital of Western Han into Luoyang the capital of Eastern Han.

Since then, the Cao Wei, Western Jin, Northern Wei, Later Tang dynasties and other regimes have successively settled their capitals in Luoyang, as had been previously established in the Sui and Tang periods. In more than 1,000 years, Luoyang had become a strategic center, as well as the starting spot of commercial and cultural exchanges between the central dynasties and the Western Regions. The Silk Road was extended with Luoyang and, so the exchanges between the East and the West were extended and deepened.

After the establishment of the Sui Dynasty, Emperor Suiyang named Luoyang as Dongjing in 604 A.D. and began to build Dongjing. Two years later, Dongjing was built well after Emperor Suiyang visited and stayed there. In 618, Tang was established with Chang'an as its capital. Emperor Gaozong renamed Luoyang as Dongdu where he lived most of his life. In the first year of Tianshou

因洛阳的存在而得以延长，交流的内容也更加广泛和深入。

隋王朝建立之后，隋炀帝于604年改洛阳为东京，开始营建洛阳，两年后东京建成，隋炀帝于当年浩浩荡荡驻跸巡视。618年唐王朝建立，定都长安，唐高宗改洛阳为东都，且大部分时间住在洛阳。天授元年（690年），武则天称帝，成为中国历史上唯一的女皇帝，她把国号改为周，把首都定在洛阳，并改名为神都。从唐高宗到武则天，洛阳取代长安，成为中国的政治、经济、文化中心，洛阳的城市建设迎来一个新的高潮，洛阳的政治地位也达到了空前的高度。洛阳作为丝绸之路东方起点的角色，这一时期表现得最为充分。

reign period (690 A.D.), Wu Zetian became the only empress in Chinese history. She changed the national name into Zhou, and set the capital in Luoyang and renamed it Shendu. From Emperor Gaozong to Wu Zetian, Luoyang, instead of Chang'an became the political, economic and cultural center of China. Luoyang's urban constructions ushered in a new climax, and its political status also reached an unprecedented heights. As the eastern starting point of the Silk Road, Luoyang has played its role very well in this period.

2. 纷纷扰扰的事与来来往往的人

汉唐时期，在这条沟通中原与外部世界的丝绸之路上，纷纷扰扰地发生了一系列大事件，来来往往地出现了一个个大人物。这些事件和人物，都不同程度地影响到了当时和后世，有些在世界历史发展进程中都起到了重要作用。

（1）政治事件与官方使节

中原王朝与西方世界开始直接交往的政治事件，以派出使节出使为标志，而其中最为著名的，莫过于张骞和班超的出使西域。前者凿通，后者经略，在两汉时期开拓西域、放眼西方的过程中具有里程碑的意义。

班超于汉明帝永平十六年（73年）出使西域，降服鄯善、于阗等国，"于阗诸国皆遣子入侍。西域自绝六十五载，乃复通焉"（《后汉书·西域传》）。次年，汉政府在西域设置西域都护府，直接行使行政管理职权。明帝驾崩后，班超受到疏勒诸国的挽留，留在西域，重新稳定了西域局势。永元六年（94年），"西域都护班超大破焉耆、尉犁，斩其王。自是西域降服，纳质者五十余国"（《后汉书·孝和孝殇帝纪第四》）。

《后汉书·西域传》记载，"永元九年（97年），都护班超派遣副使甘英出使大秦（罗马帝国），抵条支（今波斯湾一带）。临大海欲渡"，安息人（今伊朗高原一带）为垄断丝路贸易，以海事凶险、航路遥远等理由劝阻了他。中原王朝和罗马帝国的直接交往因此失之交臂。但是，班超、甘英等人"抵条支而历安息，临西海以望大秦"，"皆前世所不至，《山经》所未详，莫不备其风土，传其珍怪焉。于是远国蒙奇、兜勒皆来归服，遣使贡献"，对于汉王朝经略西域、放眼西方的意义自不待言。

2. Events and Bigwigs

During the Han and Tang dynasties, the Silk Road linked the Central Plains with the outside world and witnessed a series of great events and famous bigwigs who influenced the present and the future in different degrees, some of them even playing important roles in the development of the world history.

(1) Political Events and Official Diplomatic Envoys

The political events happened between the central dynasties and the Western Regions with the dispatch of diplomatic envoys as the mark. The most famous were Zhang Qian and Ban Chao who visited the West successively. The former farfecthed ways linking the East and the West, and the later designed the communication plans, both of which are taken as milestones in exploring the Western Regions and communicating with the West in both Western and Eastern Han.

In the 16th year of Emperor Ming's Yongping reign period of Han, Ban Chao visited the Western Regions, and surrendered Kroraina and Ku-stana to Han. The western states such as Ku-stana sent their princesses to Han for the resuming of communications with the Central Plains after the Western Regions had stopped it for sixty-five years. This event was recorded in "The Western Regions Legend" of *The History of the Later Han Dynasty*. In the following year, Han government set up General Protection Institution for the Western Regions to directly exercise administrative powers. After Emperor Ming died, Ban Chao was retained by Shulik and other states and stayed in the Western Regions, restabilizing the situation in the Western Regions. In the sixth year of Yongyuan (94 A.D.), Protection General Ban Chao destroyed the Qarasahr and Yuli states, and killed their kings. Since then the Western Regions surrendered to the Han Dynasty, and about 50 western states sent hostages to Han. This event was recorded in "The Emperor Xiaohe Legend" of *The History of the Later Han Dynasty*.

According to "The Western Regions Legend" in *The History of the Later Han Dynasty*, in the ninth year of Yongyuan reign period (97 A.D.), Ban Chao dispatched deputy Gan Ying on a mission to Cippus which covered Roman Empire, and reached ndiochia (now the Persian Gulf area). They reached the sea and planned to take a boat. Emperâturi Ashkâniân inhabitants (they lived in

归义胡王金印
Gold Seal for King of Justice

安菩墓出土的罗马金币
Roman Golden Coin Unearthed from An Pu's Tomb

永元十二年（100年），班超因年老思乡，上书请求汉和帝准许其卸任并回到中原。班超于永元十四年（102年）离开西域，回到洛阳，拜官射声校尉。一个月后即病逝。归葬洛阳邙山。今洛阳邙山岭上，班超墓封土依然高耸。

汉唐之际，有一些来自西域各部的上层人士归降中原王朝，或者直接在中原政府为官。中原王朝对待这类人物有相当的礼遇，待遇十分优渥。曹魏时，天山北路的车师后部王亦内属，"魏赐其王壹多杂守魏侍中，号大都尉，受魏王印"（徐松《汉书·西域传补注·卷下》）。洛阳博物馆收藏的一枚"归义胡王金印"属于西晋时期，说明在西晋时期沿袭了汉代以来优待归降的西域上层人士的做法——归义胡王是西晋时期对归化中原的匈奴部落首领的封号。

归义中原的西域上层在隋唐时期依然活跃。1981年，在洛阳龙门附近发掘了一座唐墓，出土文物共129件，既有中原的唐三彩，也有来自罗马的金币，为人们了解唐朝的政治、经济、文化、历史、生活等诸多方面都提供了珍贵的资料。根据墓志记载，墓主人安菩是西域昭武九姓中的安国人（今乌兹别克斯坦共和国之布哈拉），其先人为安国大首领，破匈奴后归中国。678年，唐高宗置安息州，任命安国国王为刺

the Iranian plateau) wanted to have the monopoly on the Silk Road trade, and discouraged Gan Ying from marching as maritime sinister dangers and distant routes. The direct communications between the central dynasties and the Roman Empire were therefore disbanded. However, Ban Chao, Gan Ying and other people travelled in ndiochia and Emperâturi Ashkânian, and reached mtshosngon (Qinghai Lake in English) to look forward to Cippus . Those areas they travelled were untouched before, and never described in detail in *Shanjing*. They experienced the local customs and habits, and carried back the local rare things and legendaries.

In the 12th year of Yongyuan reign period (100 A.D.), old and homesick, Ban Chao requested the permission of Emperor He to retire and return to the Central Plains. Ban Chao left the Western Regions in the 14th year of Yongyuan reign period (102 A.D.) and returned to Luoyang as Archery Commandant. A month later he died, and was buried in Mang Mountain, Luoyang where until now Ban Chao's Tomb has been still towering.

In the Han and Tang dynasties, some upper-level people from the Western Regions surrendered to the Central Plains, or directly took the official posts in central Chinese government. In the Wei Dynasty, Yi Duoza, the king of the Hou Jushi state in the northern flank of Tian Mountain surrendered their kingdom to the central government, and "was appointed as high minister, named as Commander in Chief, and granted Seal from the Emperor of Wei" (according

安菩墓出土的唐三彩盘
Tang Tri-colored Plate Unearthed from An Pu's Tomb

安菩墓出土的唐三彩胡人俑
Western Man Figure Glazed in Tang Tri-colors in An Pu's Tomb

安菩墓出土的唐三彩罐
Tang Tri-colored Pot Unearthed from An Pu's Tomb

史。安菩承袭了父亲的封号，为安国首领、定远将军。664年，安菩在长安去世，最初被安葬在长安。时隔40年，他的妻子何氏（西域人）在东都洛阳病逝。其独生子安金藏于唐景龙三年（709年）把安菩的尸骨迁到洛阳与母亲合葬。

（2）文化交流与文化使者

汉明帝永平七年（64年），皇帝做了一个奇怪的梦，梦见了一个从西方而来的身材高大的金人，在皇宫大殿里飞绕。汉明帝诏大臣问询，有人说是西方有神，其名曰佛。于是汉明帝派遣蔡愔等人沿着丝绸之路出使西域，拜佛求法，这就是佛教史上著名的"永平求法"。蔡愔等人到达了大月氏（今阿富汗阿伊哈努姆古城），见到了印度高僧摄摩腾和竺法兰，于是就邀请两位高僧到洛阳，传教弘法。两位高僧欣然前往，以白马驮经，来到洛阳，住在汉明帝专为他们安排的住所——白马寺，在此翻译出中国第一部汉文佛经《四十二章经》和其他许多汉译佛经，

to "Complementary Explanations for the Western Regions Legends" of *The History of the Han Dynasty*, Volume2, by Xu Song). Among collections in Luoyang Museum "Golden Seal for King of Justice" from the Western Jin Dynasty proved the customs inherited from Han to give surrendering kings of the Western Regions both the preferential treatments and the title of "King of Justice"—That is to say, the kings of the Western Regions surrendered to the Central Dynasty, which meant they chose justice.

The leaders and officials of the Western Regions surrendering to the Central Plains were still active during the Sui and Tang dynasties. In 1981, a Tang tomb was discovered near Longmen, Luoyang, where a total of 129 pieces of cultural relics were unearthed, including Tang tri-colored potteries of the Central Plains and golden coins from Roma, which provided valuable materials to people who are interested in the political, economic, cultural history and life of Tang. According to its epitaph, the owner of the tomb, An Pu, came from the An state, one of the nine states with Zhaowu as their surname (now Bukhara of the Republic of Uzbekistan). His ancestors, the kings of this state returned to China after being defeated. In 678 A.D., Emperor Gaozong named the An state Anxi county and appointed the king of the An state as governor of this county. An Pu inherited his father's title, as governor of the An state and Dingyuan General. In 664 A.D., An Pu died in Chang'an and was buried there. After 40 years, his wife with family name of He (a western woman) died in Luoyang. His only son, An Jincang in the third year of Jing Long reign period of the Tang Dynasty moved the bones of An Pu to Luoyang and buried An Pu with his wife.

(2) Cultural Exchanges and Cultural Messengers

In the seventh year of Emperor Ming's Yongping reign period in the Han Dynasty (64 A.D.), the emperor made a strange dream of a tall western man from the West flying around the palace hall. He asked the ministers about this dream. Some said there was a god in name of Buddha. So he sent Cai Yin and others along the Silk Road to the Western Regions to worship the Buddha. This is the famous story of "Seeking Buddhist scripture in Yongping period ". Cai Yin and others arrived at Rouzhi (now Ayhanum, Afghanistan) and met the Indian great monks Kāśyapamātanga and Dharmaratna, so they invited the two monks to Luoyang to preach the Buddhist scriptures. The two great monks agreed, and then

白马寺
White Horse Temple

并最终卒于白马寺。至今寺内仍有二高僧墓。

除此之外,还有许多西域高僧如安息国安世高、安玄,大月氏国支娄迦谶、支曜,天竺国竺佛朔,康居国康孟祥、康巨等先后居住在洛阳,在洛阳翻译佛经,对佛学的传播做出了巨大贡献,洛阳成为译经的中心。

由此可见,通过丝绸之路,起源于印度的佛教传入中国。通过洛阳这一文化中心,佛教逐渐从中原向周边地区包括朝鲜半岛和日本列岛传播。因此,洛阳不仅成为中土佛教的中心,也是东亚佛教传播的起源地。

自孝文帝迁都洛阳,至北魏末年,全国有3万多座佛寺,僧尼2百多万,而仅洛阳一地就有佛寺1,367所。在这众多的佛寺中,就有一些为"西域胡人所立"的,如菩提寺、法云寺,"佛殿僧房,皆为胡饰",由西域传来的佛骨舍利及佛牙、经像存放在这里。大批的西域高僧来洛阳传经讲法,所谓"异国沙门,咸来辐辏,扶锡持经,适兹乐土"。宣武帝专为此所立的永明寺内就有"百国沙门三千余人。西域远者,乃至大秦国,尽天地之西垂"(《洛阳伽蓝记》)。著名高僧菩提达摩、佛陀扇多、勒那摩提、菩提流支,都曾在洛阳译经讲法。白马寺、永宁寺

they reached Luoyang with Buddhist scriptures on a white horse. The hotel where they lived was specially arranged for them by the imperatorial order. This hotel was later named as White Horse Temple. They translated Buddhist scriptures *The Forty-Two Chapters of Sutra* into Chinese which were the first Chinese Buddhist scriptures and many other Buddhist scriptures. They at last died in this temple. So their tombs were also located here.

Many western great monks lived in Luoyang such as Parthamasiris and Eva Xuan from Emperâturi Ashkâniân, and Lokakema from the Rouzhi country, Hubulan from Sindhu, Kang Mengxiang and Kang Ju from Kangju country. They translated the Buddhist scriptures and made the great contribution to the Buddhism. So Luoyang had been the center for Buddhist scriptures translation.

By the Silk Road, Buddhism originating in India was introduced to China. By the cultural center Luoyang, Buddhism gradually spread from the Central Plains to the surrounding regions including the Korean Peninsula and the Japanese archipelagos. Therefore, Luoyang not only became the center of Buddhism in the Central Plains, but also the origin of Buddhism in East Asia.

From the time when Emperor Xiaowen moved his capital to Luoyang, to the later years of the Northern Wei Dynasty, there were more than 30,000 Buddhist temples all over the country, and more than two million monks and nuns, among which 1367 Buddhist temples located in Luoyang. Some temples were built for the western people such as Bodhi Temple, Fayun Temple. "Buddha Temples are of the western style" where śarīra of Buddha bone and Buddha teeth and Buddha images from the Western Regions were stored. A large number of the western great monks came to Luoyang and spread the scriptures. In the Yongming Temple, which Emperor Xuanwu set up for this purpose, there were more than 3,000 great monks. They came from the Western Regions to Qin. (This event was recorded in *Samghārāma Legends of Luoyang*) The famous great monks Bodhidharma, Buddha Fanduo, Lena Moti and Bodhi Liuzhi ever taught scriptures in Luoyang. The White Horse Temple and Yongning Temple were so great as translation fields at that time. The famous Longmen Grottoes and Gongyi Grottoes were also excavated in the Northern Wei Dynasty.

On Dong Mountain of Longmen Grottoes lies a cave named Kanjingsi Temple built in the glorious age of Tang, where stand the Arhat group sculptures

是当时主要的大寺和译经道场。著名的龙门石窟、巩义石窟也是北魏时开始开凿的。

龙门石窟东山有一盛唐时期的洞窟——看经寺，内有一组高约2米、总长31米的罗汉群像雕刻，29尊罗汉的面部，额颊方整、眉骨突出、深目高鼻，细腻入微地传达出印度人的面相特征。因此可以认为，这是盛唐时期来东都洛阳弘法传经的天竺僧侣的真实写照。

佛教之外，摩尼教、景教、伊斯兰教等来自中亚和西方的宗教文化也相继传入中原，并在洛阳建立了各自的宗教场所。

景教是基督教(天主教会)分支宗派之一。天宝四年（745年）九月，唐玄宗下诏曰："波斯经教，出自大秦，传习而来，久行中国，爰初建寺，因以为名。将欲示人，必修其本，其两京波斯寺，宜改为大秦寺，天下诸府郡置者，亦准此。"（《唐会要》）说明唐王朝专门在长安和洛阳为景教建立了寺院。

2006年，隋唐洛阳故城出土了唐代景教经幢石刻，这是唐代景教

隋唐洛阳故城出土的唐代景教经幢
Caved Stone Pillar with the Nestorianism Scriptures Unearthed in Sui and Tang Old City, Luoyang

about 2 meters high and 31 meters long. These 29 statues are of square face and cheeks, prominent eyebrows, sunken eyes and delicate nose, like the Indian countenance. So they were thought the Indian monks who spread the Buddha scriptures in Luoyang.

Therefore, beside Buddhism, Manichaeism, Nestorian Christianity, Islam and others from the Central Asia and the West came to the Central Plains successively and built their own religious fields.

Nestorianism is one of the branches of Christianity (Catholic Church). In September, the forth year of Tianbao reign period (745 A.D.), Emperor Xuanzong of the Tang Dynasty made the imperial announcement, "Persian scripture from Cippus has been studied for years in China. At the beginning of its populace in China, temples had been built. Because we want to open it for people, we should firstly mend its scriptures. The Persian temples should be renamed as the Cippus Temples in both Chang'an and Luoyang. So do for all such temples in China". (This imperial announcement was recorded in *The Laws and Regulations of the Tang Dynasty*) The announcement showed that Nestorianism temples had been established in both Chang'an and Luoyang in Tang.

In 2006, the caved stone pillar with Nestorianism scriptures in the Tang Dynasty was discovered in the old city of the Sui and Tang dynasties, Luo Yang, which has been considered the major discovery about stone carving of Nestorianism in Tang. The octahedral stone pillar was caved with the *Cippus Nestorianism Classic Scripture* and *Stone Pillar Scripture* among which the former written by Nestorianism master in the Tang Dynasty was in fact the thesis of Chinese Christian theological ontology although it has been considered as false scripture; the later recorded the time when it was built (the ninth year of Emperor Xianzong's Yuanhe reign period 814), building process and personnel attendance which had been taken as text-proofing with Dunhuang Literatures and the valuable materials for study of Nestorianism in China, cultural exchanges between the East and the West, and the links of the Silk Road to Luoyang. On such scripture pillars both the Flying Apsaras in Buddhist and the cross in Christianity were carved indicating the harmonies between Buddhism and Christianism.

In recent years, in the Longmen Grottoes the Nestorianism Grottoes were discovered, its mouth of the rectangular cross-section, the internal space in cuboid,

石刻的重大考古发现。该经幢为八面体石柱，刻有《大秦景教宣元至本经》和《经幢记》。前者是唐朝景教大师景净所自撰，被人视为伪经，实际上是一部中国化的基督教神学本体论的论文。后者记述了立幢时间（唐宪宗元和九年）、经过、人员等。此经文可与敦煌遗书互校，为研究景教在中国的传播、中西文化的交流以及丝绸之路与洛阳的关系等提供珍贵资料。经幢上，飞天与十字架并存，很形象地昭示着佛教与基督教文化之间的交融。

近年来，龙门石窟又发现了景教窟龛群，龛口横长方形，内部空间作横长方体，龛上方上阴刻一略左倾斜的近正方形十字架，与两京所见景教碑幢上的十字架形象基本接近。十字架右侧竖向刻汉字，上方汉字，似昭武九姓之"石"，显示其主人来自中亚。龙门石窟发现的这批刻有清晰十字架图案的唐代景教瘞穴，有可能是目前所知中国最早的景教墓葬遗迹。

丝绸之路上的文化传播是双向的。正如印度高僧到中原弘法一样，中原地区也有很多僧侣和学者沿着丝绸之路西行求法并传播中原文化。其中最为著名的，就是唐代高僧玄奘法师。

玄奘法师是洛阳偃师人。他自幼出家，学识渊博，很早就是得道高僧。为探究佛教各派学说分歧，玄奘于贞观元年（627年）西行5万里，经阿富汗、乌兹别克等地，历经艰辛到达印度的佛教中心那烂陀寺。在学遍当时的大小乘学说后，玄奘于唐贞观十九年（645年）自印度归国，共带回佛舍利150粒、佛像7尊、经论657部。

玄奘对中国文化乃至世界文化所做的贡献是多方面的，其中最伟大的是他对佛学典籍的翻译。归国后的20年中，他把全部的心血和智慧奉献给了译经事业。在长安和洛阳两地，玄奘在助手们的帮助下，共译出佛教经论75部，1,335卷，每卷万字左右，合计1,335万字，占去整个唐代译经总数的一半以上，为中国历史上另外三大翻译家译经总数的一倍多，而且在质量上大大超越前人，成为翻译史上的杰出典范。

and the left-slanted square cross carved in the upper part, similar to the cross in Nestorianism monuments in both Chang'an and Luoyang. The right vertical side of the cross was engraved with Chinese characters of which the upper Chinese characters like the "Shi" of the Zhaowu nine surnames show that their masters came from the Central Asia. In Longmen Grottoes these Tang Nestorianism acupoints with a clear cross pattern may be the earliest Nestorianism tomb sites in China.

The cultural communications on the Silk Road happened to both the Central Plains and the Western Regions. Just like the Indian great monks who came to the Central Plains and spread scriptures, there are monks and scholars from the Central Plains along the Silk Road westward to seek scriptures and spread Chinese culture. The most famous of them is master Xuan Zang in the Tang Dynasty.

Master Xuan Zang was born in Yanshi, Luoyang. He was a monk since the childhood, and later named as a great monk earlier than others as he was knowledgeable. In order to explore the differences among the various Buddhism schools, Xuan Zang travelled 50,000 miles westward in the first year of the Zhenguan reign period (627 A.D.), through the hardships of the Bhagyan, Uzbek and other places in Afghanistan and reached Nālandā in India, the Buddhist center. In the 19th year of the Zhenguan reign period (645 A.D.), Xuan

榆林石窟唐僧取经壁画
Xuan Zang Acquiring Scriptures Fresco in Yulin Cave

玄奘故里
Xuan Zang's Hometown

玄奘著名的著作是《大唐西域记》，记述了其亲身经历的110个和传闻所得的28个城邦、地区、国家之概况，有疆域、气候、山川、风土、人情、语言、宗教、佛寺以及大量的历史传说、神话故事等，为研究中古时期中亚、南亚诸国的历史、地理、宗教、文化和中西交通的珍贵资料，也是研究佛教史学、佛教遗迹的重要文献。晚近以来，印度那烂陀寺的废墟、王舍城的旧址、鹿野苑古刹、阿旃陀石窟等重要考古遗址的发现和发掘，都仰赖《大唐西域记》的详尽记载，这些记载亦被历史文献和文物考古所证实。

（3）商贸活动与商人

丝绸之路上来往的各色人等中，从事商贸活动的人数最多。

汉代洛阳城外专设有"胡桃宫""蛮夷邸"，款待外来商客。北魏王朝在城南洛水与伊水间筑四夷馆，以接待和安排四方来归之少数民族和异国之人。南方吴人投国者，处金陵馆；北方来归者，处燕然馆；东方来归者，处扶桑馆；西方来附者，处崦嵫馆。归附三年以后，即赐宅

Zang returned to the Central Plains. During this period he had studied various Buddhist scriptures. He brought back 150 pieces of Buddha relics, 7 Buddha statues, and 657 Buddha scriptures. He had long engaged in Buddhist scriptures translation. Xuan Zang and his disciples translated 75 books on Buddha and 1335 volumes of Buddhist scriptures.

Xuan Zang made the great contributions to Chinese culture as well as world culture, among which the greatest is the translation of the Buddhist scriptures from the Sanskrit language to Chinese. After returning to China, he spent 20 years on Buddhist translation. In both Chang'an and Luoyang, Xuanzang, with the help of his assistants, had translated a total of 75 Buddhist scriptures and 1,335 volumes with each volume of about 10,000 words, totaling 13.35 million words, which surpassed more than half of the total translations in the Tang Dynasty, and doubled the total number of the other three distinguished translators in Chinese history. Xuan Zang's translation surpassed his predecessors in quality, so his translation was taken as the outstanding example in Chinese translation history.

Xuan Zang's famous work is *The Western Regions Legends in the Tang Dynasty* in record of 110 stories and legendaries in 28 cities, regions, states and countries, covering territories, climate, mountains and rivers, civilization, languages, religions, Buddhist temples, and a large number of historical legends and mythological stories. It is valuable to study the history, geography, religion, culture and transportation of Central and South Asian countries in the middle ages, as well as Buddhist historiography and Buddhist relics. Recently, this work provides detailed records to discover and excavate the ruins of Nalanda Mahavihara in India, the old site of Rajgir, the ancient temple in Sarnath, Ajanta Caves and other important old sites. These records have been proved to be true by historical documents, cultural relics and archaeology.

(3) Trade and Trader

Among the people from different areas on the Silk Road, traders took up the most.

Outside Luoyang City in Han, there were also "Juglans regia L. palace" and "Minority nationalities mansion" to entertain the foreign businessmen. In the Northern Wei Dynasty the Siyi hotels were built between the Luoshui River and Yishui River in the south of Luoyang to receive and accomodate people from those minority nationalities and foreign countries. The surrendering southern

隋唐洛阳城定鼎门遗址
Dingding Gate Site in the Sui and Tang Dynasties

定居于四夷里。

西域胡商东来，主要集中地还是东汉的国都洛阳。当时洛阳有三个大型的集贸市场——金市、马市、南市。市内有各种交易，经营酿酒、铜铁器、纺织品、漆器、陶器、粮食等。洛阳的经济呈现出前所未有的兴盛景象，洛阳又历来被称为"天下之中"，交通发达，因此吸引了大

隋唐洛阳城定鼎门遗址中的骆驼蹄子印痕
Camel Hoof Print in Dingding Gate Site in Luoyang in the Sui and Tang Dynasties

Wu people were always treated at the Jinling Hotel; the northern comers at the Yanran Hotel; the Eastern at the Fusang Hotel; the Western at the Yanzi Hotel. After they surrendered to the central government and spent three years in Luoyang, they would be permitted to live in the Siyi hotel by the empeors of the central government .

Traders from the Western Regions gathered in Luoyang, the capital of the Eastern Han Dynasty. At that time, there were three large-scale bazaars: the Golden market, Horse market and Southern market, where various transactions were made such as sales of alcohol, copper and iron, textiles, lacquer ware, pottery and food. The economy of Luoyang had never been more prosperous. Luoyang had always been called "the center of the world" with the developed transportation, so it attracted a large number of the Western traders.

In Luoyang during the Sui and Tang dynasties, there were large-scale markets, namely the Southern Market, Northern Market and Western Market. Among them, the Southern Market was the largest. It was the distribution center of silk, porcelain and other commodities at that time, as well as the largest commerce and trade center in the eastern areas of Hangu Pass. Silk was an important export product in Tang. The silk guilds in the Southern Market and Northern Market collected silk all over the Central Plains and sold it even to the Western Regions. The perfume was the important input to Tang. It was

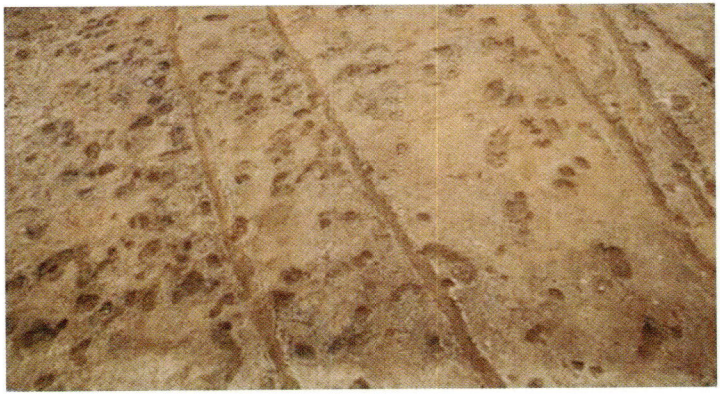

隋唐洛阳城定鼎门遗址中的人的脚印和骆驼蹄子印痕
The Western Men Footprints and Their Camels' Hoof Prints in Dingding Gate Site of Luoyang in the Sui and Tang Dynasties

龙门石窟第1,896窟北市彩帛行净土堂

Pure Earth Hall of Color Silk in the Northern Market, Cave 1, 896 in Longmen Grottoes

龙门石窟第1,504窟北市丝行题记

Inscription of Silk Guild in the Northern Market, Cave 1, 504 in Longmen Grottoes

批的西域胡人前来经商贸易。

  隋唐两代洛阳城内都建有规模庞大的市场,即南市、北市和西市。其中,南市规模最大,是当时全国丝绸、瓷器等商品的集散地,是关东最大的商业贸易中心。丝帛是唐代重要的输出品,从全国各地汇集而来的丝帛经南、北市内的丝帛行会发送到全国各地乃至西域;而香料是唐代重要的输入品,经丝绸之路从西土运到洛阳,再发送至全国各地。

  唐代墓葬出土的三彩雕塑作品中,这一题材的数量巨大,形态各异,非常形象具体地展示了唐代丝绸之路上忙碌的商人的面貌。

  在隋唐洛阳故城南部,发掘清理了一座唐睿宗时期的女性王室成员的墓葬,墓道中有两副巨大的彩绘壁画,描绘出两个高目深鼻、须发外

transported from the West to Luoyang by the Silk Road and then sold all over the country.

Among the tri-colored sculptures unearthed in the tombs of the Tang Dynasty, sculptures of trade take a large number and vary in shapes, showing merchants were busy with trade on the Silk Road in the Tang Dynasty.

In the south of the old cities of the Sui and Tang dynasties in Luoyang, the tomb of the royal female member in the Emperor Ruizong period was excavated. There are two huge painted murals of two foreigners with high bridged noses, sunken eyes, hair and beard spreading open leading camels on the ancient road. The camels are loaded with various kinds of goods on their backs such as the raw silk. Just in the site of the Dingding Gate in the Sui and Tang dynasties, not far from the tomb, human footprints and camel hoof prints were found, so the theme of foreigners with the camel on the Silk Road is confirmed by the three archaeological remains of the Tang plane paintings, three-dimensional sculptures and physical relics and vividly shows the prosperity in the Silk Road at that time.

It is particularly noteworthy that in the stone inscriptions of Longmen Grottoes, the word records of silk and perfume trade in the Tang Dynasty were retained, which specifically described the trade activities on the Silk Road among which the Chinese silk and the Central Asian perfume took the most.

唐安国相王孺人墓胡人牵驼壁画

A Wall Painting of a Western Man Leading a Camel from the Queen Tomb of the An State in the Tang Dynasty

唐三彩胡人俑　　　　　　唐三彩骆驼俑
Tang Tri-colored Western Man　　Tang Tri-colored Camel

张的胡人牵着骆驼在古道上前行的场面。骆驼背上满载着生丝等货物。恰在此墓不远的隋唐洛阳城定鼎门遗址中，有清理出来的人的脚印和骆驼蹄子印痕。这样，机缘巧合之下，胡人牵驼的丝绸之路题材通过唐代的平面绘画、立体雕塑与实物遗痕三种考古学遗存，完美地结合在一起，生动形象地展示出盛唐时期丝绸之路的繁忙景象，弥足珍贵。

特别值得注意的是，在龙门石窟的石刻题记中，保留有唐代丝绸、香料交易的文字资料，非常具体地描绘了丝绸之路上以中国丝帛、中亚香料为主要贸易内容的商贸活动。

第1,410窟（北市香行像窟）是盛唐时期开凿的一座中小型洞窟。窟西壁坛上置一佛二菩萨。北壁残存部分有一方关于此窟的题铭，系楷书，八行，行五至十七字不等，记载了永昌元年唐东都洛阳北市香行一批中外商人开凿窟龛的事迹。

第1,504窟（北市丝行像窟）位于龙门石窟西山偏南，其下即为古阳洞，亦是盛唐时期开凿的一座中小型洞窟。题铭在圆拱形窟门正中，

Cave 1,410 (perfume guild in the northern market) is a medium small-sized cave built during the glorious age of the Tang Dynasty. On the altar in the west wall of this cave are located a Buddha and two Bodhisattvas. The inscription of this cave can be found on the remains of the north wall. It is regular script, with five to seventeen characters each line, totally eight lines. It records the Chinese and foreign businessmen of perfume trade in the northern market caved the grotto in the first year of Yongchang in Luoyang.

Cave 1,504 (silk guild in the northern market) is located in the south of the west gate of the Longmen Grottoes, below which is Guyang cave, medium small-sized, built during the glorious age of the Tang Dynasty. Inscribed in the middle of the arched cave door, there are three lines of regular script, two characters in each line. In the upper north wall of its back chamber, there is one inscription of eleven lines of the regular script, ranging from three to eleven characters each line. It is known from these two inscriptions that the silk guild in the northern market was a meritorious cave made by the merchants of the silk trade in this market in Luoyang, the Tang Dynasty.

Cave 1,896 (color silk guild in the northern market) is a medium small-sized cave built in the Tang Dynasty. Inscriptions in its wall and gate prove that the cave was jointly funded to build by the merchants of the color silk and perfume trade.

The above cave inscriptions recorded the guild organizations at that time where different people took their responsibilities for guild operations with different titles such as the leader for communication and secretaries. This reflects the prosperity of the silk, silk fabrics and perfume industries. These organizations are composed of the descendants of Nine states with Zhaowu as their surname such as the An state, Kang state, He state, and other six, and the ancient Central Plains people. They engaged in trade activities as well as religious activities to promote the development of Buddhist beliefs in Longmen Grottoes. The inscriptions on the one hand reflect that there are many people who believed in Buddhism in the Western Regions and vast regions in the East, on the other hand suggest the economic and cultural communications among the ethnic groups and the Central Plains, which showed the integration among different nations.

系楷书，三行，每行两字。在后室北壁外侧上层存题记一则，也是楷书，十一行，每行三至十一字不等。从这两则题记中得知，北市丝行像窟是由唐东都洛阳北市丝行的商人所做的功德窟。

第1,896窟（北市彩帛行净土堂）是盛唐时期开凿的一座中小型洞窟。窟门及窟内有题铭，说明此窟是彩帛行和香行的商人共同出资营造的。

从以上窟铭还能了解到当时行会的组织状况，如"社官"、"录事"等职务，反映了当时丝、帛、香行业的繁荣。该组织成员中既有安、康、史、何等中亚昭武九姓的后裔，又有传统的中土人士，他们在商业贸易的同时，参与了宗教活动，推动了龙门石窟佛教信仰的发展。这说明西域和中国广大地域内信仰佛教的人很多，也反映出各民族经过经济、文化等的长期交流，呈现出民族大融合的景象。

（4）丝绸之路上的艺术家

丝路开通之后，政府间的使团往往有文艺表演者随团出访，朝贡团队也时常贡献优伶和奇技淫巧。因此，汉代以降，往来于丝绸之路上

打虎亭汉墓的角抵戏（相扑）壁画
Wrestling Portrait in Han Tomb

(4) Artists on the Silk Road

After the Silk Road was open to traffic, the central government missions often had art performers to accompany, and the tribute team from the Western Regions often contributed excellent artists and curious performances, therefore, since the Han Dynasty people from the Western Regions can be seen on the Silk Road. Some in the upper class, along with the official mission, attended the official activities, entering into the court or the official office to perform, whilst others in the middle and lower class were available to make commercial performances in officials' and rich merchants' mansions, residential areas or wine shops. Such scenes can be proved in the documents or the unearthed relics.

"The Southern Huns Legends" of *The History of the Later Han Dynasty* recorded that in the second year of Emperor Shun Han'an reign period (143 A.D.), the son of the western state in Luoyang was named as Chan Yu. On the one hand, Emperor Shun ordered escorts to send him home. On the other hand, Emperor Shun "ordered the government senior officials to gather in the outer ancestral hall of Guangyang City Gate and served them with the abundant food and acrobatics; and he came to appreciate the performances". According to " the Five Elements" of *The History of the Later Han Dynasty*, Emperor Ling liked " the suit, tent, bed, food, string instruments,

打虎亭汉墓的杂技壁画
Acrobatics Portrait of Han Tomb

的人群中，西域艺人成为一道亮丽的风景。他们中的上层，随同官方使团，配合正式活动，进入宫廷或者官署进行表演，中下层则有可能进入官员富商之家乃至里坊酒肆，进行商业性质的表演。无论是文献记载还是出土文物，都可以看到这一类群体的形象和状态。

《后汉书·南匈奴列传》记载，汉顺帝汉安二年（143年），在洛阳的匈奴国侍子被立为单于。汉顺帝一方面派人护送单于回国，一方面"诏太常、大鸿胪与诸国侍子于广阳城门外祖会，飨赐作乐，角抵百戏。顺帝幸胡桃宫临观之。"《后汉书·五行志》记载，汉灵帝更是"好胡服、胡帐、胡床、胡坐、胡饭、胡箜篌、胡笛、胡舞"，引得"京都贵戚皆竞为之"，洛阳城里一片尚胡之风。

由是，角抵百戏、乐舞杂技均成为两汉时期宫廷与豪门的娱乐观赏内容。中原地区出土的数量庞大的歌舞百戏俑中的胡人形象，其身份应

范粹墓出土的黄釉舞蹈扁壶
Yellow-glazed Dance-caved Flat Pot in Fancui Tomb

Chapter III Diversity and Wideness: Central Plains Civilizations in the Han and Tang Dynasties

汉代斗兽画像石拓片
Rubbing Picture of Fighting Beasts in Han

flute and dance of the western style ", so all the royal members followed him. The Western style was popular in Luoyang at that time.

Therefore, wrestling, acrobatics, music and dance were the entertainment contents for government officials and rich families of the Han Dynasty. The images of the western men in the vast number of acrobatic tomb figures unearthed in the Central Plains referred to the western artists in accompany with official groups. These artists not only brought exotic styles, but also spread the materialized artistic contents such as musical instruments from the Western Regions to the Central Plains, thus they were the most important messengers of cultural exchanges on the Silk Road.

During the Han and Tang dynasties, there were many rare birds and animals as the contributions of the Western Regions to the Central Plains. So were the animal trainer and the bird trainer. For example, "Biographic Sketch of Emperor Xian" from *The History of the Later Han Dynasty* recorded in the seventh year of Jian'an reign period (202 A.D.) " Ku-stana dedicated the elephant to Han". "The Western Regions Legend" from *The History of the Later Han Dynasty* described in the first year of the Emperor Zhang's Zhanghe reign period Parthian Empire asked his ambassadors to send lion and Fuba big animals, and in the thirteenth year of the Emperor He's Yongyuan reign period (101 A.D.), "the Emperor of Parthian Empire sent lions and big birds named Parthian Bird". Therefore, the western wild animal trainers in both the unearthed relics and the Han portraits can prove this exchange. The gilding elephant trainer portrait in the Eastern Han Dynasty unearthed in Yanshi, Henan is the best proof of this cultural exchange.

From Fancui Tomb of the Northern Qi Dynasty a yellow glazed dance pottery pot

该就是文献中所指称的随团来访的西域艺人。这些艺术家不但带来了风格迥异的异域风情，而且也把来自于西域的乐器等物化艺术内容传播到了中原，从而成为丝绸之路上文化交流的最重要的使者之一。

汉唐时期，西域诸国向中央王朝的进贡中，有很多珍禽异兽。随之而来的，则是驯兽人和驯鸟人。如《后汉书·献帝纪》记载建安七年（202年）"于阗国献驯象"。《后汉书·西域传》记载章帝章和元年（87年），安息国"遣使献师子、符拔"，和帝永元十三年（101年），"安息王满屈复献师子及条支大鸟，时谓之安息雀"。因此，出土文物以及汉代画像中的胡人驯兽造型，无疑应该属于这种性质。河南偃师寇店东汉窖藏出土的鎏金驯象俑，是这一文化交流现象最好的诠释。

安阳北齐范粹墓曾出土一件黄釉舞乐陶扁壶，扁壶形状类似西域皮囊壶，在壶腹两面，模印着源于西域游牧民族的胡腾舞图案。同一种造型、类似题材装饰的陶扁壶，在洛阳、宁夏等地也有出土，反映出胡腾舞这一类西域乐舞在丝绸之路沿线已经非常流行。

隋唐时期，这种景象相较于汉魏不遑多让。史载隋唐时期宫廷中胡戏表演蔚然成风，以至于蔓延整个社会。一方面，招待西域来访的使节，中原王朝会把中土的乐舞表演作为宏大的礼仪展示出来，另一方面，来访者也同样把展示自己文化特色的艺术表演呈贡给中原宫廷。所以参加表演的，实际上涵盖了中西艺人而不仅仅局限于胡人。据此，两京地区唐墓（尤其是高等级墓葬）出土的唐三彩当中乐舞表演题材的造型，应该有相当一部分属于这种性质。

河南博物院收藏的一件唐代红陶乐舞人物印模，正面浮雕四位少数民族人物形象的舞者，他们穿着不同的民族服饰，姿态各异，或踢腿甩袖，或摆首扭胯，另外两人肩扛、手捧物品作奉献状。此件器物是反映中原与西域少数民族地区经济、文化交流的一件珍贵的实物资料。

was unearthed in Anyang. Its shape is similar to the western skin pot. On both sides of the ampullae, the man-solo-dance patterns of the nomadic people in the Western Regions were imprinted. The pottery pots of the same shape and similar theme decoration were also unearthed in Luoyang and Ningxia, reflecting that the western music and dance such as solo dance by a man were very popular on the Silk Road.

During the Sui and Tang dynasties, such phenomena were almost the same as that in both Han and Wei. Western dances and operas in the courts of Sui and Tang were so precarious, even popular all over the Central Plains. On the one hand, to entertain the western envoys, the Central Plains arranged central music and dance performances in grand ceremonies. On the other hand, the western visitors also presented the artistic performances with their cultural characteristics to the Central Plains. Therefore, performance participators actually included artists both from the Central Plains and the Western Regions. Tang Tri-Color Glazed Ceramics with the theme of music and dance unearthed from Tang tombs (especially tombs of people in high status) in both Chang'an and Luoyang show such performances.

Among Henan Museum's collections, there is the red pottery dancer script with four ethnic dancers in different ethnic costumes on the front. One kicked his legs and swayed sleeves; one shook his head and hip, and the other two put contributions on their shoulders and held things in their hands. This artifact is a physical material for the economic and cultural exchanges between the Central Plains and the Western Regions.

三、贯通南北：隋唐大运河的中枢

1. 从鸿沟到隋唐大运河：中原地区运河的营建

隋唐大运河是隋代以洛阳为中心、利用既有河道开通的，唐宋金元各代均有改建并继续利用。自北向南，大运河分为永济渠、通济渠、邗沟和江南河四大段，其中的永济渠和通济渠均以洛阳为起点并流经河南西北与东南。永济渠自洛阳偏向东北，沿太行山东麓，会沁、淇、卫诸水，北达涿郡；通济渠偏向东南，从洛阳东部在黄河南岸经开封流经豫东平原，南与邗沟、江南河相连，直达余杭。唐代中期以后，大运河的偏南一支主要运输江南来的漕粮，成为维系唐帝国命脉的交通线。

大运河在河南境内沿途所经过的地区，正是中原古代文化较为发达、文物古迹分布较为密集的区域。因此，河南地区在中国古代运河研究中所处地位之重要是毋庸赘言的。

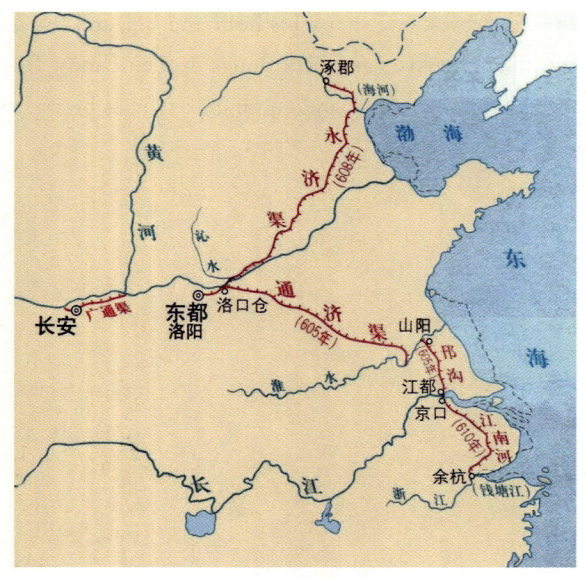

隋唐大运河示意图
Route of the Grand Canal in the Sui and Tang Dynasties

III. Linking the South and North: The Center of the Sui and Tang Grand Canal

1. From the Wild River to the Sui and Tang Grand Canal: The Construction of the Canal in the Central Plains

The Sui and Tang Grand Canal was opened with Luoyang as its center and the existing rivers as the base. This Grand Canal was rebuilt and in use successively in the Tang, Song and Jin dynasties. From the north to the south, the Grand Canal is divided into four sections: Yongji Canal, Tongji Canal, Hangou Canal and Jiangnan Canal. The first two canals started from Luoyang and flew through both of the northwest and southeast of Henan. The Yongji Canal from Luoyang toward the northeast, along the east frank of Taihang Mountains, met the Qin River, Qi River and Wei River and other rivers, and flew northward to Zhuo county; the Tongji Canal toward southeast, from the south of the Yellow River through Kaifeng and the Eastern Henan Plain, linking with the Hangou Canal and Jiangnan Canal in the south, finally reached Yuhang (now Yuhang district, Hangzhou City). After the middle of the Tang Dynasty, the southern section of the Grand Canal transported the grain from the south of the Yangtze River and became the communication line that sustained the Tang lifeline.

In Henan Province, the Grand Canal passed along the area where the ancient culture of the Central Plains developed and the cultural relics and historical sites were densely distributed. That proves the importance of Henan's position in the study of ancient Chinese canals.

In ancient China, the Central Plains, one of Chinese agricultural civilization centers, had already carried out large-scale water conservancy project constructions, including the reconstruction of natural rivers and lakes as well as excavation of the artificial lakes. In ancient China's water control history, the "River and Canal" from *The Records of the Historian* left a large amount of space to the performances of Dayu controlling the flood, many of which occurred in the Central Plains. Although many of them were legendaries, they reflected indirectly water conservancy project constructions in this period. Archaeological findings confirm that the highly developed agricultural civilization in the Central Plains

上古洪荒时期，作为中国农业文明中心之一的中原地区，即已经进行了大规模的水利工程营建，包括对自然河流湖泊的改造与人工湖的开凿。《史记·河渠书》在记述中国古代的治水历史时，用大量篇幅描绘的大禹治水的业绩，其中很多是发生在中原地区的。尽管其中很多是传说，但应该是这一时期水利工程营建的曲折反映。考古发现证实，中原地区高度发达的农业文明，使中原积累了大量营建和管理水利设施的经验。而所有这一切，均是隋唐大运河开凿与管理重要的物质与技术基础。

上古时期的一些重要的运河营建，基本可以从文物古迹和后代文献中得到不同程度的印证，其中最值得重视的，就是在中国历史上颇具影响的鸿沟。

鸿沟是中国古代最早沟通黄河和淮河的运河，有学者认为始建于春秋时期的魏惠王十年（前361年）。在秦、汉、魏晋南北朝时期，一直是黄淮间主要水运交通线路之一。

鸿沟自河南荥阳迤逦东南入淮河，连接了黄河、淮河两大水系。而黄、淮自古以来就在全国的水运系统中具有重要地位。因此，鸿沟的开凿，自应被看作中国运河营建史上具有里程碑意义的事件。隋唐大运河中的通济渠，显然就是有效利用了鸿沟的开凿、营运甚至管理的技术和经验而开通的。

学术界一般把鸿沟视为中国最古老的运河之一，加之秦汉之际著名的楚汉相争又发生在这里，鸿沟由此又承载了更多的文化史上的意义。中国象棋棋盘上对弈双方的分界线被称为楚河汉界，也是来源于此。这条目前可以确指的最早沟通黄淮的重要的运河，至少在东周时期的中原地区就已经存在了。

早在公元初年的东汉时期，政府就已经在洛阳附近完成了引洛水、谷水的水利工程，隋代开凿通济渠时引谷、洛入河的思路，应该说就是受此启发。其在短时期内完成的浩繁工程，也应该是加强了对旧有河道的有效利用，其中自然包括了两汉时期营建的水网。

had accumulated a great deal of experience in construction and management of water conservancy facilities. That is the important material and technical basis for excavation and management of the Grand Canal in the Sui and Tang dynasties.

Some important canal constructions in ancient China can basically be confirmed by cultural relics and literature. The most important thing is the influential Wild River in Chinese history.

The Wild River is the earliest canal linking the Yellow River and the Huaihe River in ancient China. The opinion has been held that this canal was built in the tenth year of King Weihui's reign period from the Spring and Autumn Period (361 B.C.). During the Qin, Han, Wei, Jin and Southern and Northern dynasties, it was one of the main water transport routes between the Yellow River and the Huaihe River.

The Wild River enters the Huaihe River from the southeast of Xingyang, Henan Province, connecting the Yellow River and the Huaihe Rivers. Since the ancient times, the two rivers have played an important role in the national water transport systems. Therefore, the excavation of the Wild River should be regarded as a landmark event in the history of the Chinese canal constructions. The Tongji Canal in the Sui and Tang Grand Canal was opened by the effective use, management, technology and experience of the Wild River.

Generally the Wild River is academically regarded as the oldest canal in China. In addition, the famous wars between Chu and Han during the Qin and Han dynasties took place here, so the Wild River witnessed the significant cultural and historical events. The dividing line between two sides of the Chinese chess board is called the Chu River at Han border, which is also derived from these wars. This is the earliest important canal linking the Yellow River and the Huaihe River, at least in the Central Plains of the Eastern Zhou dynasties.

In the early Eastern Han Dynasty, the central government completed the water conservancy projects in the Luoshui River and Gushui River near Luoyang. It was said that this inspired the idea of diverting the Gushui River and the Luoshui River into the Tongji Canal. This voluminous project was completed in a short time and took effective use of existing waterways, including the waterways networks constructed during the Western and Eastern Han dynasties.

After Emperor Guangwu of the Eastern Han Dynasty, Emperor Ming and Emperor Shun continued to improve the artificial waterway networks near

东汉光武帝以后，汉明帝、汉顺帝等继续对洛阳附近的人工水运网络进行完善。这些续建工程，完善了京师洛阳附近的防洪设施，而且已经开始强化运河的漕运功能，为后来隋代大运河的营建打下了良好的基础。所以，唐代学者认为，汉晋时期的汴渠，就是隋代大运河中通济渠的前身。

汉魏时期在中原地区的运河开凿，一方面以黄河为中心，以使新建河道能与黄河水资源配合发挥作用，一方面则综合防灾、灌溉、漕运、军备等多种功能。因此，河南境内经考古调查和发掘出的相关文物多体现出上述特点。这些遗存主要可分为两类：一类是漕运设施，如黄河岸边的栈道、题刻等；一类是为漕运服务的相关设施，如仓储遗址等。

20世纪50年代，为配合三门峡水库的建设工程，黄河水库考古队调查、勘测了三门峡附近黄河沿岸的漕运栈道，发现了大量与汉魏时期漕运相关的史迹，包括栈道、碑记、题刻、仓储遗址等多种类型。1997年开始，为配合小浪底水利枢纽工程，河南文物部门调查、发掘了汉代至唐宋时期黄河漕运有关的遗存，为研究隋唐大运河贯通之前的中原地区漕运状况和运河建设提供了重要实物资料。较为重要的发现有新安盐东汉代仓储遗址、黄河漕运古栈道遗址等。

新安盐东汉代仓储遗址
The Eastern Han Dynasty Warehousing Site, Yandong Village, Xin'an County

Luoyang. These projects have improved the flood control facilities near Luoyang, and almost strengthened the canal's function in public grain transportation, laying a sound foundation for the construction of the Grand Canal of Sui. Therefore, some scholars of Tang believed that the Tongji Canal of the Grand Canal in the Sui Dynasty grew out of the Bian Canal in the Han and Jin dynasties.

During the Han and Wei dynasties, the canals excavated in the Central Plains took the Yellow River as theirs center on the one hand, so that the waterways newly built could cooperate with the Yellow River water resources to play their roles; on the other hand, the canals were of diverse functions such as comprehensive disaster prevention, irrigation, transportation, and military. Therefore, the above-mentioned characteristics of the canals had been proved by the archaeological investigations and cultural relics in Henan. The remains of canals can be divided into two types of facilities, one for public grain transportation, such as the plank roads and inscriptions on the banks of the Yellow River, the other in the service of public grain transportation, such as warehouse sites.

In the 1950s, in order to serve the Sanmenxia Reservoir construction, the Yellow River reservoir archaeological team investigated and surveyed the plank road for public grain transportation along the Yellow River near Sanmenxia, and found a large number of historical sites related to public grain transportation in the Han and Wei dynasties, including plank roads, tablets, inscriptions, and warehousing ruins and others. Since 1997, in order to serve the Xiaolangdi Water Control Project, Henan cultural relics departments investigated and discovered the remains of public grain transportation on the Yellow River from the Han to the Tang and Song dynasties, providing important materials for studying public grain transportation in the Central Plains and the canal constructions before the Sui and Tang Grand Canal was open. More important discoveries include the warehousing site of Eastern Han in Yandong Village of Xin'an County and the ancient plank road ruins along the Yellow River.

The warehousing site of the Eastern Han Dynasty in Yandong Village of Xin'an County was located on the Yellow River bank, near the Hangu Pass in the Han Dynasty. In the middle of the site, the base of the building with a length of 179 meters and a width of 35 meters was excavated. The stone column foundation

新安盐东汉代仓储遗址位于黄河岸边，地近汉代函谷关。在遗址中部发掘清理出长179米、宽35米的建筑基址，石质柱础保存完好，排列有序，基址四周有夯土墙。这是一处规模宏大、功能齐备的黄河漕运设施。这处仓储建筑与位于汉新安县城附近的函谷关共同构成水陆联运体系，是汉代漕运系统的重要网络。

黄河古栈道位于小浪底大坝上游，是关中地区和洛阳之间的交通要冲。在黄河两岸2,000多米长的峭壁上，发现了众多的牛鼻孔、路面、造像、题刻等重要文物，证明这段栈道形成于汉代、兴盛于三国，唐宋时期仍继续使用。实际上，这段黄河漕运遗存，与三门峡以及山西平陆、夏县、垣曲等地发现的同类遗存属同一个整体，共同反映出长安与洛阳之间、关中与关东之间漕运的具体情况，并间接提供了当时运河航运的素材，具有重要的学术价值。

曹魏正始九年题刻记述了魏国贺将军率五千人修建栈道的重要史实："贺晃领师五千人治此道，天大雨。正始九年正月造。"这处重要题记的发现，与文献中曹魏时期以军队为主开凿运河、实施漕运的记载恰相印证。

黄河古栈道遗迹
The Ancient Plank Road Built along the Yellow River Bank

was well preserved and arranged in order, and the base site was surrounded by rammed earth walls. This is a large-scale, comprehensively functional Yellow River public grain transportation facility. This warehouse building together with Hangu Pass only near Xin'an County formed water-land transportation system, which was an important network of public grain transportation system.

Located on the upper reaches of the Xiaolangdi Dam, the ancient plank road on the Yellow River is the traffic hub between central Shaanxi and Luoyang. On the 2,000-meter-long cliffs on both sides of the Yellow River, many important cultural relics such as bull nostrils, pavements, statues, and inscriptions were discovered. This proves that this plank road was built in the Han Dynasty and developed in the Three Kingdoms. It continued to be in use during the Tang and Song dynasties. In fact, the remains of public grain transportation on the Yellow River together with those found in Sanmenxia in Henan Province and Pinglu County, Xia County and Yuanqu County in Shanxi Province are in the same waterway system. They reflected the public grain transportation between Chang'an and Luoyang, central Shaanxi and eastern Shaanxi, which indirectly provided the material of the canal transportaion at that time, and enjoyed the important academic value.

Engravings of the ninth year of Zhengshi reign period of the Wei Kingdom recorded the important historical facts that General He from Wei led 5,000 workers to construct the plank road. "He Huang led 5,000 workers to reconstruct this road, and it was raining heavily. It was built in the first month of the ninth year of Zhengshi period." The discovery of this important inscription is in line with the documentary record of the canal construction mainly by the army in the Wei Kingdom and the implementation of public grain transportation.

2. 通济渠与永济渠：作为大运河枢纽的洛阳

通济渠是隋唐大运河中的核心部分，它的开通，强化了洛阳的枢纽地位。一方面，江南地区供应京师的物资经江南运河北上，要经通济渠运抵洛阳，再由洛阳经漕渠运抵长安。另一方面，涿郡等河北诸郡与长安的水上交通也必须从洛阳中转。换言之，洛阳作为大运河中通济渠与永济渠的节点，已成为大运河的枢纽，实际上也成为京师长安的门户。

从文献记载中可以看出，通济渠分二段凿成：一段自今河南洛阳西的隋帝宫殿"西苑"开始，引谷、洛二水达于黄河；一段自河南的板渚(今河南荥阳市氾水镇东北17.5公里处)，引黄河水经荥阳、开封间与汴水合流，然后东南而行，会泗水后入淮河。通济渠的这种走向，显然充分利用了汉魏以来已经开通的旧有河道，所以能在短时期内即可贯通。据《隋书》记载，隋炀帝在大业元年八月十五日即率文武百官乘龙舟巡行江都，而此时距开始开凿通济渠不过171天。

永济渠在黄河北岸，长约1,000多公里，是隋代运河系统中华北地区最重要的干渠之一。它的开凿也是利用了曹魏时期的旧渠，从而沟通了黄河与海河两大水系。与通济渠一样，永济渠也是主要分为南北二段。南段的主干在河南境内。经过唐代的维修和疏凿，永济渠南段的水面扩大到宽56.67米，深8米，保持了航道的畅通。

隋唐以后，东京汴梁成为运河航运中心的中枢。开封境内唐宋金元时期的运河遗存，如北宋州桥遗址、水门遗址、仓储遗址、汴河故道遗址等，成为研究中国运河发展史不可或缺的材料。

因此可以说，自鸿沟开通以来，中原地区的运河水利工程逐步纳入国家政权的基本政务，中央及个地方政权多设有专门机构负责营建与管理。降及秦汉，制度化的倾向更为明显，水运网络基本形成。魏晋南北朝时期，则损益有差，或踵事增华，或时有湮废。所有这一切，从对区域水网的认识、兴修运河的经验与技术、管理与修缮制度等，都为隋炀帝开通纵贯南北的大运河奠定了良好基础，隋唐大运河也由此成为古代

2. Tongji Canal and Yongji Canal: Luoyang as the Hub of the Grand Canal

The Tongji Canal is the core of the Grand Canal, which has strengthened the hub function of Luoyang. On the one hand, the supplies for capital from southern area of the Yangtze River through the canals in these areas are transported to Luoyang via the Tongji Canal, then through Luoyang and finally reached Chang'an. On the other hand, waterway transportations in counties of Hebei Province such as Zhuojun County and Chang'an also transferred from Luoyang. In other words, Luoyang as the epicenter of the Tongji and Yongji canals plays the roles of both the hub of the Grand Canal, and the gateway to Chang'an.

It can be found in literature that the Tongji Canal was divided into two sections: one from the Xiyuan Garden of the Sui Emperor's Palace in Luoyang leading the Gu River and Luo River to the Yellow River, and the other from Banzhu (17.5 kilometers northeast of Sishui Town, Xingyang County, Henan Province), leading the Yellow River water through Xingyang and Kaifeng, then together with the Bianshui River toward southeast to the Huaihe River with the Sishui River. This flow direction of the Tongji Canal clearly made full use of the old river ways opened since the Han and Wei dynasties, so it can open in a short time. According to *Sui Records,* Emperor Yang of Sui was on the 15th of the first year of Daye reign period led the civil officials and military officials to patrol Jiangdu by dragon boat after 171 days since the excavation of the Tongji Canal.

On the north bank of the Yellow River, the Yongji Canal in the length of more than 1,000 kilometers is the most important main channel in North China region of the Sui Canal System. Its excavation also utilizes the old canals of the Wei Kingdom, thus linking the Yellow River and the Haihe River. Like the Tongji Canal, Yongji Canal is also divided into two sections, the North and the South. The main section of the southern section was in Henan. The Yongji Canal was repaired and dug in the Tang Dynasty, and its southern water surface was expanded to 56.67-meter width and 8-meter depth, keeping the waterway unblocked.

After the Sui and Tang dynasties, Bianliang (now Kaifeng) as the capital became the hub of the Canal Shipping Center. Over the years, archaeological investigations, excavations and studies on the remains of canals in the Tang, Song and Jin dynasties in Kaifeng, such as the Northern Song Dynasty Bridge Site, the

中国历史乃至人类历史上最为浩大恢弘的人工水运系统之一。

随着政治经济中心的转移，大运河逐步东移，现今帆樯相望的京杭大运河在古老中原已不复存在。只有深埋地下的众多考古遗存，在默默记录着已逝的辉煌。但是，河南在中国运河史上的重要地位是有着文献和考古实物的坚实支撑的。

作为人工水利设施，运河的主要功能包括防治水患、灌溉农田、漕粮运输、军队与军需物资的交通等诸多方面。中原地区从上古时期以降，逐步将这些功能相结合，发展出了较为成熟的技术和管理制度，为隋唐大运河的开通积累了宝贵经验。

隋唐大运河自建立之日起就是以洛阳为核心的。洛阳作为当时的政治、经济、文化中心之一，承载着调度、中转南北漕运的中枢功能，同时也成为出入关中、拱卫西京长安的最重要的门户之一。隋唐洛阳城遗址中水利工程以及含嘉仓等重要遗存的发现，证实了洛阳乃至中原地区在隋唐大运河中的枢纽地位。

大运河·卫河永济渠浚县段
The Xun County Section of the Grand Canal: The Wei (Yongji) Canal

Water Gate Site, the Warehousing Site, and the Bianhe River Site, have become indispensable materials for studying the Chinese canal development history.

Therefore, it can be said that since the opening of the Wild River, the canal water conservancy projects in the Central Plains have gradually been incorporated into the basic government affairs. The central and local governments have set specialized agencies responsible for construction and management of the canals. Until the Qin and Han dynasties the institutionalization of water conservancy projects had the obvious tendency, and the waterway network was basically formed. During the Wei, Jin, and Southern and Northern dynasties, there were profits, loss, improvement and decadence in this network. All of these including regional waterway networks knowledge, the experience and technology of the canal construction, and the management and repair systems laid sound foundations for the opening of the Grand Canal by Emperor Suiyang. The Grand Canal is thus considered as the most ambitious artificial waterway transport system in human history.

With the transfer of the political and economic center, the Grand Canal had gradually moved eastward. The Beijing-Hangzhou Grand Canal has not existed in the old Central Plains. Only a large number of archaeological remains buried deeply underground silently recorded its past glory. However, the important position of Henan in Chinese canal history can be supported by the literature and archaeological objects.

As an artificial water conservancy facility, the main functions of the Canal include prevention and control of floods, irrigation of farmland, public grain transportation, transportation of military and military supplies, and many other aspects. Since the ancient times, the Central Plains had gradually combined these functions together and developed the relatively mature technologies and management systems, which accumulated valuable experience for the opening of the Sui and Tang Grand Canal.

Since the establishment of the Grand Canal of the Sui and Tang dynasties, Luoyang had been the core section. As the political, economic and cultural centers at that time, Luoyang carried the central function of north-south public grain dispatching and transshipment. Simultaneously, it also became the most important gateway to reach central Shaanxi and protect Chang'an. The key position of Luoyang and even that of the Central Plains in the Grand Canal of the Sui and Tang dynasties were confirmed by the water conservancy projects

丝绸之路融汇了东西方不同传统的文明，大运河沟通了中国南北方不同区域的物产。这两个文化和商贸交流的线性世界文化遗产，在古老的中原大地、在中华文明的腹心地带的河南交汇在一起，形成了华夏文明的十字架，这种在中国独一无二的文化现象，其实是一种历史的必然，是对古老中原在华夏文明体系乃至世界文明体系中所扮演的重要角色的肯定和彰显。

in Luoyang City site of the Sui and Tang dynasties and the important remains including Hanjia Granary that was the Tang national granary.

    The Silk Road links different traditional civilizations from the east and the west. The Grand Canal communicates products between the north and south of China. These two linear cultural heritages in the world separately play the roles of cultural and commercial exchanges. Both the Silk Road and the Grand Canal take Henan, the heart of Chinese civilization, as their important section, which is in the Central Plains and the heart of Chinese civilization. So they form a cross of Chinese civilization, which is the unique cultural phenomenon in China. This historical inevitability confirms and manifests the importance of the Central Plains in Chinese civilization even world cultural civilization.

第四章

东京梦华：中世纪的国际都会

Chapter IV

A Dream of Splendor in the Eastern Capital:

A Metropolis of the Middle Ages

960年，宋太祖赵匡胤建立了北宋王朝。北宋的都城汴京城位于今天的河南省开封市。据文献记载，汴京城人口达137万，是当时世界上最大的城市之一，即使按照今天的标准也是一个大都会。不仅如此，由于海上丝绸之路的兴盛，汴京城通过汴河等水运网络与扬州、泉州甚至广州等港口城市建立联运体系，北宋王朝的对外交流更为频繁和深入。正因如此，汴京城成为当时中外文化交流的中心。

北宋的社会生活尤其是都城汴京城的繁荣景象，可以从一幅著名的画和一本著名的书中得到非常形象的体现。

这幅画名叫《清明上河图》，画家名叫张择端。张择端是北宋时期的艺术家，他在《清明上河图》中描绘的场景，是他本人的亲历亲见，呈现给观众的，是形象具体的人物和场景。

这本书名叫《东京梦华录》，它的作者是文人孟元老。孟元老作为一位由北宋进入南宋、经历过家国之变后的文人，在晚年时对自己年少时的京都生活进行了回忆。从笔端流露出的，既有其本人的亲身经历和所见所闻，也有他本人对国破山河在的感情投入。因此，留给读者的，既有具体事件、具体人物、具体过程的描绘，也有风闻、回忆和想象的成分。

这一幅画和一本书，基本上描绘和勾勒出了北宋社会的上层生活和市井百态。

In 960 A. D., Zhao Kuangyin, Emperor Taizu, established the Northern Song Dynasty, whose capital, Bianjing, was located in today's Kaifeng, Henan Province. Records show that the population of Bianjing was as many as 1.37 million, so it was one of the biggest cities in the world at that time, and also a metropolis even by today's standards. Furthermore, thanks to the thriving Maritime Silk Road, Bianjing was engaged in a joint transport system with port cities such as Yangzhou, Quanzhou and even Guangzhou through the water transport network such as the Bian River, which enabled more frequent and deeper foreign exchanges in the Northern Song Dynasty. Therefore, Bianjing was also the center of cultural exchanges between China and foreign countries at that time.

The prosperity of the social life, especially in the Capital Bianjing in the Northern Song Dynasty, is vividly reflected in a famous painting and a famous book.

The painting is the *Landscape in the Qingming Festival along the Bian River* by Zhang Zeduan, who was an artist of the Northern Song Dynasty. The content of the painting, which presents concrete figures and scenes, reflects what he experienced and saw.

The book is entitled *A Dream of Splendor in the Eastern Capital* by Meng Yuanlao, a man of letters who witnessed the changes from the Northern Song Dynasty to the Southern Song Dynasty, and wrote the memoirs in his old days according to his life in Bianjing when he was young. The book shows both his personal experiences and his own emotions towards the Northern Song Dynasty overthrown by the minority kingdom. Therefore, it offers readers not only descriptions of specific events, persons and processes, but also hearsay, memories and imagination.

The painting and the book basically depict the upper life and the folk life in the Northern Song Dynasty.

一、张择端的《清明上河图》

北京故宫有一件闻名遐迩的镇院之宝,也是在中国妇孺皆知的传世名画,就是北宋时期宫廷画家张择端的名作《清明上河图》。

《清明上河图》宽24.8厘米、长528厘米。作品以长卷形式,采用散点透视构图法,生动记录了中国12世纪北宋都城东京的城市面貌和当时社会各阶层人民的生活状况,是北宋时期都城东京繁荣的见证,也是北宋城市经济情况的写照。在5米多长的画卷里,共绘了数量庞大的各色人物,牛、马、骡、驴等牲畜,以及车、轿、船只、桥梁、房屋、城楼等,生动形象地展现了北宋都城的市井生活,具有很高的历史价值和艺术价值。

《清明上河图》的开始部分,描绘了小溪旁边的大路上有一溜驼队远远地从东北方向汴京城走来。显然,这是来自西北乃至西域的丝绸之路上的商客。不远处紧邻大道旁,则是货码头与货运栈。货运栈四周街道四通八达,南边紧靠深水港湾,有好几艘船只停泊在港湾里依次装卸货物。再不远,又有一个客运码头,客船上的二十多人正在紧张地

《清明上河图》局部
Part of *Landscape in the Qingming Festival along the Bian River*

I. *Landscape in the Qingming Festival along the Bian River* by Zhang Zeduan

The painting *Landscape in the Qingming Festival along the Bian River* by Zhang Zeduan is one of the most valuable and well-known relics in the Forbidden City in Beijing, as well as a classic masterpiece that is well known to all the Chinese people.

In the form of a scroll, *Landscape in the Qingming Festival along the Bian River*, 24.8 cm wide and 528.7 cm long, vividly depicts the city appearance and the living conditions of the people of all walks of life in Bianjing in the 12th century of the Northern Song Dynasty through scatter-point perspective composition method. The painting reflected the prosperity in Bianjing, and also the urban economy in the Northern Song Dynasty. The scroll has included a large number of figures, livestock such as cattle, mules and donkeys, transport vehicles such as carriages, sedan-chairs, boats and ships, and buildings such as houses, bridges, and towers with their own characteristics. It presents a vivid picture of the city life in Bianjing, thus enjoying a high historic and artistic value.

At the right end of the scroll, a camel caravan on the road beside a stream, who apparently are merchants from northwest China or even the Western

《清明上河图》局部

Part of *Landscape in the Qingming Festival along the Bian River*

工作，船顶的几位船工正在收帆放桅，有的船工正在接收从虹桥上抛下的缆绳，准备把客船牵引到码头，再拴牢在岸上的栓船柱石上。舱体与舱面有封闭与阻隔，并有舱门便于客人进出，船没停稳之前舱门决不打开，安全措施相当严谨，可以断定是一艘安全性能良好的长途客船。显然，这些是通过水路来到中原的南方乃至南洋的客商和货物。汴河作为大运河的黄金水道，以及东京汴梁城作为中外商贸和文化交流中心的地位，在画面中得到了充分的体现。

Regions through the Silk Road, come to Bianjing in the distance from northeast. Not far away, beside the road is a cargo dock and several freight stations, the streets around which extend in many directions, and the south side of which is close to a deep-water harbor, where several ships are stationed to load and unload in sequence. Not far away is a passenger dock: more than 20 people on the passenger ship are busy with their work, and several boatmen on the top of the ship are taking in the sails and laying down the mast, and some boatmen are catching cables dropped from the Rainbow Bridge to pull the ship to the dock and moor it to the stone on the strand. Between the body and the wall of cabins are sealed, and there are cabin doors for passengers to come in and out, which will not open before the ship comes to a complete stop, so the ship is with tight security, and thus it can be said a long-distance passenger ship with good safety performance. Obviously, these merchants and goods from Southern China and even Southeast Asia come to the Central Plains through the waterway. That the Bian River is the golden waterway of the Grand Canal and that Bianjing is the center of Chinese and foreign exchanges on trade and culture have been fully manifested in the painting.

二、孟元老与《东京梦华录》

所有对这幅画和这本书略有涉猎的人都会说,《清明上河图》是绘图本的《东京梦华录》,而《东京梦华录》是文字版的《清明上河图》。两者分别从各自的视角和关注点,选取了北宋东京城从上层社会到普通市井生活的方方面面,立体多元地呈现出了12世纪前后一个鲜活的东方大都会的文化内涵和生活主题。比如,《东京梦华录》所记述的内容,从人物身份上看,上到帝王将相,下到贩夫走卒;从题材上看,有饮食起居和岁时节令,有歌舞曲艺和婚丧习俗;从地点上看,有皇宫官署,也有勾栏瓦肆,如此等等,恰好和《清明上河图》互为补正。由此,以东京汴梁城为代表的北宋社会的经济状况、文化生活、典章制度和民间习俗等,几乎都可以从中管窥。

孟元老在该书的开始部分就清楚地记述了汴梁的城市布局,尤其注

开封北宋天清寺塔
The Po Pagoda at the Tianqing Temple in Kaifeng, the Northern Song Dynasty

II. *A Dream of Splendor in the Eastern Capital* by Meng Yuanlao

Anyone who knows the painting, *Landscape in the Qingming Festival along the Bian River*, and the book, *A Dream of Splendor in the Eastern Capital*, would agree that the painting is the pictorial version of the book, and the book the written version of the painting. From their own perspectives and concerns, the two masterpieces select all the aspects of the upper life and the folk life in Bianjing to represent the cultural connotations and life themes of an oriental metropolis in the 10th-11th centuries in various ways. For example, the contents described in *A Dream of Splendor in the Eastern Capital* coincide with *Landscape in the Qingming Festival along the Bian River*, as seen not only in the identities of the characters ranging from the royal members and down through to the underdogs, but also in the subject matter of daily diets, festivals, songs, dances, and customs of wedding and funerals, and again in places as the royal residence, the administrative offices, and the public areas for entertainment. Therefore, the economic situation, cultural life, system of rules, and folk customs of the Northern Song Dynasty, represented by Bianjing, can all be seen from the painting and the book.

In the beginning of the book, Meng Yuanlao clearly describes the city layout, such as the outer city, the inner city, the rivers, the bridges, the distribution and location of the government office buildings inside and outside the palace, the streets and markets inside the city, shops, hotels and restaurants, paying particular attention to the rivers and the names of each bridge, from which we can learn that Bianjing had the palace walls, and the inner and outer walls, dividing the city into several districts. The palace walls were also called the imperial walls, which were 2500 meters long, with three gates in the south wall, but only one gate in the east, west and north walls respectively. Between the east gate and the west lies a street, on the south of which were the central government agencies, and on the north of which was the residing area for the emperor. Such descriptions are still precious documents for the study of the capital of the Northern Song Dynasty. Even now, the Henan Provincial Institute of Cultural Heritage and Archaeology still regards *A Dream of Splendor in the Eastern Capital* as a required reference

意河道和每座桥的桥名这样的坐标点。京城的外城、内城及河道桥梁，皇宫内外官署衙门的分布及位置，城内的街巷坊市、店铺酒楼等无所不备。据此，我们可以知道，开封有宫、里、外三道城墙，把这个城市化为若干区域。宫城即皇城，周长五里，南面三门，东、西、北三面各仅一门，东西门之间有一横街，街南为中央政府机构所在地，街北为皇帝居住生活区。这一类的记述，成为后世研究北宋都城的珍贵文献。包括今天河南省文物考古研究院对开封城的考古发掘，也把孟元老的记载作为必读书目和参考坐标。该书的历史价值由此可见一斑。

　　孟元老少时周游全国，宋徽宗崇宁二年（1103年）定居于汴京。20多年后，1127年，北方的金兵南下攻占汴京，宋徽宗、宋钦宗父子二人被一同俘虏而去，北宋王朝覆亡，史称"靖康之变"。孟元老与很多中原人士一样随朝廷南下，寓居江南日久，故国故乡之思渐浓，诚如宋人周辉《清波别志》云："绍兴初，故老闲坐，必谈京师风物。"《东京梦华录》就是在这一历史背景下，于南宋绍兴十七年（1147年）撰成问世的。书中所记内容，大多是宋徽宗崇宁到宣和年间（1102—1125年）北宋都城东京开封的情况。该书问世之后，被学术界称为北宋社会研究的百科全书。

for the archaeological excavation in Kaifeng. This is another piece of evidence that indicates the book's great historic value.

Meng Yuanlao traveled around the country in his childhood, and he settled down in Bianjing in 1103 and grew up in the capital city. Over 20 years later, in 1127, the Jin soldiers of the north sieged the city, captured Emperor Huizong and Prince Qinzong, and since then the Northern Song Dynasty was thus ended. This was called the Jingkang Incident. Meng Yuanlao, like many people in the Central Plains, fled southward with the rest of the royal family. He lived in the south for a long time, but with the passage of time, he missed the north and the old times very much, just as what his contemporary Zhou Hui described in *Qing Bo Bie Zhi (Essays in Reflection)*: "In their early life in the south, it was inevitable to mention Bianjing and the old days wherever they gathered to chat." It was under such a background that Meng Yuanlao wrote his *A Dream of Splendor in the Eastern Capital* in 1147. The book was mostly the records and reflections of Bianjing from the year of 1102 to 1125. As soon as the book was discovered, it was regarded by the scholars as an encyclopedia for social studies of the Northern Song Dynasty.

开封北宋开宝寺塔

The Iron Pagoda at the Kaibao Temple in Kaifeng, the Northern Song Dynasty

三、北宋皇陵：一个王朝的夕阳

北宋王朝的首都在开封，北宋皇室的陵园却在开封和洛阳之间的巩义。

北宋共有九个皇帝，除徽、钦二帝被金兵掳去死于五国城外，其余七个皇帝以及开国皇帝赵匡胤的父亲赵弘殷，都葬在这里。再加上皇帝的后妃和宗室亲王、王孙，还有寇准、包拯、杨六郎、赵普等功臣名将也葬于帝陵旁，这里便集中了北宋王朝皇室亲贵的陵墓近千座，总面积达156平方公里。

与众多依山而建、拾阶而上的皇室陵园迥异，北宋皇陵坐北面南，南高北低，是中国陵寝建筑史上的孤例。它南靠嵩山北坡，东依青龙山一线，南有洛河，西为伊洛平原。七帝八陵以统一的"倒悬"制式集中分布在这片丘陵地带，整体来看是东南穹之、西北垂之。加上附近分布的近千座皇族墓和文武大臣墓之围拱，构成一个规模宏大的皇陵区，其

北宋皇陵
The Imperial Mausoleums of the Northern Song Dynasty

III. The Mausoleums of the Northern Song Dynasty: The Sunset of a Dynasty

The capital of the Northern Song Dynasty was located in Kaifeng, while the imperial tombs were in Gongyi, a county between Kaifeng and Luoyang.

There were nine emperors in the Northern Song Dynasty, and except Huizong and Qinzong who were captured, seven others, together with Zhao Hongyin, father of the founding Emperor Zhao Kuangyin, were all buried in Gongyi. In addition, the emperors' concubines, princes and their descendants, important officials and generals such as Kou Zhun, Bao Zheng, Yang Liulang, and Zhao Pu, were also buried next to the imperial tombs. There are nearly 1,000 tombs of the royal family of the Northern Song Dynasty, covering an area of 156 square kilometers.

Distinguished from other imperial tombs that lay on the mountains and facing the river on the south, with descending staircases, those of the Northern Song Dynasty were the only tombs that lay with the river in the back, facing

北宋皇陵石像生

The Stone Figures in the Imperial Mausoleums of the Northern Song Dynasty

气势之恢宏，史上也绝无二例。

这种皇家墓葬建制，源自当时流行的一种堪舆学说"五音姓利"，就是把人的姓氏分为宫、商、角、徵、羽五音，再将五音分别与阴阳五行中的土、金、木、火、水对应，如此便可在地理上找到与其姓氏相应的最佳埋葬方位。北宋皇陵就是按此思想，坐北朝南，东南高，西北低，呈"倒悬"制式。

永昭陵是北宋第四代皇帝宋仁宗赵祯的陵墓，保存有完整的60件石像生，还有经过考古发掘后修复的鹊台、乳台、宫墙、阙楼的等建筑基址，这是皇陵的上宫部分。沿着东南向西北方向延伸，还建有负责陵区祭奠、保卫等管理事宜的宫殿式建筑群——下宫。

与前朝皇陵石像生种类、数目、陈放位置缺乏定制不同，北宋皇陵有严格的定制。北宋皇陵神道石像生排列的顺序及数目，加上宫城四神门外两座狮子、南神门内两位宫人、陵台前两位内侍，共计60件。此外，在神道和下宫还有4块上马石。经历千年，石像生的保存状况还算完好。

石像生们今天依然伫立在田野之上，不过田野已不再荒凉。与北宋石人石象相依偎的是巩义百姓种在田里的庄稼，石像们或立于田埂，或扎在田间，历史的苍凉感与田里庄稼绿油油的蓬勃气息混搭在一起——这就是宋太祖赵匡胤的永昌陵。

石象与驯象人在前——当年宋皇室的大驾卤簿，也就是仪仗队，打头阵的正是这安南进贡的象与象奴，披着东南亚异国风采的装饰缓缓地走在大街上，引领着豪华的皇室仪仗队伍，那情形必然相当壮观。然后是雕刻着瑞禽的石屏，此瑞禽马头、禽身、凤尾、鹰爪，是宋皇室御用匠人的创新之作，为北宋皇陵独有，更是中国皇陵中空前绝后的珍品，据说其艺术构思受到唐乾陵鸵鸟像的启迪，代表威猛、祥瑞和正义。接下来是一位名叫甪（lù）端的神兽，这种神兽可日行9,000公里，通晓四方语言，而且只陪伴明君，专为英明帝王传书护驾，所谓"如身使

the mountains. All those tomb gardens were set with the southern and eastern parts higher than the northern and western ones. They were all built with Mount Songshan in the south, Mount Qinglong in the east, the Luo River in the north and the Yiluo Plains in the west. The eight tombs, of the seven emperors and Emperor Zhao Kuangyin's father, are now still lying there neatly with the same unique unconventional style of "inversion". Together with the nearly 1000 tombs of other royal members and ministers, the whole area presents itself as a unique scene of the imperial magnificence.

The construction system of the imperial tombs was originated from a popular geomancy theory, "Wu Yin Xing Li", which divided the surnames into five tones: Gong, Shang, Jue, Zhi, and Yu, and matched them respectively with Soil, Gold, Wood, Fire, and Water in the system of the Yin-yang and Five Elements, so that the best burial-place in accordance with the surname could be found. The tomb designs of the Northern Song Dynasty followed this idea in a strict sense, which explains the reason for the unconventional style with its southeast higher than its northwest.

In the Yongzhao Ling, the tomb garden of the fourth Emperor Zhao Zhen of the Northern Song Dynasty, there are 60 complete stone figures and building bases restored after archaeological excavations, such as Quetai, Rutai, Palace Walls and Quelou, and these are the Upper Palace. The Lower Palace, a complex of buildings designed for sacrifice, management and other functions, is also seen extending from the southeast to northwest.

Different from the stone figures in the tombs of other dynasties in style, number and location, the tombs of the Northern Song Dynasty have adopted strict rules of design. There are altogether 60 stone figures, including those on the pathway to the tomb, two stone lions, two stone maids, and two stone eunuchs. In addition, there are four pieces of stepping stones on the tomb pathway in the Lower Palace. After nearly a thousand years, the stone figures are still fairly well preserved.

Today, the stone figures are standing on the fields with the crops planted by local farmers. The desolation of history is mixed with the flourishing atmosphere of the green crops, and this is the Yongchang Ling of the founding Emperor Zhao Kuangyin.

In front of the stone figures stands a stone elephant and its trainer from

永定陵神道及西侧石刻
The Holy Pathway in the Yongding Ling and the Stone Figures on Its West

臂，如臂使指"。仪仗中的马与控马官后面跟着威风的石虎和安顺的石羊。

　　石像生队伍中最有特色的是客使，即外国使节，宋以前的帝王陵石像生中，设客使并不是定制，但北宋开始制度化了。永昌陵的客使身材矮小、面目严肃、戴头盔、蓄长须，显然不是汉人打扮，双手托一圆盘，盘中盛一方形物，应该是进贡之宝物。专家研究认为，宋陵客使手中所托的宝物相当稀有珍贵。还有客使手托宝瓶的，瓶乃七宝金瓶或者琉璃瓶，瓶中装的是蔷薇水，就是阿拉伯玫瑰香水。中国自古薰香多用香丸、香饼、香膏，这种蒸馏制成的香水在宋时可是极为奢侈的消费品。此外还有贡珊瑚的、奉犀角的，四夷来朝的大宋天朝气象在客使石像上可见一斑。宋代以后，随着中国南方的进一步开发和经济重心的南移，从广州、泉州、杭州等地出发的海上航路日益发达，航线已然从南洋、阿拉伯海，发展到非洲东海岸，政府还在沿海各地设立市舶司专门管理海外贸易，这条海上丝绸之路的繁荣发展当

永泰陵石像生
The Stone Figure in the Yongtai Mausoleum

Annam as tributes, both dressed in exotic Southeast Asian style. They seemed to be leading a grand team of the imperial honor guards. It must be a very grand and spectacular scene on the street. Behind them was a stone screen engraved with an auspicious lucky bird with a horse head, a poultry body, a phoenix tail and eagle claws, which was a unique innovation of the royal craftsmen in the Northern Song Dynasty, representing fierceness, auspiciousness and justice. This is a rare and unprecedented treasure excavated in the Chinese tombs. It was said that the creation of the lucky bird was inspired by the ostrich in the Qianling tomb of the Tang Dynasty. Behind the stone screen was a holy beast called Luduan, who could travel 9,000 km a day and speak all languages. It was said that the holy beast would accompany and protect, and serve only the wise and enlightened emperor. This is the image of a perfect companionship. Following the stone horse and the horseman in the guard of honor was an imposing stone tiger and an obedient stone sheep.

The most striking stone figure is that of the foreign envoys. Before the Song Dynasty, such a stone figure was not custom-made; it was a tribute, instead. But

然带动了北宋的对外交流。

　　从东京汴梁城的繁华喧嚣，到巩义宋陵的日暮安静，北宋王朝完成了一个历史的轮回和王朝的更替，也给中原古代典章礼仪和艺术创作注入了新的内容。无论是汴河巍峨的虹桥，还是宋陵里孤独的翁仲，都是北宋这个富有人文气息的王朝故事的讲述者。北宋王朝的夕阳，也在黄河岸边皇家陵园的围墙下，沉沉落下。

since the Northern Song Dynasty, customized stone foreign envoy figures have begun to be made as a regular practice. The stone foreign envoys in the Yongchang Ling, the tomb of the founding Emperor Zhao Kuangyin, were short and serious-looking. They wore helmets and long hairs, which were not of the Han style. They held a plate with both hands, on which lay a square object, which, according to experts, must be a precious treasure of tribute. Some stone envoys held precious bottles in their hands, which are believed to be colorful gold bottles or glass bottles, which must be filled with the Arabian rose perfume. Since ancient times, the Chinese have been using the incense pills, cakes and cream, and the perfume, made through distillation, was a rare luxury in the Song Dynasty. In addition, articles of tribute such as coral and rhinoceros horns could also be seen on the stone envoy figures. After the Song Dynasty, the center of the Chinese economy started to shift to the south, and the sea routes began to flourish, extending from cities such as Guangzhou, Quanzhou, and Hangzhou to the Southeast Asia, the Arabian Sea, and the east coast of Africa. The imperial government also established the Customs in coastal areas to manage overseas trade. It was certain that such a thriving Maritime Silk Road promoted the exchanges with foreign countries in the Northern Song Dynasty.

From the bustling capital of Bianjing to the quiet imperial tombs of the Northern Song Dynasty in Gongyi, the Northern Song Dynasty completed a historical cycle and witnessed a change of dynasties. It also injected new contents into the ancient regulations and rituals and artistic creations in the Central Plains. Both the lofty Rainbow Bridge over the Bian River and the lonely stone figures in the tomb gardens are the narrators of the stories of the Northern Song Dynasty, which seem to be of cultural essence. The sun of the Northern Song Dynasty also sets behind the walls of the tombs on the banks of the Yellow River.

第五章

巧夺天工：河南古陶瓷的技术和艺术成就

Chapter V

Exquisite Workmanship: The Technical and

Artistic Achievements of Ancient Pottery and

Porcelain in Henan Province

一、瓷器摇篮：古朴浑厚的河南夏商周原始瓷器

中国是瓷器的故乡，瓷器是中国的国粹。而古老的中原，就是中国瓷器的摇篮。

早在20世纪中期，郑州商城遗址中就出土了质地坚硬、外表有一层青色薄釉的器物，当时学术界普遍称之为"釉陶"。但研究者认为，这种的所谓"釉陶"已经具备了瓷器的基本特质，可以称为原始瓷器，是中国乃至世界上已知的最早的瓷器之一，中国瓷器的起源也因此应可上溯至商代。这一发现和研究成果可谓石破天惊，并逐渐为陶瓷考古界普遍接受，具有超凡发立的意义。近年来，郑州小双桥商代遗址、鹿邑长子口商末周初大墓、洛阳庞家沟西周墓、北窑西周墓等一批商周原始青瓷器的出土，提供了更新、更丰富的资料，也为中国早期瓷器更深入的研究创造了条件。

殆至2002年，在河南偃师二里头遗址的贵族墓葬中，出土了原始青瓷，属于盉的口沿部位，表面有一层薄薄的青绿色釉，根据科学的测试结果，其胎体是高岭土，烧结温度在1,100摄氏度以上。它的出土，把

世界上最早的瓷器：二里头遗址出土的原始青瓷

The Earliest Porcelain in the World: Primitive Cyan Glazed Porcelain Unearthed from the Erlitou Site in Yanshi

I. The Cradle: Simple and Vigorous Protoporcelain of Xia, Shang and Zhou Dynasties in Henan Province

China is the home of porcelain, and porcelain is the quintessence of China. The ancient Central Plains (Henan Province) is the cradle of Chinese porcelain.

As early as the middle of the 20th century, some artifacts, with hard texture and a thin layer of cyan glaze, were unearthed at the Shang City Ruins in Zhengzhou (the capital ruins of the early and middle Shang Dynasty (1600-1046 B.C.)), which were generally called "glazed pottery" by academics at that time. However, researchers think that this so-called "glazed pottery", already with the basic characteristics of porcelain, can be called protoporcelain, i.e. the earliest known porcelain in China and even the world. Therefore, the origin of Chinese porcelain should be traced back to the Shang Dynasty. This discovery and research findings with extraordinary significance shocked the ceramics and archaeology circle, and gradually accepted by them. In recent years, with the excavation of some ruins, such as the Shang Dynasty ruin of Small Double Bridge (Xiaoshuangqiao) in Zhengzhou, the Zhangzikou Tomb of Luyi County in eastern Henan (the end of the Shang Dynasty and the beginning of the Zhou Dynasty), the Pangjiagou Western Zhou Tomb in Luoyang, and the Beiyao Western Zhou Tomb in Luoyang, a batch of primitive cyan glazed porcelain made in the Shang and Zhou dynasties were unearthed, providing newer and richer information and creating conditions for in-depth study of Chinese early porcelain.

In 2002, the primitive cyan glazed porcelain was unearthed at the royal tombs of the Erlitou site in Yanshi City, the central and western city of Henan Province, which had a thin layer of cyan glaze and was fragments of the mouth part of He (wine container). According to scientific tests results, the porcelain body is Kaolin and its sintering temperature is above 1,100 degrees Celsius. That is the earliest known porcelain in China and even the world, therefore, the birth of porcelain could be traced back to the 18th B.C., one century before the Shang Dynasty, and the significance was extraordinary.

郑州商城出土的原始青瓷
Primitive Cyan Glazed Porcelain Unearthed from the Shang Dynasty Capital Ruins in Zhengzhou

人类发明瓷器的年代从商代向前提到了前18世纪，意义非同凡响。

商周时期原始瓷器的出土和确认，是中国古代手工业史上划时代的事件。这种胎体厚重、釉色晶莹、造型古朴、风格特异的新产品，是自新石器时代以来制陶手工业的一个革命性成果。自此，人类的生活用具中开始出现了一种全然不同于以往的新品种，拥有3,000余年悠久历史的中国瓷器制造业，从此踏上了漫漫旅程。

洛阳庞家沟西周墓出土的原始青瓷
Primitive Cyan Glazed Porcelain Unearthed from the Pangjiagou Western Zhou Tomb in Luoyang

The excavation and confirmation of primitive porcelain made in the Shang and Zhou dynasties was an epoch-making event in the history of ancient Chinese handicraft industry. This new kind of porcelain with thick body, crystal-clear glaze color, simple shape and unique style is the revolutionary result of pottery handicraft industry since the Neolithic Age. Henceforth, some completely new life utensils have begun to appear in human beings life. The Chinese porcelain manufacturing industry with a long history of over 3,000 years has also embarked on a long journey.

二、盛世华章：富丽华美的中原汉唐陶瓷

汉代和唐代是中国古代历史上政治、经济和文化高度发达的两座高峰。中国传统的陶瓷业也在这种得天独厚的大环境下取得了新的成就，在陶瓷史上写下了浓墨重彩的一章。

汉代制陶业最伟大的成就之一是低温铅釉陶的发明。它秉承了商周以降原始瓷器施釉或装饰工艺，又影响了唐宋时期三彩器的产生和发展，所取得的技术革新成就对此后的中国陶瓷艺术产生了重要影响。河南地区发现的汉代釉陶所采用的复色釉工艺、二次上釉工艺、釉上绘彩工艺等，均是陶瓷史上的开山之作，代表了汉代陶瓷艺术的最高水平，奠定了后世陶瓷的工艺基础。关于中国铅釉的起源以及与地中海沿岸铅釉器物、玻璃器物的关系等问题，则又关乎中国汉代的中西交通与文化交流的研究，具有重要的学术意义。

汉代低温铅釉陶鸮尊
Low-temperature Lead-glazed Pottery of the Han Dynasty

II. Prosperous Times: Magnificent and Colorful Pottery and Porcelain of the Central Plains in the Han and Tang Dynasties

The Han Dynasty(25-220 A.D.) and the Tang Dynasty (618-907A.D.) witnessed highly developed politics, economy, and culture in the history of ancient China. Chinese traditional pottery and porcelain industry has also achieved new achievements in this advantaged environment and, as such, has left an indelible mark.

One of the greatest achievements of the Han Dynasty pottery industry was the creation of low-temperature Lead-glazed pottery. It has adhered to the glazing or decoration craft of protoporcelain since the Shang and Zhou dynasties, and affected the production and development of the tri-color glazed pottery in the Tang and Song dynasties. Its technical innovations have had an important influence on the Chinese art of pottery and porcelain after the Han Dynasty. The glazed pottery of the Han Dynasty excavated from Henan Province all showed us unprecedented craftsmanship, such as the fancy glaze, the secondary glaze, and over-glaze decoration, which represented the highest level of pottery and porcelain art in the Han Dynasty and laid foundation for later generations. The question about the origin of Chinese Lead-glazed craft and its relationships with Lead-glazed objects and glassware on the Mediterranean coast is related to the study of transportation and cultural exchanges between the Han Dynasty and Western countries, which has important academic significance.

Tang tri-color glazed potteries (Tang Sancai) were more gorgeous and graceful with rich hues like yellow, brown, green, blue, white, and black. In particular, the use of cobalt not only made the blue tri-color glazed pottery precious, but also laid technical foundations for the creation of the blue-and-white porcelain. So far, the earliest blue-and-white porcelain fragments were unearthed at the Huangye Tang Sancai kiln site in Gongyi, a central city in Henan. Thus the birth of blue-and-white porcelain was advanced from the Yuan Dynasty to the Tang Dynasty, and helped to find the place of origin of the early blue-and-white porcelain unearthed in Yangzhou and other places.

北朝青瓷莲花尊
Northern Dynasty Celadon Lotus Zun

唐三彩呈现出黄、褐、绿、蓝、白、黑等丰富的色调，更加缤纷华丽，雍容大气。尤其是钴元素的应用，不仅使蓝釉三彩成为名贵品种，而且为青花瓷器的发明奠定了技术基础。巩义黄冶唐三彩窑址出土了迄今所知年代最早的青花瓷片，从而把青花瓷器的发明从元代提早至唐代，并为扬州等地出土的早期青花瓷器找到了产地。

河南唐三彩以其复杂的工艺、艳丽的外表、华贵的气韵和奇异的造型成为世人倍加推崇的艺术品，其影响远播东瀛、西域、南洋，日本的奈良三彩、朝鲜半岛的新罗三彩以及在中东、东南亚等地出土的中国三彩，都是河南唐三彩作为文化使者的最好物证。

Chapter V Exquisite Workmanship: The Technical and Artistic Achievements of Ancient Pottery and Porcelain in Henan Province

隋张盛墓出土的瓷器
Porcelain Excavated from the Zhangsheng Tomb of the Sui Dynasty

With its complex craftsmanship, gorgeous appearance, luxurious charm and fantastic shape, Henan Tang Sancai has become a work of art admired by the world and its influence far spread to Japan, the Western Regions, and Southeast Asia. Japan's Nara Sancai, the Korean Peninsula's Silla Sancai, as well as the Tang Sancai unearthed in the Middle East, Southeast Asia and other places strongly indicated that the Henan Tang Sancai was the cultural ambassador between China and other countries.

Since the Northern Dynasty (386-581 A.D.), Henan's porcelain industry has been further developed. Porcelains, unearthed from the Jin Dynasty (266-420 A.D.) Tomb in Luoyang, the Yuanshao Tomb of the Northern Wei Dynasty (386-534 A.D.) in Luoyang, and the Fancui Tomb of the Northern Qi Dynasty (550-577 A.D.) in Anyang, the Zhangshang Tomb and the Buren Tomb of the Sui Dynasty (581-618 A.D.) in Anyang, and the General Liyun Tomb of the Northern Qi Dynasty in Puyang, represent the intermediate link of the development of porcelain industry in the Central Plains from the Han Dynasty to the Tang and Song dynasties, connecting the past with the future.

唐三彩兽首执壶
Tri-color Glazed Pottery of the Tang Dynasty (Tang Sancai)

北朝以降，河南制瓷业不绝如缕。洛阳晋墓、北魏元邵墓，安阳北齐范粹墓、隋张盛墓和卜仁墓以及濮阳北齐李云墓出土的瓷器，代表了中原地区由汉晋到唐宋制瓷业发展的中间环节，具有承上启下的意义。

在安阳洹河之滨发现的相州窑遗址是河南境内发现的年代最早的瓷窑遗址之一，为寻找前述北朝及隋代墓葬出土瓷器的产地提供了极为重要的线索。张盛墓出土的白瓷，形象地描述了中原北方地区白瓷的兴起和南青北白格局形成的具体途径。而以鲁山段店窑、郏县黄道窑为代表的唐代花瓷，使人们得以管窥唐代瓷业的缤纷。

Chapter V Exquisite Workmanship: The Technical and Artistic Achievements of Ancient Pottery and Porcelain in Henan Province

汉代低温铅釉陶壶
Low-temperature Lead-glazed Pottery of the Han Dynasty

The Xiangzhou kiln site excavated on the bank of the Huan River in Anyang is the earliest porcelain kiln site discovered in Henan, providing an extremely important clue for searching the original place of the aforementioned porcelains of the Northern Dynasty and of the tombs of the Sui Dynasty. The white porcelain from the Zhangsheng Tomb vividly describes the rise of white porcelain in the northern Central Plains and the specific formation way of the southern blue and northern white situation. People can roughly see the flourishing of Tang porcelain industry through the Tang Dynasty Jun porcelains represented by the Duandian Kiln in Lushan County (Pingdingshan City in Henan) and the Huangdao Kiln in Jia County (Pingdingshan City in Henan).

三、大雅大俗：宋元时期生机盎然的民窑与典雅深邃的官窑

如果说艺术作品有"大雅之雅"与"大俗之雅"两种极致的话，那么北宋时期的官窑作品和宋金元时期的民窑瓷器对此做出了最恰当、最完美的诠释。汝窑、官窑和钧窑作品，深深浸润着北宋文人士子超然洒脱、清秀典雅的风尚，体现出"物我两忘"的深邃意境。以汝州严和店窑、新密西关窑、登封曲河窑、修武当阳峪窑、鹤壁集窑、禹州扒村窑等为代表的一批宋金元时期的民用瓷窑，则向世人展示了民间瓷业直抒胸臆、服务现实生活的大众情怀，与官窑瓷器的阳春白雪、曲高和寡一起，描绘了宋元时期瓷器制作业"大雅"与"大俗"两种艺术风格的极致，构成了宋元时期河南陶瓷考古的全景图像。

河南古代瓷业最辉煌的篇章是北宋时期的官窑御用瓷。后人乐道的宋代汝、钧、官、哥、定五大名窑中，前三者均在河南境内。

汝窑遗址瓷片出土现场
Porcelain Ruins Unearthed from the Ru Kiln Site

III. Aristocratic and Popular: The Elegant Official Kiln and the Vibrant Folk Kiln During the Song and Yuan Dynasties

If the works of art have two kinds of extreme of "the beauty of elegance" and "the beauty of vulgarity", then the official kiln arts of the Northern Song and the folk kiln works of the Song, Jin, and Yuan dynasties made the most appropriate and perfect interpretation. The porcelains of the Ru kiln, the Northern Song official kiln and the Jun kiln deeply showed a kind of transcendent and elegant characteristics brought by the northern and southern scholars and reflected the chaste artistic space. A batch of the folk kiln of the Song, Jin, and Yuan dynasties, represented by the Yanhedian kiln in Ruzhou City, the Xiguan kiln in Xinmi City (southwest of Zhengzhou), the Quhe kiln in Dengfeng City, the Dangyangyu kiln in Xiuwu County, the Hebiji kiln, and the Bacun kiln in Yuzhou City, showed public expects for the folk porcelain industry that products can not only express people's feelings directly, but efficiently serve the real life. While the official kiln was too elegant to be appreciated by the masses, the two kinds formed a panoramic image of Henan pottery and porcelain archaeology in the Song and Yuan dynasties together with two ideal styles of the " the great elegant" and " the popular ".

The most glorious chapter of Henan's ancient porcelain industry was the porcelains for emperors produced by the Northern Song official kiln. Among the five famous kilns in the Song Dynasty, i.e., the Jun kiln, the Ru kiln, the Guan kiln (official kiln), the Ge kiln, and the Ding kiln in the Song Dynasty, the former three kinds were all located in Henan.

钧窑瓷茶具
Porcelain of the Jun Kiln: Porcelain Tea Set

五大名窑中，"汝窑为魁"，因其以玛瑙为釉且流入民间的数量极少，全世界各大博物馆典藏的汝窑瓷器也不过70余件，因此视其为瓷中极品，并非溢美之词。近年来，在清凉寺窑址发掘出大规模保存较好的作坊、窑炉以及数量众多的汝官瓷片。这些瓷器造型简洁洗练，釉面均匀亮泽，釉色素静雅致，再现了北宋宫廷御用汝瓷的典雅韵致以及蕴含其间的宋代士林孜孜以求的无我之境。这些特征与传世的汝官窑瓷器几无二致，据此，汝官窑这一长期困扰学术界的千年悬案遂趋尘埃落定。

　　汝州张公巷窑址出土的与汝窑造型相似、风格接近的一批质量上乘、工艺考究的瓷器，是继清凉寺窑址后陶瓷考古的又一项重要发现。同汝窑一样，北宋官窑也一直笼罩在迷雾中，人们只知道才华横溢的风流皇帝宋徽宗在京师自设官窑烧造青瓷，却不知真正的官窑瓷器究竟为何物，更不知这官窑设在何处。不过人们有理由相信，以宋徽宗之才情和审美情趣，以宫廷不计工本的皇家气度，北宋官窑成就之高当不在汝

汝瓷天青釉刻花鹅颈瓶
Porcelain of the Ru Kiln: Azure Glazed Gooseneck Bottle

钧窑瓷碗
Porcelain of the Jun Kiln: Porcelain Bowl

Among the five well-known kilns, "the Ru kiln ranks first", for it was glazed with agate. Few private collectors owned the Ru porcelains, even the number of the Ru porcelain in the major museums around the world is just around 70. Therefore, it is no exaggeration to regard it as the best in porcelain. In recent years, large-scale well-preserved workshops, kilns and a large number of fragments of the Ru kiln have been excavated in the Qingliang Temple kiln site. These porcelains, with simple shape, sleek glaze, and elegant color, re-showed the elegant charm of the Ru porcelain for the Northern Song Royal Palace, as well as the "Ego-absent realm" constantly pursued by scholars in the Song Dynasty. These

汝瓷莲瓣熏炉
Porcelain of the Ru Kiln: Porcelain Furnace with Lotus Petals

白瓷净瓶
White Porcelain Bottle

窑之下。不少学者认为,张公巷窑所显示的艺术风格和工艺特征,与北宋官窑颇多吻合,极有可能就是"众里寻他千百度"的北宋官窑。

同样,禹州钧台窑与神垕窑出土的陈设类瓷器,与传世的故宫等大博物馆藏品毫无二致,釉色有天蓝、月白、海棠红、玫瑰紫、鹦哥绿等极富诗意的称呼。这诸多斑斓的色彩,缘自钧窑创造性地发明了高温铜红釉并得以灵活自如地应用。在高温状态下,各种颜色釉料互相交流渗透,肆意地流泻挥洒,形成变幻莫测、神妙奇诡的艺术效果,"绿

白地黑花瓷碗
Porcelain Bowl with Black Decoration on White Ground

青瓷炉
Celadon Furnace

characteristics are the same as those of the official porcelains which were handed down from generation to generation. According to this, questions related to the Ru kiln have been cleared up, which have long plagued academia.

The excavation of the Zhanggongxiang kiln site was another significant discovery after the Qingliang Temple kiln site, wherein a batch of high-quality, well-crafted porcelains were similar to the Ru porcelain in shape. Just like the Ru kiln, little was known about official kilns of the Northern Song Dynasty. People only know that the talented Emperor Huizong set up official kilns to produce the cyan glazed porcelain in Dongjing, capital of the Northern Song dynasty (today's Kaifeng City in Henan), but do not know what the real official porcelain is and where it is located. However, people have reason to believe that its achievements would not be under the Ru kiln, because of the talent and aesthetic taste of Emperor Huizong as well as the generosity of royal family. Many scholars believe that the artistic style and craft features displayed by the Zhanggongxiang kiln site are quite consistent with the official kiln of the Northern Song Dynasty, and it is very likely that it is the official kiln we are looking for.

Meanwhile, some porcelain—mainly for exhibitions and appreciation-unearthed from the Juntai kiln and the Shenhou kiln in Yuzhou City could completely rival to those collected in the large museums as the extant Forbidden

如春水出生日,红似朝霞欲上时","峡谷飞瀑兔丝缕,夕阳紫翠忽成岚"。窑变工艺也因此成为钧窑的标志性技术成就。

宋代的官窑瓷器如同一幅立意高远、清幽典雅的文人画卷,而民用瓷器则像一张张散发出"柴米油盐酱醋茶"芳香的木版年画。磁州窑系的白地黑花、刻花、剔花、珍珠地作品,钧窑系色彩斑斓的窑变釉作品,临汝窑系印花、刻花作品,无不反映出宋金元时期普通民众乐观向上、渴求富足、祈求安宁的心态和愿望,其不拘陈规的造型、洒脱洗练的笔触和密切贴近现实生活的产品结构,使之成为研究当时物质文化生活的一部百科全书。

白地黑花瓷枕
Porcelain Pillow with Black Decoration on White Ground

红绿彩蹴鞠人物
Red and Green Cuju Figure

City. Besides, the glazing color has some poetic nicknames such as sky blue, moon white, begonia red, rose purple, and parrot green. Due to the innovative invention and flexible application of high-temperature copper-red glaze of the Jun kiln, those porcelains wore gorgeous and colorful garments. Through mutual reaction and penetration of various hues under the high-temperature state, unpredictable and mysterious artistic effects as well as subtle change of accidental coloring appeared in the kiln. The color and shape transformation workmanship of porcelain, named "Yaobian", in the kiln has thus become the technical landmark of the Jun kiln.

The official porcelain in the Song Dynasty is like the a literati painting with high-spirited and elegant styles, while the folk porcelain looks like a woodcut New Year painting that records our daily life and sends forth a delicate fragrance. The decorative techniques of Cizhou kiln (in today's Heibei) include black flowers glazed on white porcelain body (also called rust coloured glaze), carved flowers, scratch, and pearl-ground scratch; the decorative techniques of Jun kiln include the works of " Yaobian "; and the decorative techniques of the Linru kiln include printing and engraving works; all the three kinds reflect the optimism, eagerness for wealth, and pray for peace and happiness of the general people in the Song and Jin dynasties. The unconventional style, free and easy brushwork, and structures close to real life make it an encyclopedia for people to study the material and cultural life at that time.

第六章

火的精魂：灿烂的中原古代冶金

Chapter VI

The Spirit of Fire: The Splendid Ancient Casting Technology of the Central Plains

早在龙山文化晚期，中原地区就开始了青铜的冶炼和铸造。在登封王城岗遗址的龙山文化遗存中，就发现有小件青铜器。这是目前所知中国最早的青铜文物之一，也被学术界认定龙山文化晚期已经进入文明时代的重要证据。二里头文化继承并发展了龙山时代的技术成就，已经可以铸造出结构复杂的腔体容器，冶铸技术已臻成熟。

中国古代青铜冶铸技术的顶峰是商周时期。已经发掘出土的商周青铜器不可胜数，其中既有武器、乐器和日用器具，更有组合完备的祭祀礼器；既有个体较小的器物，更有伟形巨制的大型用品。最能代表这一时期工艺成就的，非"司母戊"青铜方鼎莫属。

"司母戊"青铜方鼎重达832.84千克，是世界上现存最大的单体青铜器。由于器身巨大，铸造时需要有容量巨大的熔炉，采用地槽流注工艺浇铸，庞大的鼎身和四条圆柱状实足为一次浇铸而成，然后再于其上安模、翻范、浇注铜液，做出两个直立的大耳，工艺流程十分复杂。整个鼎所需铜料在1,000千克以上，模具和范芯多达几十块，人力数以百计。不仅需要明确的分工协作，还必须具备对铜、锡、锌、铅等金属原

二里头文化网格纹青铜鼎
Gridded Bronze Tripod Unearthed from Erlitou Ruins

Chapter VI The Spirit of Fire: The Splendid Ancient Casting Technology of the Central Plains

As early as the late Longshan culture, the Chinese people of the Central Plains started the smelting and casting methods to make bronze. Small bronze wares were discovered at the Wangchenggang site in Dengfeng, which belonged to the Longshan culture. These are regarded as one of the earliest bronze relics known in China, and also as important evidence for the academics to prove the late Longshan culture's entry into the civilized era. The Erlitou culture inherited and developed the technical achievements of the Longshan era, and made mature the smelting and casting technology to make complex cavity containers.

The peak of bronze smelting and casting technology in ancient China appeared during the Shang and Zhou dynasties. Innumerable bronze wares in the two dynasties were unearthed, including weapons, musical instruments, sets of ritual vessels, and articles for everyday use. The size of these bronze wares varied greatly, ranging from small ones to those grand and spectacular. And the most representative of the technological achievements in this period was no doubt the huge Simuwu Rectangular Ding.

The four-legged bronze cauldron, 32.84 kg in weight, was the largest bronze vessel in the world. Its huge size required a large-capacity melting smelter, and a very complicated process, including the ground trough injection to cast the huge body with four columnar legs at one shot, mold setting, mold shifting and liquid copper casting to make two erect handles. The whole process required over 1,000 kilograms of cupriferous materials, dozens of molds and cores, and hundreds of

淅川下寺春秋楚墓云纹铜禁

Bronze Jin with Cloud Design, Unearthed from a Chu State Tomb at Xiasi, Xichuan County, the Spring and Autumn Period

料熔点、性能、成分配比的精确认识，以及对火候控制、成型加工技术的严格掌握。这一系列技术问题的解决，使商代的青铜冶铸技术达到了当时的高峰。

郑州商城和安阳殷墟都发现了商代青铜铸造的作坊遗址，为研究了解其复杂的工艺流程提供了较为完备的考古资料。

楚国的青铜冶铸也取得了很高的技术和艺术成就。淅川下寺春秋楚国贵族墓葬中出土的王子午鼎、云纹铜禁等大型青铜器是其代表作品。这一时期，铸造、焊接、锻打甚至车床一类的技术手段都已经得到发明并成功运用，尤其是翻模铸造和失蜡法铸造工艺，即使以现代眼光来评判，也是相当先进的。现代金属冶铸业中，这类技术仍然在继续使用。

由于技术手段先进，东周时期的许多青铜器不仅造型美观，具有较高的艺术价值，而且功能先进，有些至今仍可以使用。如信阳长台关楚国贵族墓葬出土的青铜编钟音律齐备，中国第一颗人造地球卫星上播放的乐曲《东方红》就是由其演奏的；新近发掘出土的铜镜依然光可鉴人，几十件酒器金光灿灿，历经2,000多年没有丝毫生锈。所有这些，都是当时技术成就的生动体现。

中国古代的冶铁业虽然比青铜冶铸业起步较晚，但在青铜冶铸业的

商代青铜鸮卣
Owl-shaped Bronze Jar of the Shang Dynasty

craftsmen. The process required not only the specific division of labor, but also a clear knowledge of the exact melting points, properties, and proportions of copper, tin, zinc, lead and other metals. It was also fundamental to have a strict mastery of temperature control and the molding process technology. With the solution of this series of technical problems, the bronze smelting and casting technology of the Shang Dynasty reached the peak at that time.

Bronze casting workshop sites of the Shang Dynasty have been found in the Shang Dynasty capital site of Zhengzhou and Yin ruins of Anyang, both providing relatively complete archaeological data for the study and understanding of its complicated technological process.

The bronze casting of the State of Chu also attained high technical and artistic achievements. The large bronze wares such as the Sheng-ding for Prince Wu and the bronze Jin, were the most representative of those relics unearthed at Xiasi in Xichuan, from the aristocrats' tombs of the Chu State in the Spring and Autumn period, when the casting, welding and forging technology were adopted, and even the lathe invented and used. In particular, the mold-casting and lost-wax casting processes were quite advanced even if judged by modern standards. And these technologies are still employed in the modern metal smelting and casting industry.

郑州出土商代乳钉青铜方鼎
Bronze Rectangular Ding of the Shang Dynasty in Zhengzhou

西周青铜尊

Bronze Zun of the Western Zhou Dynasty

技术基础上，一经产生就达到了相当的高度。实际上，早在商代，中原地区就已经开始利用天然的陨铁制作金属兵器；到了西周晚期，已经开始人工铁器的制造。三门峡虢国贵族墓葬出土的玉柄铁剑，是目前中原地区所见最早的人工炼铁制品之一。自此以降，中原地区到春秋晚期基本完成了由技术发明到实际生产和应用的转化，战国晚期铁器已得到初步普及，古代铁器工业基本形成。发展至两汉，铁器基本完成了对石器和青铜器的取代过程，成为社会生产的主要推动力，并影响到了当时的

三门峡虢季墓玉柄铁剑

Iron Sword with a Jade Handle Unearthed from the Guoji Tomb at Sanmenxia

洛阳战国错金银铜鼎

Warring States Bronze Ding Engraved with Gold and Silver in Luoyang

Due to the advanced technology, many bronze wares were not only beautiful in appearance, great in artistic value, but also advanced in function and some of them can still be used today. The bronze chime-bells unearthed from the tombs of the Chu aristocrats at Changtaiguan in Xinyang had complete musical scales, and were used to play the music on China's first man-made satellite. The newly excavated bronze mirrors were still in good condition, and dozens of wine vessels were free of rust, and glittered as they did over two thousand years ago. All this presented a vivid reflection of the remarkable technological achievements of the time.

Although the iron casting industry in ancient China started later, it reached a considerable height on the basis of the bronze casting industry since it was produced. In fact, as early as the Shang Dynasty, the Central Plains had begun to use the natural iron meteorite to make metal weapons, and by the late Western Zhou Period, people had started to produce iron wares. The Jade-handled Iron Sword unearthed in the aristocrats' tombs of the Guo State in Sanmenxia, for example, was the earliest artificial iron-made artifact in the Central Plains. Since then, the Central Plains had completed the transformation from technical invention to actual production and application by the late Spring and Autumn Period. The iron ware of the late Warring States Period was popularized in the preliminary sense, and the ancient iron ware industry had finally come into

生活方式、文化艺术等方方面面。两汉时期凿山为陵的王室大墓、遍及中原的艺术瑰宝画像砖和画像石，均是古代中原铁器冶铸业的物证。

河南境内已发现的战国两汉时期的冶铁遗址多达数十处。以南阳瓦房庄、巩义铁生沟、郑州古荥镇、鲁山望城岗、泌阳下河湾为代表的汉代冶铁遗址，出土了炼炉、炼渣、模具、矿石原料等大批与冶炼工艺相关的遗存，并有许多铁器。正是有了这批丰富的实物资料，我们得以认识到，从春秋战国经两汉到魏晋时期，中原地区已经发展出脱碳钢、炒钢、球墨铸铁、锻打等一系列先进的生产工艺。其中的球墨铸铁、锻打工艺现代工业中仍在使用。

由于铁器的广泛应用已涉及社会生产生活的方方面面，铁器冶铸也成为关系国计民生的重要行业，因此从汉代开始，中央政府实行了铁器的国家专卖制度。河南境内出土有很多相关文物，反映出当时中央和地方政府已在河南建立了组织完备、管理制度严格的铁官体系。此后的历代王朝，基本继承了汉代的这一制度。

焦作嘉禾屯出土的汉代五凤铜熏炉
Bronze Incense Burner with Five Phoenix in the Han Dynasty

form. In the Han Dynasty, iron wares had basically completed the process of replacing stoneware and bronze vessels: it became the main driving force of social production development, and affected the way of life, culture and art and other aspects at that time. The royal tombs dug in the mountain in the Han Dynasty and the painted bricks and stones throughout the Central Plains, are all the physical evidence of the iron casting industry in the ancient Central Plains.

Dozens of iron casting foundry ruins of the Warring States Period and Han Dynasty have been found in Henan. A large number of smelting furnaces, slag, molds, ore raw materials and other remains of casting technology as well as iron wares have been unearthed from the iron casting sites, represented by Wafangzhuang in Nanyang, Tieshenggou in Gongyi, Guxing in Xingyang, Wangchenggang in Lushan and Xiahewan in Qinyang. It is with the rich amount of physical materials that we have realized that from the Spring and Autumn Period and the Warring States Period to the Wei and Jin dynasties, the Central Plains region had developed a series of advanced production technologies such as decarburizing the iron to make steel, heating the steel, casting irons with nodular, and forging. Among them, the nodular cast iron process and forging process are still used in the modern industry.

Since the extensive application of ironware has involved all aspects of social production and life, ironware smelting and casting has also become an important industry related to the national economy and people's livelihood so, from the Han Dynasty, the central government had implemented the national monopoly system of ironware. Many related cultural relics unearthed in Henan reflect that at that time, the central and local governments had established the iron official system in Henan with complete organization and strict management system, and the subsequent dynasties basically inherited this system of the Han Dynasty.

第七章

河南的世界文化遗产

Chapter VII

World Cultural Heritage in Henan

一、龙门石窟

1. 龙门石窟普遍的突出的价值

龙门石窟是北魏和唐朝盛期两代皇家经营的造像艺术，1961年被国务院列为全国重点文物保护单位，2000年被联合国教科文组织列为世界文化遗产，是中国石窟艺术极为重要的组成部分，也是世界石窟艺术5世纪末至8世纪中叶间最为辉煌壮美、璀璨绚烂的篇章。这些艺术品以佛教为创作题材，代表了中国石刻艺术的最高峰。

龙门石窟开凿于北魏孝文帝迁都洛阳之际（494年），北魏以降，经东魏、北齐、西魏、隋、唐等朝代，历时历经400多年才得以完成。其中5世纪末至8世纪中叶最为兴盛，是中国这一时期石窟艺术的典范。两山窟龛造像数量多，规模大，题材多样，雕刻精美，以北魏和唐代造像最具代表性。

龙门石窟延续时间长，跨越朝代多，所处地理位置优越，自然景色幽美，是其他许多石窟难以比拟的。龙门石窟以大量的实物形象和文字资料从不同侧面反映了中国古代政治、经济、宗教、文化等许多领域的发展变化，对中国石窟艺术的创新与发展做出了重大贡献。龙门石窟的历史、艺术、科学和鉴赏价值，使其成为石窟艺术系列中不可缺少的主

龙门石窟西山远眺
An Overlook of the West Hill of the Longmen Grottoes

Ⅰ. The Longmen Grottoes

1. Universal and Prominent Value of the Longmen Grottoes

Representative of the sculptural art in the charge of the royal families at the peak of the Northern Wei Dynasty and the Tang Dynasty, the Longmen Grottoes were listed as the national key cultural relics protection unit by the State Council in 1961 and the world cultural heritage by UNESCO in 2000. The Longmen Grottoes are not only indispensable to the Chinese art of stone carving but also the most brilliant and glorious in the art of the worlds' caves and niches from the end of the 5th century to the mid-8th century. Taking Buddhism as their subject matter, these works of art represent the climax of Chinese stone carving.

The construction of the Longmen Grottoes began when Emperor Xiaowen of the Northern Wei Dynasty moved the capital to Luoyang in 493 and continued in the following 400 years and more which witnessed the Eastern Wei Dynasty, the Northern Qi Dynasty, the Western Wei Dynasty, the Sui Dynasty, the Tang Dynasty, and so on. Among them, the grottoes were the most highly developed from the end of the fifth century to the middle eighth century, hence the masterpiece of Chinese grotto art in this period. The caves and statues in the two hills are known both at home and abroad for their large number, massive scale, variety of subjects as well as delicacy in carving. Among them the statues in the Northern Wei Dynasty and the Tang Dynasty are the most representative.

The Longmen Grottoes are superior to other grottoes in terms of the length of history, the time of construction which spanned a number of dynasties, and the advantageous location as well as the scenic beauty. Quantities of artifacts and documents have reflected from different perspectives the development and changes of politics, economy, religion and culture in ancient China, and have made great contributions to the innovation and development of Chinese stone carving art. With the value in history, art, science and appreciation, the Longmen Grottoes have become a crucial representative in the series of stone carving artifacts and as such the cultural heritage shared by all mankind.

Buddhism was introduced to China in the early first century B.C., while the art of grottoes, which originated in ancient India, began to thrive along the

要代表作之一，是全人类共同的文化遗产。

佛教于前1世纪初传入中国，而源于古印度的石窟艺术，约3世纪始在丝绸之路上勃兴。到了5世纪和7世纪前后(魏晋至盛唐时期)，中国北方先后形成了北魏和唐代两次开窟营造高峰，龙门石窟就是这两次造像高峰的典型范例和伟大的杰作。

以龙门石窟为代表的北魏和隋唐时期石窟艺术，表现出印度文化与中国文化融合的特点，使中国的石窟艺术更加民族化、世俗化，形成了典型的中原风格。这是一种具有划时代意义的发展变化，在题材内容、艺术形式、雕刻技巧、审美情趣等方面较之以往都有很大突破，对全国和域外(朝鲜、韩国、日本)的石窟与佛教造像都产生了深远的影响。因此，龙门石窟既不同于巨大造像的云冈石窟，也不同于以彩塑、绘画为主的敦煌莫高窟，又不同于生活化的大足石刻。

Silk Road only around the 3rd century. By the fifth century and around the 7th century (from the Wei and Jin dynasties to the heyday of the Tang Dynasty), two peaks of stone carving were seen with one after the other in northern China, respectively in the Northern Wei and Tang dynasties. The Longmen Grottoes are the typical example and the great masterpiece in these two peaks of statue carving.

  The art of stone carving developed during the Northern Wei, the Sui and Tang dynasties, as represented by the Longmen Grottoes, reflected the integration of Indian and Chinese cultures and, with the Chinese stone carving more localized and mundane, developed a style typical of the Central Plains. Such epoch-making development and changes led to major breakthroughs of tradition in terms of subject matters, artistic forms, carving skills and aesthetic tastes, hence far-reaching influences on the carving of grottoes as well as Buddhist statues in and out of the country (in such foreign countries as North Korea, South Korea and Japan). Therefore, the Longmen Grottoes differ from the Yungang Grottoes featuring giant statues, from the Mogao Grottoes characterized by the painted sculptures and murals and from the Dazu Rock Carvings which are close to daily life.

2. 龙门石窟的内容

石窟集中分布在古都洛阳之南伊河两岸峭壁上，现存窟龛2,137个、造像近10万尊、碑刻题记3,680种。整个石窟规模宏大，气势磅礴，雕刻精美，内容丰富，是世界上最伟大的古典艺术宝库之一。

两山造像依岩开凿，窟龛密如蜂房，南北绵延1公里，其西山大、中型洞由北向南依次有潜溪寺、宾阳三洞、敬善寺、摩崖三佛龛、万佛洞、老龙洞、莲花洞、普泰洞、赵客师洞、破窟、魏字洞、唐字洞、奉先寺、药方洞、古阳洞、火烧洞、皇甫公窟、路洞、极南洞等50余个，多系北魏和唐代皇家或王公大臣出资营造。涉及佛教宗派有法相宗、华严宗、三阶教、净土宗、密宗等，另外有道教造像。

奉先寺卢舍那佛特写
Close-up of Buddha Vairocana of the Fengxian Temple

2. Statues of the Longmen Grottoes

The Longmen Grottoes, flanking the Yihe River to the south of the ancient capital of Luoyang, Henan Province, comprise 2,137 caves and niches carved into the steep limestone cliffs, housing more than 100,000 statues as well as 3,680 steles and inscriptions. The grottoes are massive in scale, great in momentum, exquisite in carving techniques and rich in contents. They have been known as one of the world's greatest treasure houses of classical art.

The statues in the two hills are all carved into rocks, and the niches stand close to each other like beehives in a stretch extending one kilometre from the south to the north. There are more than 50 large and medium-sized caves in the West Hill, including the Qianxisidong Cave (the Hidden Stream Temple Cave), the Binyangsandong Cave (the Three Binyang Caves), the Jingshansidong Cave (the Kindness-worship Temple Cave), the Moyasanfokan Niche (the Moya Three Buddha Niche), the Wanfodong Cave (the Ten-thousand Buddha Cave), the Laolongdong Cave (the Old-dragon Cave), the Lianhuadong Cave (the Lotus Cave), the Putaidong Cave (the All-peace Cave), the Zhaokeshidong Cave (the Scholar Zhao Cave), the Poku Cave (the Shattered Cave), the Weizidong Cave (the Character Wei Cave), Tangzidong Cave (the Character Tang Cave), the Fengxiansidong Cave (the Ancestors-worship Temple Cave), the Yaofangdong Cave (the Prescription Cave), the Guyangdong Cave (the Guyang Cave), the Huoshaodong Cave (the Fire-burning Cave), the Huangfugongku Niche (the Duke Huangfu Niche), the Ludong Cave (the Cave by the Road), and the Jinandong Cave (the Southernmost Cave), as they stand in the sequence of order from the north to the south. Most of these niches were cut with funds from the imperial families or senior officials of the Northern Wei and Tang dynasties. Besides Taoist statues, there are Buddhist ones, including the Dharmalaksana Sect, the Avatamsaka Sect, the Three Stages Sect, the Pure Land Sect and the Tantrism Sect.

The Guyangdong Cave is the first excavated and at the same time has the greatest variety of sculptures. As a typical example of grotto statue in the 6th century, the Binyangzhongdong Cave is the most gorgeous. The Giant Niche in the Fengxiansidong Cave is the largest in scale. The main statue of Buddha Vairocana is 17.14 meters in total height. Taken as a whole, the statue is clear in

奉先寺菩萨与弟子
Bodhisattva and the Disciples of the Fengxian Temple

其中，古阳洞开凿最早、佛教内容最丰富、书法艺术成就最高；宾阳中洞最为富丽堂皇，是6世纪石窟造像的典范；奉先寺大像龛规模最大，主尊卢舍那佛高达17.14米，整个雕像主次分明，比例适度，浑然一体，对比、夸张、烘托、渲染运用得恰到好处，既追求形式美，又注重准确表达思想内容，具有永恒的艺术魅力，是7世纪石窟造像最完美的杰作之一。

东山窟龛亦依岩开凿，且深入万佛沟内，曲折绵延亦为1公里。其大、中型洞窟有擂鼓台三洞、高平郡王洞、西方净土变龛、千手千眼观音龛、看经寺、二莲花洞、四雁洞等20余个，主要为唐代王公大臣和佛

奉先寺北壁天王力士
Vaisramana on the North Wall of the Fengxian Temple

the differentiation of its primary and secondary parts, appropriate in proportion and integral in composition. Artistic methods such as contrast, exaggeration, highlighting have all been used to their best both to create a formal beauty and to express ideas in precision. With a never-evading artistic appeal, it is a perfect masterpiece of stone sculpture in the 7th century.

The niches in the East Hill are excavated along the cliffs and zigzag for one kilometre deep into the Wanfogou Valley (the Ten-thousand Buddha Valley). There are more than 20 large and medium-sized caves here, including the Leigutaisandong Cave (the Three Drum-playing Platform Caves), the Gaopingjunwangdong Cave (the Cave of Gaoping's Governor), the Xifangjingtubiankan Niche (the Western Pure Land Niche), the Qianshouqianyanguanyinkan Niche (the Thousand-arm and Thousand-eye Avalokitesvara Bodhisattva Niche), the Kanjingsi Cave (the Sutra-reading Cave), the Erlianhuadong Cave (the Cave of Two Lotuses) and the Siyandong Cave (the Cave of Four Cranes). Most of them are excavated by the emperors, senior officials and believers in Buddhism of the Tang Dynasty. The subject matters include the Zen Sect, the Tantrism Sect, and the Pure Land Sect. The Dawanwufodong Cave (The Grand Ten-thousand Buddha Cave) at the Leigutai Platform (the Drum-

教信徒所开凿，题材内容有禅宗、密宗、净土宗等。其中擂鼓台的大万伍佛洞内容涵盖广博，雕饰华丽殊别，且在三壁壁基雕25尊罗汉像，是7世纪石窟艺术的典型范例。看经寺内，一壁雕29尊与真人等身的罗汉像，俨然是瑰丽的人物画廊，长达30多米。人物塑造形神兼备，性格迥异，无不透视出各个不同的内在情趣，为石窟造像艺术中所罕见。

以《龙门二十品》为代表的碑刻题记可谓一部刻在石头上的史书，具有重要的历史价值，是石窟考古断代分期的依据，也为书法史增添了光辉的篇章。龙门石窟的碑刻题记共30多万字，其数量居世界石窟之冠。它主要是出资开窟造像功德主的发愿文。这些功德主的身份有皇室贵族、显达官吏、寺院僧侣，以及外国的佛教信徒等。文字还包括有历代帝王、文人、士大夫等游览龙门时留下的铭刻。这些碑刻题记往往被书法家所推崇，其中《龙门二十品》最受人青睐，为魏碑书体之精华。碑刻题记中还刻有佛经、药方，内容广涉政治、经济、军事、宗教、地理、民族、姓氏、民俗、艺术、医药、中外文化交流等，无不具有补史之阙、证史之误的重要价值。它不仅是龙门石窟历史沿革的文字记录，还是一部涵盖多种学科的石刻史料。龙门石窟许多有纪年的题记，不唯是龙门石窟考古断代与分期的绝好佐证和标尺，而且在一定程度上也是中国石窟考古的准绳和圭臬。

playing Platform) involves an extensive range of sculptures and is gorgeous and special in its carved ornaments. Moreover, 25 statues of Arhats are carved at the bases of its three walls, creating a typical example of the art of stone carving in the 7th century. In the Kanjingsi Temple, 29 statues of Arhats as tall as human beings are carved into one wall. Stretching for more than 30 meters, they seem to form a magnificent gallery of portraits. The figures, expressive in shape and spirit and different in temperament, tell their different inner tastes, hence a rarity in the art of stone carving.

The steles and inscriptions represented by the "20 Masterpieces of Longmen" can be said to be "history written on stones'. With an important historic value, they not only provide the basis for the division of history into different periods in speleological archeology, but also add a glorious chapter into the history of calligraphy. In the Longmen Grottoes, there are steles and inscriptions containing over 300,000 Chinese characters, which rank first among its kind in the world so far as their quantity is concerned. Most of these steles and inscriptions are the vows of those who had donated funds to the cutting of the grottoes. Among these people, there are the members of imperial families, high-ranking officials, monks, and Buddhist believers from foreign lands. Some of these steles and inscriptions have been left by emperors, scholars and senior officials of various dynasties when they visited the grottoes. These steles and inscriptions have often been held in esteem by calligraphers. The "20 Masterpieces of Longmen" from the inscriptions of the Northern Wei period have been much favored and held as the model of calligraphy developed in those days. These steles and inscriptions are also about Buddhist sutras and prescriptions, in such fields as politics, economy, military affairs, religion, geography, national affairs, names, folkways, art, medicine and cultural exchanges. They are all valuable because they can either fill in gaps or correct mistakes in history. These steles and inscriptions are not only the written records of the historical course of the Longmen Grottoes, but also history carved in stone, covering various branches of study. Moreover, many of the grottoes here have inscriptions recording the time of their excavation. They serve not only as the most ideal evidence and yardsticks for the archeological division of history and development phases of the Longmen Grottoes, but also as the criteria and standard, to some extent, for the archeological study of grottoes in China.

3. 龙门石窟的艺术风格和历史意义

龙门石窟以自身系统独特的艺术语言，揭示了雕塑艺术的创作法则。它远承印度石窟艺术，近继大同云冈石窟风范，与魏晋洛阳和南朝先进而深厚的汉族历史文化相融合。所以龙门石窟的造像艺术一开始就有"改梵为夏"的倾向，呈现出了中国化、世俗化的趋势。其造像的神态气质、衣着服饰、雕刻手法为之一新。造像特征表现出一种"褒衣博带"、"秀骨清像"、表情温和、潇洒飘逸且富有生机、健康和力度的风格。入唐以后，造像雍容华贵、富丽健美、面相丰润、隆胸细腰、典雅端丽，达到了形似完美的高峰。这两种划时代的中原风格，既遵循经典，又突破了宗教仪轨，对不同人物赋予不同的性格特征，人神交融，美丑、善恶对比强烈，写实、夸张运用适度，具有更强的艺术感染力和社会教化作用，堪称中国古代民族雕塑艺术完整的集中代表。它一经形成，便迅速风行全国甚至域外。其周围众多的中小型石窟，远及云冈晚期造像、乐山大佛、甘肃炳灵寺大弥勒佛以及敦煌莫高窟的造像也概莫能外，就连朝鲜、韩国、日本的石窟艺术和佛教造像也不同程度地受到龙门石窟的影响。

龙门石窟是北魏、唐代皇家贵族发愿造像集中的地方，也可以说它主要是皇家意志和行为的体现，具有浓厚的国家宗教色彩。如古阳洞、宾阳三洞和奉先寺大像龛，分别为北魏孝文帝、宣武帝和唐高宗、女皇武则天所开凿。龙门石窟的不少大型洞窟雕像是把皇室宫廷和上层社会披上宗教的外衣，从宫廷官署移到了佛场。又如古阳洞、莲花洞、皇甫公窟、宾阳三洞、敬善寺、万佛洞、极南洞以及未竣工的摩崖三佛龛、高平郡王洞等，都是皇帝、后妃、贵族大臣的祈福之所。

正是由于统治者的直接经营，才能不惜人力、物力营造出如此规模宏大且璀璨绚烂的洞窟。因此龙门石窟的兴衰嬗变，不仅反映了中国历史上5至10世纪皇室崇佛信教的盛衰变化，而且因与众多的重要人物和历史事件有关，也在某些侧面披露了中国历史上一些政治风云的动向和

3. Artistic Style and Historical Significance of the Longmen Grottoes

With their own special artistic expressions, the carvings of the Longmen Grottoes have revealed the laws of sculptural creation. By inheriting the art of stone carving developed in as far as India and the style of the Yungang Grottoes in as close as Datong, the Longmen Grottoes are assimilated with the advanced and profound history and culture developed by the Han Nationality in Luoyang during the Wei and the Jin dynasties as well as in the Southern Dynasty. For this reason, the art of stone carving demonstrated in the Longmen Grottoes has at the very beginning shown the tendency of transforming the style of the Buddhist sculptures from what is Indian into what is Chinese, hence more localized and secular. This is why the statues created here are original in terms of their outlook, clothing and methods of carving. What can be seen in these statues are scholarliness, elegance, mildness, unrestraint, liveliness and vigor. Since the Tang Dynasty, the statues have featured dignified outlook, plump bodies, round faces, full breasts, slim waists and graceful manners. As a result, the works have achieved a likeness not only in appearance but also in spirit, thus attaining the peak of perfection. These two epoch-making styles developed in the Central Plains have both stayed in line with what is classical and broken the limitations of religious traditions. By endowing the statues with different temperaments and characteristics, the sculptors have tried to integrate human beings with gods by putting into contact the beautiful and the ugly, the good and the evil, and by achieving ever greater artistic appeal and social edification through appropriate application of various artistic techniques such as realistic creation and exaggeration. The Longmen Grottoes as they are are worthy of being called an exclusive representative of the art of stone carving developed by ancient Chinese. As soon as they were completed, the Longmen Grottoes began to be imitated both at home and abroad. They have influenced numerous medium-sized and small grottoes around them as well as the late appearing grottoes at Yungang, the Giant Buddha at Leshan, the Giant Buddha Maitreya in the Bingling Temple in Gansu and the Mogao Grottoes at Dunhuang. The art of stone carving and creation of Buddhist statues in Korea and Japan have to some extent also followed suit.

The Longmen Grottoes have been where the royal families and nobles of the Northern Wei and Tang dynasties had taken as the best choice to make vows and

龙门石窟之宾阳中洞
The Binyangzhongdong Cave of the Longmen Grottoes

龙门石窟之莲花洞
The Lianhuadong Cave of the Longmen Grottoes

社会经济态势的发展。

  龙门石窟是佛教众多宗派的集成。在中国佛教史上，由于信仰的神祇和义理不同而出现了许多宗派。龙门石窟就聚集了佛教众多宗派的造

carve statues. Reflecting the will and decisions of the imperial court, the Longmen Grottoes have become the symbol of state religion. For instance, the Guyangdong Cave, the Binyangsandong Cave, the Giant Niche in the Fengxiansidong Cave have been respectively excavated by Emperor Xiaowen and Xuanwu of the Northern Wei Dynasty as well as by Emperor Gaozong and Empress Wu Zetian of the Tang Dynasty. With the transfer of regime from the imperial palace to the Buddhist sites, many of the large niche statues in the Longmen Grottoes have symbolized the wills of the feudal court and the upper class in religion. Similar examples can be found in the Guyangdong Cave, the Lianhuadong Cave, the Huangfugongku Niche, the Binyangsandong Cave, the Jingshansidong Cave, the Wanfodong Cave, the Jinandong Cave as well as the unfinished Moyasanfokan Niche and the Gaopingjunwangdong Cave where the emperors, the empresses, the nobles and the senior officials pray for the blessings from Heaven.

It is exactly because of the direct supervision by the state rulers that manpower and materials could have been assembled to create such massive and splendid grottoes. As the situation stands, the rise and fall of the Longmen Grottoes have reflected the ups and downs of the enthusiasm in and respect for Buddhism by the imperial courts from the 5th century to the 10th century in Chinese history. In the meantime, related with a variety of important historical figures and events, the Longmen Grottoes have also revealed from a certain perspective the political, social and economic trends in Chinese history.

The Longmen Grottoes are an integration of diverse Buddhist sects different in their worship and doctrines and have thus housed multifarious Buddhist statues. For instance, the Giant Niche in the Fengxiansidong Cave belongs to the Avatamsaka Sect, the relief Arhats in the Dawanwufodong Cave and the Kanjingsi Cave in the East Hill have a direct link with the Zen Sect, and the Jingtutang Hall (the Pure Land Hall) in the West Hill and the Xifangjingtubiankan Niche in the East Hill are related with the Pure Land Sect. Besides, the 11 Avalokitesvaras on the upper-south wall of the Wanfodong Cave in the middle of the West Hill, the Qianshouqianyanguanyinkan Niche, the Qianshouguanyinku Cave (the Thousand-arm Avalokitesvara Bodhisattva Cave) and the Leigutaibeidong Cave (the North Cave of the Drum-playing Platform) on the north cliff of the Wanfogou Valley (the Ten-thousand Buddha Valley) are

像。如奉先寺卢舍那佛属华严宗，东山大万伍佛洞和看经寺的罗汉浮雕群像与禅宗有直接联系，西山的净土堂和东山的西方净土变龛同净土宗有关。西山中段万佛洞南上方的11面观音，东山万佛沟北崖的千手千眼观音龛、千手观音窟以及擂鼓台北洞为密宗窟龛。西山40余尊优填王造像与法相宗有关。老龙窝北侧的地藏菩萨龛属三阶教造像等。在一处石窟中聚集了如此众多的佛教宗派造像，在全国石窟中极为罕见。这就大大地丰富了石窟造像的题材内容，反映了龙门石窟初、盛唐时期的中心地位，也为研究佛教宗派的活动及其仪轨提供了实物形象资料。

all Tantrist caves and niches. More than 40 statues of King Udayana in the West Hill are realted with the Dharmalaksana Sect. And the Bodhisattva Ksitigarbha Niche at the north of the Laolongwo Cave falls into the Three Stages Sect. It is rare to see in China the concentration of the statues of so many Buddhist sects in a single site of grottoes. These have greatly helped to enrich the subject matters and contents of the grotto statues and reflected the central position of the Longmen Grottoes in the early and peak Tang Dynasty. In addition, they have also provided visible evidence for the study of the activities of various Buddhist sects and their tracks of rituals.

二、安阳殷墟

1. 殷墟概说

位于河南省安阳市西北洹河两岸的殷墟，是中国第一个有文献记载并经甲骨文及考古发掘所证实的商代晚期都城遗址，也是前14世纪至前11世纪世界青铜文明的重要代表。

前1300年，商王盘庚迁都于殷，历经8代12王，共255年。这一时期的商王朝疆域辽阔，国力空前强盛，开创了中国上古史的新纪元。作为商代晚期的国都，殷墟依托洹河，地理位置优越，形成了以宫殿宗庙区为中心的环形、分层、放射状分布的总体规划形式，体现出一个高度繁荣都城的宏大气派。

位于洹河南岸的宫殿宗庙建筑群以土木为主要建筑材料，形制多样，对西周及以后的宫殿宗庙建筑产生了重要的影响。位于洹河北岸的13座王陵大墓和2,000余座陪葬墓、祭祀坑与车马坑，组成了中国目前已知最早的王陵区。

殷墟甲骨文是中国目前已知最早的成体系的文字，也是世界上古老文字之一。甲骨文的发现印证了中国商代历史的可信性，使中国的信

安阳殷墟
The Yin Ruins in Anyang

II. The Yin Ruins in Anyang City

1. Introduction to the Yin Ruins

The Yin Ruins, situated on the banks of the Huan River in the northwest of Anyang City, Henan Province, is the first ruin of the late Shang Dynasty in China, documented by oracle bone inscriptions and archaeological excavations. It is also important representative of the world bronze civilization from the 14 B.C. to 11 B.C.

King Pan Geng of the Shang Dynasty moved his capital from Yan to Yin around 1300 B.C., and went through eight generations and twelve kings for a total of 255 years. During this period, the Shang Dynasty with vast land and unprecedented national strength created a new era of Chinese ancient history. As the capital of the late Shang Dynasty, the Yin Ruins on the bank of the Huan River took a superior geographical position. It formed a circular stratified and radial distribution of the overall planning with palaces and the ancestral temples in the center, reflecting the grandness of a highly prosperous capital.

The palaces and ancestral temples with diverse structures on the south bank of the Huan River employed earth and wood as the main materials, which exerted an important influence on the palace and ancestral temple architectures in the Western Zhou Dynasty and later dynasties. Located on the north bank of the Huan River, the mausoleum of Emperor Shang is more than 10 meters deep in a large scale with great amount of human sacrifice and numerously exquisite funerary objects, which is the earliest and most complete imperial mausoleum in China.

The oracle bone inscription of the Yin Ruins is one of the earliest known written system in China and one of world's oldest writing systems, which confirms the credibility of Shang history in China and has pushed Chinese credible history forward nearly a thousand years. The Yin Ruins is also famous for its large number of unearthed oracle bone inscriptions. The various bronzes unearthed from the Yin Ruins are exquisitely crafted, delicately decorated and widely used. These rare art treasures enjoy a high reputation across the world. The jade carvings in the Yin Ruins in great number with the exquisite craft formed a climax of the production

史上推了近千年。殷墟也因大量且集中出土甲骨文而名扬天下。殷墟出土的各种青铜器制作精美、纹饰细腻、用途广泛,是不可多得的艺术珍品,在世界上享有极高的声誉。此外,殷墟出土的玉器数量巨大、工艺精湛,形成了中国古代玉器制作与使用的一次高潮。殷墟的手工业空前发达,门类齐全,技术先进。殷墟丰富的文化遗存表明,它不仅是一个地下文物宝库,而且是华夏文明的发祥地之一。殷墟以其重要的历史、文化、科学和艺术价值,书就人类文明史上不可或缺、辉煌壮美、璀璨绚丽的一页,成为人类文明进程中一个重要的里程碑。

安阳殷墟出土的司母戊鼎

The Simuwu Rectangle Ding Unearthed from the Yin Ruins in Anyang

and use of ancient Chinese jade. The handicraft industry of the Yin Ruins had unprecedentedly developed, with complete categories and advanced technologies. The rich cultural heritage of the Yin Ruins shows that it is not only a treasure house underground, but also one of the birthplaces of the Chinese civilization. With its important historic, cultural, scientific and artistic values, the Yin Ruins has become an indispensable, glorious and beautiful page in human civilization history, as well as an important milestone in human civilization.

安阳殷墟出土的甲骨文
Oracle Bone Inscriptions of the Yin Ruins

2. 殷墟的突出价值

殷墟是中国第一个有文献记载并经考古发掘所证实的商代都城遗址。甲骨文的发现和殷墟发掘，确证了商王朝的存在，重新构建了中国古代早期历史的框架，使传统文献记载的商代历史成为信史。

殷墟甲骨文以象形为基础，发展出4,500个以上的单字，并形成了较为固定的语法结构。源于殷墟甲骨文的中国汉字，其书写形式虽然经过了3,000多年的演变，但是以形、音、义为特征的文字和基本语法保留了下来，至今仍为世界上近四分之一的人口使用，对中国文化的形成与发展产生了深远的影响。同时，还影响到周边国家，乃至整个亚洲和全世界。

以青铜器、玉器为代表的殷墟文物，制作精美、工艺精湛、纹饰神秘，是沟通人神关系的祭祀礼器。以司母戊鼎为代表的殷墟青铜器达到了古代东方青铜铸造技术的高峰。以妇好墓玉器为代表的殷墟玉器，采用圆雕、俏色、双勾阴线等主要技法，表现出栩栩如生的人物、动物形

殷墟车马坑展厅
The Carriage Pit Hall of the Yin Ruins

2. The Outstanding Value of the Yin Ruins

The Yin Ruins is the first Shang Dynasty ruins in China documented and confirmed by archaeological excavations. The discovery of oracle bone inscriptions and the excavation of the Yin Ruins confirmed the existence of the Shang Dynasty and reconstructed the early history framework of ancient China, helping to confirm the credibility of Shang history recorded in the traditional documents.

Oracle bone inscriptions are the earliest known developed writing in China. The inscriptions on pictograms include more than 4,500 words and form a relatively fixed grammatical structure. The Chinese characters derive from oracle bones inscriptions. Their writing forms experienced over 3,000-year changes, but their characters with unique form, sound and meaning as well as their basic grammar have been preserved until now. Those characters used by a quarter of the world's population influenced deeply the form and development of Chinese culture, even on its neighboring countries, the whole Asia and the world.

The Yin Ruins cultural relics represented by bronze vessels and jade carvings are exquisitely crafted with exquisite craftsmanship and mysterious ornamentation. They are the rituals for communication between humans and the

妇好墓
Fuhao Tomb

安阳殷墟出土的玉器
Jade Figure of the Yin Ruins

象,堪称世界玉雕艺术宝库中的精华。现存的铜器、玉器作坊遗址和出土的数量惊人的青铜器、玉器等,成为古代东方发达的青铜文化和艺术成就的杰出见证。

以宫殿宗庙建筑为代表的殷墟建筑,采用黄土、木料等建筑材料,夯筑高大厚实的台基,房架用木柱支撑,墙用夯土版筑,具有浓郁的中国古代宫殿建筑特色。以宗族为单位的民居,成片分布,并铺设了陶制排水管道,其聚族而居、聚族而葬的形式,一直延续至今。

以M1001等为代表的13座商代王陵大墓深埋地下,形制壮阔,墓室宏大,棺椁极尽奢华,随葬品极多且精美,人殉、人牲数量惊人,为中国历史上最早、最完整的王陵墓葬群,代表了中国古代早期王陵建设的最高水平。

以人祭、人殉、车马殉葬、兽祭等为代表的殷墟丧葬习俗,记录了中国早期独特的文化现象。这种人祭、人殉、车马殉葬、兽祭的丧葬习

妇好墓出土的玉凤
Jade in Form of Phoenix in Fuhao Tomb

gods. The Yin Ruins bronze vessels among which the Simuwu Rectangle Ding is considered as the representative have reached the peak of ancient eastern bronze casting technology. The Yin Ruins jade carvings especially unearthed from Fuhao Tomb use as the main techniques the round carving, pretty color, and double-hook shade line, showing the vivid characters and animal images, which is the essence of the world jade carving treasure house. The existing bronze vessels, jade carving workshops and an amazing number of unearthed bronzes and jade carvings have become the outstanding witnesses to the developed ancient bronze culture and art in the East.

The palace and royal ancestral shrine area of the Yin Ruins use loess, wood and other building materials to form a tall and thick plat base. The frame is supported by wooden pillars and the wall built with earthenware. It presents rich characteristics of ancient Chinese palace architecture. The residences of the clan are distributed in parts, and the drainage channels of ceramics are laid. The custom of gathering living and burying has been employed until today.

Thirteen royal mausoleums of the Shang Dynasty represented by M1001

俗，延续到春秋时期发展为制作陶俑或木俑等殉葬的方式。

殷墟是中国现代考古学的摇篮。1928年开始的殷墟考古发掘，是中国国家学术机构第一次全面负责、中国学者独立主持的考古发掘，是中国现代考古学诞生的标志。

因此，国际古迹遗址理事会(ICOMOS)认为，殷墟符合世界文化遗产的四条标准：

标准Ⅱ，殷墟是商代晚期的都城，它显示了各种重要影响力的相互交流以及中国古代青铜文化发展的最高水平，包括文字体系。

标准Ⅲ，殷墟的文化遗存为商代晚期的文化传统提供了独特的证据，并且是诸如阳历、阴历体系等许多科技成果和创造发明的见证。

标准Ⅳ，殷墟的宫殿、宗庙和皇家陵墓是中国古代早期建筑的杰出代表，它们具有重要的意义，树立了早期中国宫殿建筑群和皇家陵墓群的典范。

标准Ⅵ，殷墟的实物遗存被视为具有杰出的全球价值的中国文字和语言体系的早期历史、古代信仰、社会体系以及重大历史事件提供了物质证据。

2006年7月，在联合国教科文组织第30届世界遗产大会上，安阳殷墟被列入世界文化遗产。

have been deeply buried underground. The tombs are extremely luxurious with numerous funerary objects and the amazing number of buried living people and sacrifices. They are the earliest and most complete royal tombs known in China, representing the highest level of royal tomb construction in ancient China.

The funeral custom of the Yin Ruins with human sacrifices, living people, car and horse, and animal sacrifices, recorded the unique cultural phenomena of China in ancient times. Such funeral custom had been inherited until the Spring and Autumn Period in the form of pottery or wooden figurines as sacrifices.

The Yin Ruins is the cradle of modern Chinese archaeology. The archaeological excavation of the Yin Ruins since 1928 has been the first comprehensive archaeological excavation of Chinese national academic institutions and independently hosted by Chinese scholars. It is the symbol of the birth of modern Chinese archaeology.

Therefore, according to ICOMS, the Yin Ruins meets four criterions of world cultural heritage.

Criterion (ii). The Yin Ruins, capital of the late Shang Dynasty, exhibits an exchange of important influences and the highest level of development in China's ancient bronze culture, including the system of writing.

Criterion (iii). The cultural remains at the Yin Ruins provide exceptional evidence of cultural traditions in the late Shang Period, and are testimony to many scientific and technical achievements and innovations, such as the solar and lunar calendar system, and the earliest evidence of systematic written Chinese language in oracle bones.

Criterion (iv). The palaces, ancestral shrines and the royal tombs of the Yin Ruins are outstanding examples of early Chinese architecture. They have great significance in establishing the early prototypes for Chinese palace architecture and royal tomb complexes.

Criterion (vi). The material remains discovered at the Yin Ruins provide tangible evidence of the early history of the system of Chinese writing and language, ancient beliefs, social systems, and major historical events, which are considered of outstanding universal significance.

In July 2006, UNECO in 30th session of the World Heritage Committee announced that the Yin Ruins was inscribed into World Heritage List.

三、登封"天地之中"历史建筑群

登封"天地之中"历史建筑群位于河南省会郑州所辖登封市境内。嵩山在古代中国被认为是具有神圣意义的中岳。围绕嵩山的这些古代建筑历经9个朝代，作为世界文化遗产的8组11项历史建筑包括太室阙和中岳庙、少室阙、启母阙、嵩岳寺塔、少林寺建筑群（常住院、初祖庵、塔林）、会善寺、嵩阳书院、观星台。它们不仅以不同的方式展示了"天地之中"的概念，还体现了嵩山作为虔诚的宗教中心的力量。登封"天地之中"历史建筑群是古代建筑中用于祭祀、科学、技术及教育活动的典范。

嵩山是中国历史名山，居五岳之中，其主体由太室山和少室山组成，海拔在300米到1,512米之间。自古以来，嵩山以其地处京畿的优势地理位置，以及自然景观和人文景观的完美结合，成为中华文明最早、最重要的一座圣山。在嵩山主体太室山和少室山区域内的40平方公里范围内，汇集时代跨度如此之长、种类数量如此之多、价值如此之高的古代建筑，堪称举世罕见的独特文化现象。

由于嵩山被认为是万山之祖和神仙居住之地，在"君权神授"的古代，嵩山就成了历代帝王接天通地、永固江山、昌盛国运的祭祀、封禅对象。据铸造于西周初年的《天亡簋》铭文记载，周武王在灭商后"祀于天室（即太室山）"，举行封天祭地的大典，开创了中国盛大、高等级的封禅礼制的先河。秦、汉之后，帝王祭祀嵩山连绵不断。据统计，从周武王开始至清末，历史上有史可查巡狩、祭祀、封禅嵩山的帝王就有68位。

嵩山地区自新石器时代开始，一直是中国史前文化交流的十字要冲。高度发达的史前文化和独特的文化交流格局，使得嵩山地区诞生了中国最早的国家文明，是夏、商、周三代的建都之地、立国中心。《史

III. Historic Monuments of Dengfeng at "the Centre of Heaven and Earth"

The historic monuments at "the Centre of Heaven and Earth" are situated at the foot of Mount Songshan within the borders of Dengfeng in Zhengzhou City, the capital of Henan Province. With 11 sites in 8 clusters, these historic monuments, nominated as the property of the world cultural heritage, include the Taishi Que Gates and the Zhongyue Temple, the Shaoshi Que Gates, the Qimu Que Gates, the Songyue Temple Pagoda, the architectural complex of Shaolin Temple (the Kernel Compound, the Chuzu Temple, the Pagoda Forest), the Huishan Temple, the Songyang Academy of Classical Learning and the Observatory. These buildings have not only revealed what it means to be "the Centre of the Heaven and Earth", but also demonstrated the importance of Mount Songshan as the symbol of religious piety. The building clusters of Dengfeng have best exemplified how the ancient Chinese buildings are used in religious rituals, science, technology and education.

Historically significant, Mount Songshan, largely made up of Mount Taishi and Mount Shaoshi, is the center of the Five Sacred Mountains, with an altitude of 300 to 1,512 metres. With its proximity to ancient capitals and a nice combination of both the natural and cultural landscapes, it has become one of the earliest and most important sacred mountains in Chinese civilization. It is very rare to see in the world that such a large number of highly diversified ancient buildings that span a wide range of ages have coexisted within an area of 40 square kilometres between Mounts Taishi and Shaoshi.

Since Mount Songshan is seen as the place where the god of mountains and the immortals have dwelled, it is used by the emperors of different dynasties to offer sacrifices to Heaven and Earth, to pray for the stability and prosperity of their monarchy and to conduct imperial mountain-top worship in times when the belief of "monarchical power delegated by God" was widely preached by the rulers and assumed by people. According to the inscriptions on a bronze vessel named Tianwanggui made at the early Western Zhou Dynasty, King Wu of the Zhou Dynasty, after his conquest of the Shang Dynasty, offered sacrifices to Heaven and Earth on Mount Taishi, the grandest and most prestigious of this kind in China. Ever since the Qin and Han

记·封禅书》载:"昔三代之居,皆在河洛之间,故以嵩高为中岳。"司马迁的这一记述,得到了中国现代考古学成果的证实。嵩山脚下的登封王城岗遗址和偃师二里头遗址是中国第一个国家——夏的建都之地。位于嵩山东麓的郑州商城遗址和嵩山北麓的偃师商城遗址则是商前期的重要王都。位于嵩山西麓的洛阳成周遗址、东周王城遗址分别是西周的东都洛邑和东周国都。

夏、商、周三代是中华民族形成的重要时期。这一发生在嵩山脚下的波澜壮阔的历史进程,使得嵩山地区不仅成为当时中国文明的中心,也在民族文化心理上刻下了"天地之中"的深深印记。至迟在西周初年,嵩山地区已被称为"中国"(西周初《何尊》铭文)。《周礼·地官·司徒》也记载,周公为了寻找"天地之中"营建东都,在嵩山脚下的阳城"以土圭之法,测土深,正日影,以求地中"。现存登封观星台院内的周公测景台虽为唐人所立,但也从一个侧面反映了嵩山地区为"天地之中"的历史传承。

王城岗遗址地貌
The Wangchenggang Site at Dengfeng

dynasties, religious rituals on the top of Mount Songshan have been unremitting. Statistics show that from King Wu of the Zhou Dynasty to the end of the Qing Dynasty, 68 emperors as seen in historical records went hunting, performed religious worship or offered sacrifices to Heaven and Earth on Mount Songshan.

Since the Neolithic period, the region of Mount Songshan has always been the hub of prehistoric cultural exchanges. The highly developed prehistoric culture and the unique cultural exchanges lead to the birth of the earliest state civilization in China, which makes this region the capital and political centre of the Xia, Shang, and Zhou dynasties. According to the chapter of sacrifice offering in *The Records of the Historian* written by Sima Qian (145-90 B.C.), "people of the three dynasties have all lived between the Yellow River and the Luohe River, hence Mount Songshan as the center of the five mountains". What was stated by Sima Qian has been confirmed by modern archaeological research. The capital of Xia—the first empire in China—was located at the two sites of Wangchenggang of Dengfeng and Erlitou of Yanshi at the foot of Mount Songshan. The site of Shang Capital in Zhengzhou at the eastern foot of Mount Songshan and Shang Capital in Yanshi at the northern foot are where the influential royal capitals were located in the early Shang Dynasty. The site of Chengzhou in Luoyang and Wangcheng in the Zhou Dynasty at the western foot of Mount Songshan are respectively the Eastern Capital of Luoyi of the Western Zhou Dynasty and the Capital of the Eastern Zhou Dynasty.

The Xia, Shang, and Zhou dynasties have constituted a crucial period in which the Chinese nation came into being. What happened in the foothills of Mount Songshan has not only made the region the hub of ancient Chinese civilization but also embedded the notion of "the Centre of Heaven and Earth" in the national and cultural psyche. By the early Western Zhou Dynasty, the region of Mount Songshan has become known as "Zhongguo", or the Center of Land (according to the inscriptions on the ritual wine vessel of He Zun made at the beginning of the Western Zhou Dynasty). Recorded in "The Chancellor" from *The Rites of the Zhou Dynasty*, in Yangcheng City at the foot of Mount Songshan, the Duke of Zhou, in order to locate the capital at the "the Centre of Heaven and Earth", used a sundial to measure the depth of earth and shadow of sunlight at Yangcheng City in the foothills of Mount Songshan. The Zhougong

佛教于汉代传入中国后最初的数百年里，嵩山地区便集中创建了多座寺院，包括嵩岳寺、少林寺、会善寺等。其后，随着禅宗初祖达摩在少林寺传法故事的渲染及禅宗的广传，嵩山成了佛教的繁荣圣地。嵩山地区同样在道教发展史上扮演过重要角色。

正是在这样的历史文化背景下，伴随着原始宗教的发展，嵩山也由于地邻京畿和"天地之中"的文化心理优势，最早完成了从原始的山岳崇拜对象到圣山崇拜对象的转换，确立了民族文化心理上的圣山地位，也汇聚了各类建筑的精华。

登封"天地之中"历史建筑群历经东汉、北魏、唐、五代、宋、金、元、明、清等，至今2,000多年，是中国历史建筑群保存种类最多、修建时间跨度最长、历史文化内涵最丰富者。登封"天地之中"历史建筑群的创建和兴盛，与历代帝王或大臣巡狩、封禅、祭祀中岳，与人们的嵩山为"天地之中"文化心理有密切的联系。登封"天地之中"历史建筑群深受嵩山的地理环境、历史文化、礼制文化、宗教文化、教育文化、科技文化、建筑文化、社会状况的历史进程影响。除了历代帝王亲自或遣使到嵩山巡狩、祭祀之外，还有众多文人学士、高僧名道来嵩山游览讲学、隐居修身，在这里留下了大量与之相关的建筑和遗迹。

Sundial Platform in the courtyard of the Observatory in Dengfeng, though built in the Tang Dynasty, reveals the historical origin of the region's status as "the Centre of Heaven and Earth".

In the first few centuries after Buddhism was introduced to China in the Han Dynasty, a great many Buddhist temples were established in the region of Mount Songshan, including the Songyue Temple, the Shaolin Temple, the Huishan Temple, and other temples. Later, with the story of how Bodhidharma the Master of the Zen Sect of Buddhism spread the Buddhist truth at the Shaolin Temple as well as the popularization of the Zen beliefs, Mount Songshan has become recognized as a sacred place for the spread of Buddhism and the same importance has been seen in the development of Taoism.

Against such a historical and cultural background and with the development of the earliest religion, Mount Songshan, taking its cultural and geographical advantage of being next to the capital and situated at "the Centre of Heaven and Earth", becomes the first to be worshiped as the sacred mountain other than an ordinary one. With the integration of the essence of various architectural forms, the divinity of Mount Songshan has been well acknowledged in the national and cultural consciousness of the Chinese civilization.

Spanning over 2,000 years, the historic monuments have witnessed such dynasties as Eastern Han, Northern Wei, Tang, the Five Dynasties, Song, Jin, Yuan, Ming, Qing, as well as the Republic period. These building clusters have been supreme in their variety, in the span of the time of their construction and in their historical and cultural significance. Their construction and prosperity are closely related with the fact that Mount Songshan is frequented by emperors and ministers in their huntings, religious worship or sacrifices made to Heaven and Earth, and with the recognition of the mountain as "the Centre of Heaven and Earth". The monuments are deeply influenced by the mountain in many ways, not only by its geographic environment, history, ritual systems, religion, education, science and architecture, but by the evolution of society. Emperors of different dynasties have offered sacrifices to the mountain in person or through their deputies, whilst many men of letters, scholars, eminent monks and Taoists have come to the mountain to give lectures or to live in seclusion or self-cultivation, leaving behind them buildings or other cultural relics.

1. 太室阙和中岳庙

太室阙是中岳庙前身太室祠前的神道阙，位于太室山黄盖峰下中岳庙天中阁前600余米处的中轴线上，是历代中岳庙前导空间的重要建筑。太室阙始建于汉安帝元初五年（118年），以青灰色块石砌筑，分为东西2阙，间距6.75米，相对如门，是太室祠的象征性大门。阙身平面呈长方形，上有出檐的四阿顶，为石质仿木结构，东西2阙分别由母阙和子阙组成，各通高3.96米，长2.13米，厚0.7米，子阙比母阙低1.31米。阙身四周雕饰有反映汉代社会风俗和信仰的画像，保存较好的有50余幅。阙的题额阳刻在西阙南面上部，仅存"中岳太室阳城"6字。铭记阴刻在西阙北面，计27行，每行7字，内容主要是赞颂中岳神君的灵应和阳城县长吕常等建阙的缘由。太室阙是我国现存最早的一座庙阙，是古代祭祀太室山神的重要实物见证，亦是中国古代祭祀礼制建筑的典范。

中岳庙位于太室山南麓，南距太室阙600米，坐北朝南。中岳庙前身是太室祠，至迟在汉武帝时已经存在，原为祭祀嵩山太室山神的场所。中岳庙历史上几经重修，现存建筑格局至少可以上溯到金代，建筑

登封"天地之中"历史建筑群之太室阙
Taishi Que Gates of the Historic Monuments of Dengfeng at "the Centre of Heaven and Earth"

1. The Taishi Que Gates and the Zhongyue Temple

The Taishi Que Gates are situated on the central axis 600 meters from the Tianzhong Pavilion of the Zhongyue Temple at the foot of the Huanggai Peak of Mount Taishi. They were originally a pair of structures flanking the sacred pathway leading up to the Taishi Shrine—the precursor of the Zhongyue Temple—and later became important architectural elements in front of the temple. These structures were first built in the fifth year of Yuanchu during the reign of Emperor An of the Han Dynasty (118 A.D.). Standing 6.75 meters apart with the east and west gate on either side, they form a symbolic entrance to the Taishi Shrine. Although made of gray stone, the structures resemble wooden gates. Measuring 3.96 meters high, 2.13 meters long and 0.7 meter thick, they each have a rectangular surface and an overhanging hipped roof and are composed of the major gate in the east and the minor gate in the west, 1.31 meters lower than the major one. The gates are ornamented on the four sides with carvings that reflect

登封"天地之中"历史建筑群之太室阙西阙

West Taishi Que Gate of the Historic Monuments of Dengfeng at "the Centre of Heaven and Earth"

登封"天地之中"历史建筑群之太室阙东阙

East Taishi Que Gate of the Historic Monuments of Dengfeng at "the Centre of Heaven and Earth"

登封"天地之中"历史建筑群之中岳庙
Zhongyue Temple of the Historic Monuments of Dengfeng at "the Centre of Heaven and Earth"

多复建于清代。中岳庙南北长650米，东西宽166米，面积107,900平方米。

  中岳庙依山势而建，自南向北，渐次升高，前后高差37米。庙中有殿、宫、楼、阁、亭、廊等建筑39座近400间。中岳庙具有中国传统官式建筑风格，建筑依中轴线左右对称，纵深多进。中轴线上共有11进建筑，是中岳庙的主体建筑。前6进为门、坊建筑，组成深远神圣的中轴甬道。自峻极门向后为主殿宇。中轴线建筑高大宏伟，多用琉璃瓦顶，雕饰彩绘华丽，至峻极殿构成庙宇中心。峻极殿建筑在高台之上，面阔9间，进深5间，重檐庑殿，覆以黄琉璃瓦，雕梁画栋，高达23米，面积920平方米，前有广阔月台，雄伟辉煌，是供奉和祭祀中岳神的主殿，是五岳中最大的殿宇。两侧分布四岳殿等多组院落，建筑以单层布瓦色调陪衬主体建筑，是道士举行祀典和生活的地方。庙内尚有古代碑刻73品，有汉代到清代古柏330余株。

the social customs and beliefs of the Han Dynasty, among which over fifty are well preserved. Of the inscriptions, only the six characters of "Zhong Yue Tai Shi Yang Cheng" carved in relief on the upper part of the southern side of the western gate are legible. The 27 lines (with seven characters in each line) carved in intaglio on the other side of the gate contain a eulogy to the magic power of the God of Zhongyue (Central Sacred Mountain) and recount why Lv Chang, the magistrate of Yangcheng, among others, built the gates. The Taishi Que Gates are the oldest temple-side structures to be found in China. They provide important evidence of the ancient practice of offering sacrifices to the God of Mount Taishi, and are notable as a typical example of official architectural style in ancient religious worship.

Facing south, the Zhongyue Temple is situated at the southern foot of Mount Taishi, 600 meters south of the Taishi Que Gates. Its precursor, the Taishi Shrine, built during the reign of Emperor Wudi of the Han Dynasty at the latest, is a place for offering sacrifices to the God of Mount Taishi. The Zhongyue Temple has been rebuilt several times throughout history. The present layout of the temple can be traced back to no later than the Jin Dynasty, and most of its components were rebuilt in the Qing Dynasty. The temple measures 650 meters from the south to the north and 166 meters from the east to the west, covering an area of 107,900 square metres.

The Zhongyue Temple is built along the mountain slope, ascending gradually from the south to the north, with a 37-meter elevation difference. Thirty-nine buildings or nearly 400 rooms such as halls, palaces, towers, pavilions, and corridors are lying in the temple. The Zhongyue Temple features traditional Chinese official buildings, as they are built on the central axis from the north to the south, with bilateral symmetry and courtyards stretching in depth. On its central axis lie eleven buildings, which are the main body of the Zhongyue Temple. The first six buildings from the south are gates and archways, forming a deep and sacred pathway of the central axis. Behind the Junji Gate are the main palaces. The buildings on the central axis are towering and magnificent, most with glazed tile roofs, exquisite carvings and colored drawings or patterns. These buildings, together with the Junji Palace on the other end, are where the temple center is. The 23-meter-high Junji Palace, covering an area of 920 square meters, is constructed on a high terrace, with

登封"天地之中"历史建筑群之中岳庙峻极殿
Junji Palace of the Zhongyue Temple of the Historic Monuments of Dengfeng at "the Centre of Heaven and Earth"

完整的建筑布局使中岳庙成为一座主次分明、错落有致、布局紧凑、色调和谐的庞大建筑群。由太室阙和中岳庙构成的礼制建筑群，是古代祠庙建筑群空间处理的优秀范例。中岳庙是五岳中现存最大的历史建筑群，是清代官式建筑的代表和古代山岳崇拜的实物见证。

nine chambers in width and five ones in depth, each with double-eave hip roofs and covered with yellow glazed tiles. Ahead of it is built a broad platform, grand and splendid, which is the main palace for enshrining and worshiping the gods of the Zhongyue Temple: it is also the largest palace among the Five Mountains of China (Wu Yue). On both of its sides scatter multiple-unit courtyards such as the Siyue Palace (the Palace of Four Mountains). The buildings are in a single-layered black color against the color of the main architecture. It is where the Taoists live or hold worship ceremonies. Inside the temple are left 73 types of ancient steles, and about 330 ancient cypresses planted between the Han Dynasty and the Qing Dynasty.

The complete architectural composition renders the Zhongyue Temple a giant, well-proportioned architectural complex with a clear distinction between the main buildings and the minor ones, compact layout as well as harmonious tonal matching. The architectural complex composed of the Taishi Que Gates and the Zhongyue Temple is an excellent example in space design of the ancestral temple architectural complex. As the largest existing historic architectural complex among the Five Mountains, the Zhongyue Temple represents the official buildings of the Qing Dynasty and witnesses the worship of the mountains in ancient times.

登封"天地之中"历史建筑群之中岳庙镇库铁人
Iron Generals of the Zhongyue Temple of the Historic Monuments of Dengfeng at "the Centre of Heaven and Earth"

2. 少室阙

少室阙是少室山庙前的神道阙，位于少室山下，面对太室山，少溪河从背后潺潺流过。少室阙始建于汉安帝延光二年（123年），少室山庙现已无存。少室阙以青灰色块石砌筑，其结构和太室阙基本相同。少室阙东西两阙间距7.6米，相对如门，是少室山庙的象征性大门。东阙通高3.37米，西阙通高3.75米，各长2.12米，厚0.7米。阙身画像剥蚀较为严重，保存较完整的有60余幅。其中具有突出价值的画像有马戏、月宫图、蹴鞠等。阙铭为篆书，刚劲俊逸，和启母阙铭风格相同。少室阙是古代祭祀少室山神的重要实物见证，也是中国古代祭祀礼制建筑的典范之一。

登封"天地之中"历史建筑群之少室阙东阙
East Shaoshi Que Gate of the Historic Monuments of Dengfeng at "the Centre of Heaven and Earth"

2. The Shaoshi Que Gates

The Shaoshi Que Gates, or the Shendao Que Gates, flanking the approach to the now demolished Temple of Mount Shaoshi, are located at the foot of Mount Shaoshi, facing Mount Taishi, with the Shaoxi River flowing behind. The Shaoshi Que Gates were firstly built in the second year of Yanguang of Emperor An of the Han Dynasty (123 A.D.), and the Temple of Mount Shaoshi is out of existence now. The Shaoshi Que Gates are constructed with green and grey block stones, its structure being almost the same with that of the Taishi Que Gates. The east and west Ques are 7.6 meters apart, facing each other like two gates, which are also the symbolic gates of the Temple of Mount Shaoshi. The east Que gate is 3.37 meters high and the west 3.75, each with the length of 2.12 meters and the thickness of 0.7 meter. The drawings on the Que gate bodies have been seriously corroded over time, with only 60 ones remaining well-preserved. Among them, the drawings with notable value are those of the Circus, the Moon Palace and Cuju (ancient game of soccer). The inscriptions on the Que gates are of seal character, bold and elegant, in the same style as the inscriptions on the Qimu Que Gates. The Shaoshi Que Gates have witnessed the worship of the gods of Mount Shaoshi in ancient times. They are also representative of the official architectural style in ancient religious worship.

登封"天地之中"历史建筑群之少室阙西阙

West Shaoshi Que Gate of the Historic Monuments of Dengfeng at "the Centre of Heaven and Earth"

3. 启母阙

启母阙是启母庙前的神道阙，位于嵩山万岁峰下山坡上，北距启母石190米。启母庙今已无存。据阙铭记载，启母阙亦建于汉安帝延光二年。阙以青灰色块石砌筑，其结构和太室阙相同，东西2阙间距6.8米，相对如门，是启母庙的象征性大门。现存西阙高3.17米，东阙高3.18米，各长2.13米，厚0.7米。阙身画像保存较完整的有60余幅，具有突出价值的雕刻画面有夏禹化熊、启母化石、幻术、斗鸡等。启母阙的铭文为篆书，堂溪协撰写，字体俊逸刚劲，计35行，每行12字，是3阙铭记中保存较好者，内容主要是赞颂夏禹治水的功绩和"三过家门而不入"的忘我精神。另一段铭记为隶书，记述堂溪协之子中郎将堂溪典来嵩山祈雨的情况。

启母阙与太室阙、少室阙并称"汉三阙"，其画像的雕刻技法，主要是浅浮雕加阴线刻，以线写形，以形传神，用粗犷古拙的形象，显现

登封"天地之中"历史建筑群之启母阙

The Qimu Que Gates of the Historic Monuments of Dengfeng at "the Centre of Heaven and Earth"

3. The Qimu Que Gates

The Qimu Que Gates, or the Shendao Que Gates, flanking the approach to the now demolished Qimu Temple, are located at the foot of Peak Wansui of Mount Songshan, 190 meters away from the Qimu Stone to its north. The Qimu Temple is nowhere to be seen now. According to the inscriptions on the Qimu Que Gates, they were built in the second year of Yanguang of Emperor An of the Han Dynasty. The Qimu Que Gates are constructed with green and grey block stones, its structure being almost the same as that of the Taishi Que Gates. Its east and west Ques are 6.8 meters away, facing each other like two gates, which are also the symbolic gates of the Qimu Temple. The existing west Que gate is 3.17 meters high and the east 3.18. Both are 2.13 meters wide and 0.7 meter thick. About 60 drawings on the bodies of the Que gates are well-preserved. Among them, the engraved drawings with notable value are about the transformation of King Yu of the Xia Dynasty into a Bear and about the mother of King Qi into a Statuary Stone. Along with those are also Magic-playing, Cockfight and so on. The inscriptions on the Qimu Que Gates are seal characters by Tangxi Xie. They are bold and elegant, with 35 lines in total and 12 characters in each line. They are better preserved among the three Que Gates of the Eastern Han Dynasty, namely, the Shaoshi Que Gates, the Taishi Que gates and the Qimu Que Gates. The inscriptions are mainly the eulogies of Yu, the Founder of the Xia Dynasty, concerning his achievements in controlling the floods and how he has sacrificed himself by neglecting his own home while bypassing it three times. Another part of the inscriptions are official scripts describing Tangxi Dian, the commander of imperial corps and the son of Tangxi Xie, about how he has come to Mount Songshan to pray for rains.

The Qimu Que Gates, together with the Taishi Que Gates and the Shaoshi Que Gates, are called the "Three Han Que Gates". The engraving techniques of their paintings are mainly bas-relief plus incised carvings. Lines are applied to build up the figures which in turn have reflected the overall style, coarse but plain and simple. The majestic images have reflected the bold creativeness of the Han artists. Simple and unadorned, the "Three Han Que Gates", as the rare remains of the ancient buildings of the Han Dynasty, not only have the classical features of stone buildings, but also show the characteristics of wooden structure

出磅礴雄浑的气势，是汉代艺术家的大胆艺术创造。汉三阙作为极少的汉代建筑遗存，造型朴拙，既具有石构建筑的典型面貌，又在屋顶等细部上反映了木构建筑的若干特点，其上的画像和铭文十分精美，形态夸张，富有浪漫气息，是汉代艺术风格的集中反映。汉三阙的建筑形式和画像内容是研究建筑史、美术史和东汉社会史的珍贵资料。

启母阙蹴鞠画像
Painting of Cuju (folk soccer game two thousand years ago) on the Qimu Que Gates

in such specific places as the roof. The paintings and inscriptions are both bold and romantic, hence the display of the artistic style of the Han Dynasty. The architectural designs and paintings of the "Three Han Que Gates" are all valuable in studying the history of architecture, art and society of the Eastern Han Dynasty.

启母阙玉兔捣药画像
Painting of Rabbit of the Moon Palace Ramming Medicine on the Qimu Que Gates

4. 嵩岳寺塔

嵩岳寺塔为12边形密檐式筒体结构砖塔，位于登封市区北5公里的嵩岳寺内，背靠太室诸峰，西傍西灵台山，东依东灵台山，南面山坡漫缓开阔，数十里之外，即遥遥可望。寺东溪水潺潺，山清水秀，林木葱郁，环境清幽。嵩岳寺塔体量高大，外呈米黄色，是为纪念佛祖释迦牟尼而建。

嵩岳寺原是北魏宣武帝的离宫，始建于北魏永平年间（508—511年）。现在的嵩岳寺塔院只是原嵩岳寺的一个部分，现存建筑除嵩岳寺塔外，还有大雄宝殿、伽蓝殿和六祖殿。嵩岳寺塔是该寺留存至今最具建筑艺术和景观价值的代表性建筑。

登封"天地之中"历史建筑群之嵩岳寺塔
Songyue Temple Pagoda of the Historic Monuments of Dengfeng at "the Centre of Heaven and Earth"

4. The Songyue Temple Pagoda

The Songyue Temple Pagoda is a dodecagonal-structured brick tower with a roof of densely overlapping eaves. It is located in the Songyue Temple, 5 km north of Dengfeng City, with the peaks of Mount Taishi at its back, West Lingtai Mountain on the west and East Lingtai Mountain on the east. Its southern slopes are open and wide, with the range of views stretching slowly for dozens of miles. To the east of the temple are streams and lush woods among the mountains, creating a tranquil environment. The Songyue Temple Pagoda is tall and exhibits a cream color outside. It is built to commemorate Sakyamuni the Buddha.

The Songyue Temple was originally the provisional palace of Emperor Xuanwu of the Northern Wei Dynasty. It was built in the Yongping Period of the Northern Wei Dynasty (508-511 A.D.). The current courtyard of the Songyue Temple Pagoda is only a part of the original Songyue Temple. In addition to the Songyue Temple Pagoda, the Daxiongbaodian Hall (the Main Hall), the Jialandian Hall (the Garan Hall) and the Liuzudian Hall (Hall of the Sixth Master of the Zen Sect of Buddhism) are also among the existing buildings. As the representative building that has survived, the Songyue Temple Pagoda has the greatest value of architectural art and landscape viewing.

嵩岳寺塔作为佛教鼎盛时期的北魏遗存，在佛塔的类型上有极大的开创性，塔身上段的抛物线形轮廓，下段塔门采用的火焰券形门洞和壶门狮子的装饰等，是中国建筑艺术和西域建筑交流的产物。塔的整体刚劲挺秀，细部制作精致质朴，达到了极高的艺术水平，同时也表现出高超的造塔技术，成为高层筒体结构的先驱。后来的唐代方塔，如小雁塔、香积寺塔等，均脱胎于此。在建筑史上，嵩岳寺塔极为重要。嵩岳寺塔为佛塔中密檐式塔的重要例证，从整体造型到细部雕饰均有明确的宗教文化含义，是佛教文化传播与演变在建筑上的重要体现。

The Songyue Temple Pagoda is the relic of the Northern Wei Dynasty in which Buddhism was in its prime. It has great pioneering feature in the type of stupa. The parabolic contour of the upper part of the body, the flame-shaped door of the lower section and the decoration of the lion of the kunmen altar are the results of the exchanges between the art of Chinese architecture and that of the Western one. In all, the pagoda is sturdy, tall and straight. The details are not only exquisite and plain, reaching a very high level of art, but also showing superb pagoda-building technology, hence making the pagoda a pioneer in the high-rise cylinder structure. Later square pagodas of the Tang Dynasty, such as the Small Wild Goose Pagoda and the Xiangji Temple Pagoda, are all descended from this. This is extremely important in the history of architecture. As an important example of the Buddhist pagodas with densely overlapping eaves, the Songyue Temple Pagoda carries clear religious and cultural message from the overall shape to the detailed carvings. It is the very epitome of the spread and evolution of Buddhist culture in architecture.

5. 少林寺建筑群（常住院、初祖庵、塔林）

少林寺建筑群位于登封市区西北13公里处的少室山阴，现存历史建筑包括少林寺常住院、初祖庵、塔林等。其中，初祖庵是寺僧为纪念佛教禅宗初祖菩提达摩而营建的纪念性建筑。塔林为少林寺历代高僧的墓塔群。少林寺自古以来，被称为"天下第一名刹"，不仅是中国佛教禅宗的祖庭，还是中国武术最大流派——少林派的发源地，有"天下功夫出少林"的美誉，是一处禅、武结合的圣地。少林寺建筑群规模宏大，遥遥望去，红墙绿瓦，绿树掩映，呈现出"深山藏古寺，碧溪锁少林"的清幽意境。

少林寺常住院坐北朝南，背依五乳峰，面对少室山，少溪河从门前潺潺流过，常住院山门距少溪河65米。北魏太和十九年（495年），孝文帝元宏为安顿天竺僧人跋陀传教而敕建少林寺。寺院天王殿、大雄宝殿、藏经阁、方丈室、立雪亭、千佛殿等7进建筑，阶梯升高，高差22.61米。其明、清建筑多为单檐琉璃瓦，硬山、歇山、庑殿间而有

登封"天地之中"历史建筑群之少林寺
Shaolin Temple of the Historic Monuments of Dengfeng at "the Centre of Heaven and Earth"

5. Architectural Complex of the Shaolin Temple (the Kernel Compound, the Chuzu Temple, and the Pagoda Forest)

The Architectural Complex of the Shaolin Temple is located in the north of Mount Shaoshi, 13 kilometers northwest to Dengfeng City. The existing historic monuments include the Kernel Compound, the Chuzu Temple, the Pagoda Forest, the surrounding ancient pagodas and so on. Among them the Chuzu Temple is the monument constructed by the monks of the Shaolin Temple to commemorate Bodhidharma, the ancestor of the Zen Sect of China's Buddhism. The Pagoda Forest is the cluster of tomb pagodas of the Shaolin Temple for the burial of the great monks. Since ancient times, the Shaolin Temple has been called "the first temple in the world". It is not only the ancestral temple of the Zen Sect of China's Buddhism, but also the birthplace of the Shaolin School, the largest branch of Chinese martial arts. As a holy place which sees the combination of Buddhism and martial arts, the Shaolin Temple has been honored with the praise that "the world's martial arts come from Shaolin". Tranquil and private, the grand Shaolin Temple complex, visible from the distance, presents a painting of red walls and green glazed tiles among the shady lush trees. And here goes the saying that "an ancient temple hides itself in the deep mountains and a green stream surrounds the Shaolin Temple".

The Kernel Compound of the Shaolin Temple is located in the north while facing the south, with Peak Wuru at its back and Mount Shaoshi ahead, the Shaoxi River flowing right in front of it. The gate to the Compound is 65 meters away from the Shaoxi River. In the 19th year of Taihe of the Northern Wei Dynasty (495 A.D.), Yuanhong, or Emperor Xiaowen, built the Shaolin Temple for the Indian monk Batuo to spread his teachings. Along the central axis of the Compound, there are seven buildings, which are the Tianwandian Hall, the Daxiongbaodian Hall, the Sutra Depository, the Abbot Room, the Lixue Pavilion and the Qianfodian Hall (the Thousand Buddha Hall). As the steps stretch upwards, the buildings rise up to a height of 22.61 meters. Most of the buildings in the Ming and Qing dynasties are decorated with glazed tiles with single eave. Except for the Qianfodian Hall, the sizes of all the buildings are quite moderate. The Qianfodian Hall is seven-room wide, and the walls inside the hall are covered with the precious murals of more than 300 square meters. On both sides of the

登封"天地之中"历史建筑群之少林寺大雄宝殿
The Daxiongbaodian Hall (The Main Hall) of the Historic Monuments of Dengfeng at "the Centre of Heaven and Earth"

之,除千佛殿外,体量适中。千佛殿面阔7间,殿内墙壁满绘壁画达300多平方米,甚为珍贵。中轴线两侧有钟楼、鼓楼、六祖堂、紧那罗殿、东西寮房、文殊殿、普贤殿、白衣殿、地藏殿等附属建筑,其中白衣殿绘有少林拳谱、十三武僧救秦王、紧那罗御红巾等反映少林武术、历史的壁画。再外,西有塔院,东有禅堂、僧房等。常住院内还保有宋代释迦塔、下生弥勒佛塔,历代碑碣174品以及秦槐和树龄超过1,500年的银杏等古树名木,共同构成了一座深山之中僧人从事佛事活动、习武和生活的著名佛教寺院。常住院内现存碑碣、壁画是少林寺发展的历史见证,也是研究历史、文化、武术、宗教、建筑、书法、雕刻、美术乃至寺院与域外文化交流等极为珍贵的实物资料。少林寺作为禅宗祖庭和少林武术的发源地,在佛教界和中国武术界有崇高地位并享有盛名。

初祖庵位于少林寺常住院西北2公里处的龟背形山丘上,它背连五乳峰,周围丘洞环抱,陡崖绝壑,古木参天,北距达摩洞1,800米。初

central axis are the Bell Tower, the Drum Tower, the Liuzutang Hall (the Sixth Patriarch Hall), the Jinnaluodian Hall (the Kinnara Hall), the East and West Monk's Apartments, the Wenshudian Hall (the Manjusri Hall), the Puxiandian Hall (the Samantabhadra Hall), the Baiyidian Hall (the White Robe Hall), the Dizangdian Hall (the Ksitigahba Buddhisattva Hall) and the other annexes. Among them, the Baiyidian Hall has murals on its walls which exhibit the skills and history of Shaolin Martial Arts, which are about either the chart of Shaolin martial arts or how the thirteen warrior monks saved Emperor Li Shimin of the Tang Dynasty and how the Kinnara resisted the Red Turban Rebellions. Outward, there are pagoda courtyards in the west, meditation halls and monk's dormitories in the east. In the Kernel Compound, there are also the Shijiata Pagoda (Pagoda of Sakyamuni Buddha) of the Song Dynasty, the Xiashengmilefota Pagoda (Pagoda of Maitreya Buddha's Birth), 174 types of steles in the past dynasties, and precious ancient trees such as the pagoda tree of the Qin Dynasty and the ginkgo tree which is more than 1,500 years old. Together, they contribute to a famous Buddhist monastery in the deep mountains, in which the Buddhist monks are engaged in Buddhist activities, martial arts and daily rituals. The existing steles and murals in the Monastery are not only the historical witnesses of the development of the Shaolin Temple but also extremely valuable evidence for the study of history, culture, martial arts, religion, architecture, calligraphy, sculpture, fine arts and the cultural exchanges between the temple and outside. As the temple of the Master of the Zen Sect and the birthplace of Shaolin martial arts, the Shaolin Temple maintains a supreme status in the Buddhist world and enjoys a respectable reputation in the Chinese martial arts field.

  The Chuzu Temple is located on the turtle-shaped hill, 1,800 meters northwest of the Kernel Compound of the Shaolin Temple. Nestled in hills and streams, it is connected to Peak Wuru at its back, surrounded with cliffs and ancient trees. A naturally-formed stone cave, the Dharma Cave, close to Peak Wuru, was built to commemorate Buddha Dharma. With an area of 3,418 square metres, the courtyard of the Chuzu Temple is 88.28 meters long from the north to the south and 38.72 meters wide from the east to the west. On the central axis, there are the Gate, the Main Hall and the Qianfodian Hall, with the Mianbiting Pavilion (Wall-facing Pavilion), the Shenggongshengmuting Pavilion (the

登封"天地之中"历史建筑群之少林寺塔林
Pagoda Forest of the Shaolin Temple among the Historic Monuments of Dengfeng at "the Centre of Heaven and Earth"

祖庵院落南北长88.28米，东西宽38.72米，面积3,418平方米。中轴线上分布着山门、大殿、千佛阁等3座建筑，两侧有面壁亭、圣公圣母亭等。初祖庵大殿建于宋代，出檐深远，斗栱硕大，雕饰精美，反映出宋代木构建筑优美的造型和精致的工艺。初祖庵大殿的建造年代与中国古代建筑科学巨著《营造法式》的成书年代相近，其斗栱、梁架、雕饰多与《营造法式》的制度相符合，是宋代木构建筑技术的重要例证，在木构、石雕方面的技术做法甚至可称为孤例，为今人理解《营造法式》提供了独特的实物展示。此外，现在庵院中还保存有历史建筑5座，宋、金以后碑碣49余品，以及唐代"六祖手植柏"等。

少林寺塔林位于少林寺常住院以西280余米处的山坡上，占地面积约2万平方米，南临少溪河，北靠五乳峰，依山傍水，环境优美。这里古塔丛立，势如密林，故有"塔林"之称。塔林及周边地区保存唐、五代、宋、金、元、明、清7个朝代（791—1803年）的古塔，其中唐代6座，五代1座，宋代2座，金代8座，元代44座，明代143座，清代14座，建年不详23座，共计241座。大多塔上都有石质或砖质塔铭。塔林内还

Pavilion of Dharma Parents) and the other monuments on both sides. The Chuzu Temple was built in the Song Dynasty. It has long, overhanging eaves and a giant bracket system. Delicately carved, it reflects the beautiful shape and exquisite craftsmanship of the wood architecture of the Song Dynasty. The construction date of the Chuzu Temple is close to the completion of *Mode of Construction*, the ancient Chinese architectural science masterpiece. Its brackets, beams and carvings are consistent with what the book has decreed, which has significantly illustrated the wood structure construction technology in the Song dynasties. The technical practice in wood structure and stone engraving can be regarded as a unique case, which provides a special physical display for today's understanding of *Mode of Construction*. In addition, there remain five historical buildings in the monastery, more than 49 types of steles after the Song and Jin dynasties and the "the Cypress Planted Personally by the Sixth Patriarch" in the Tang Dynasty.

  The Shaolin Temple Pagoda Forest is a cluster of sacred tomb pagodas of eminent monks of the past dynasties. It is located on the slope 280 meters from the west of the Kernel Compound of the Shaolin Temple. Bordering the Shaoxi River in the south and Peak Wuru in the north, it covers an area of about 20,000 square metres. Surrounded with mountains and rivers, it is endowed with a pleasant natural landscape. Here, the ancient pagodas stand densely like a forest, which explains why the "Pagoda Forest" has been taken as its name. In the Pagoda Forest and its surroundings are preserved the ancient pagodas of the seven dynasties (791-1803 A.D.) of Tang, Five Dynasties, Song, Jin, Yuan, Ming and Qing. Among the pagodas six are from the Tang Dynasty, one from the Five Dynasties, two from the Song Dynasty, eight from the Jin dynasties, 44 from the Yuan Dynasty, 143 from the Ming Dynasty, and 14 from the Qing Dynasty. The year of construction of some other 23 pagodas remains unknown. In total, there are 241 pagodas, most of which have stone or brick inscriptions. Fourteen types of steles are also kept in the Pagoda Forest. It has displayed the changes in the shape and artistic style of tomb pagodas in different periods since the Tang Dynasty. It shows the exchanges between and the integration of Zen Buddhism and the other different cultures in history. As a pagoda cluster, the Shaolin Temple Pagoda Forest has the largest number of ancient pagodas in China. Known as the "Ancient Pagoda Art Museum", the Pagoda Forest is a treasure trove of physical materials

有14品碑刻。塔林为人们展示了自唐以来不同时期墓塔造型、艺术风格的变化，表现出了历史上佛教禅宗文化与多种文化的交流与融合。少林寺塔林是中国现存古塔数量最多的塔群，被称为"古塔艺术博物馆"，是综合研究中国建筑、雕刻艺术和宗教发展史的实物资料宝库。

少林武僧练武场面
Monks of the Shaolin Temple Performing Martial Arts

for comprehensive research in the history of not only Chinese architectural development, but also engraving art and religious development.

6. 会善寺

会善寺位于登封市区西北6公里处的太室山积翠峰下，左倚龙山，右傍虎山，林木葱郁，风光旖旎。会善寺前身是北魏孝文帝元宏的一所离宫，魏亡后舍宫为寺。会善寺坐北朝南，常住院南北长65.06米，东西宽57.53米，占地3,743平方米，中轴线保存有照壁、山门、大殿东西配房等，两侧有东西配房等8座历史建筑。山门前照壁上嵌有"天中山"和"天光云影"刻石。大殿建筑在广阔的月台后部，斗栱硕大，结构严谨，保存完整。会善寺大殿是嵩山地区现存唯一的元代木结构建筑。

会善寺是嵩山地区著名的寺院，是古代嵩山地区僧人受戒中心，和少林寺、法王寺、嵩岳寺并称为嵩山四大寺院。著名高僧普寂、元珪、净藏、惟宽及著名天文学家僧一行（俗名张遂）等皆出自该寺。

登封"天地之中"历史建筑群之会善寺大雄宝殿
Main Hall of the Huishan Temple of the Historic Monuments of Dengfeng at "the Centre of Heaven and Earth"

6. The Huishan Temple

The Huishan Temple is located at the foot the of Jicui Peak of Mount Taishi, six kilometers northwest of Dengfeng City. Leaning against the Longshan Mountain (the Dragon Mountain) on its left and the Hushan Mountain (the Tiger Mountain) on the right, it is surrounded by spectacular scenery and lush woods. The Huishan Temple was formerly a provisional palace of Emperor Xiaowen of the Northern Wei Dynasty. After the fall of the Wei Dynasty, the palace was discarded and transformed into the temple. The Huishan Temple is located in the north while facing the south. Its kernel compound is 65.06 meters long from the north to the south and 57.53 meters wide from the east to the west, covering an area of 3,743 square meters. Along the central axis are eight historical buildings, namely, the screen wall, the gate, the east and the west wing rooms of the main hall. The "Mountain amidst Clouds" and "Brightness of the Sky and Shadows of the Clouds" are engraved on the stones embedded in the screen wall in front of the gate. Built behind the vast terrace, the main hall displays a huge system of brackets, rigorous structure and fine preservation. The main hall of the Huishan Temple is the only existing Yuan Dynasty wooden structure in the area of Mount Songshan.

The Huishan Temple is one of the most famous monasteries in the area of Mount Songshan: it represents the very place where the monks of Mount Songshan are initiated into monkhood. The Huishan Temple, along with the Shaolin Temple, the Fawang Temple and the Songyue Temple, are known as the Four Great Temples of Mount Songshan. Such eminent monks as Pu Ji, Yuan Gui, Jing Zang, Wei Kuan and the famous astronomer Seng Yixing (also known as Zhang Sui) are all from this temple.

7. 嵩阳书院

嵩阳书院位于嵩山太室山峻极峰下,坐北朝南,东、北、西三面峰峦环拱,溪水围合,南面开阔平缓,距双溪河165米。书院前身为建于北魏太和八年(484年)的嵩阳寺,五代后唐时改为书院。南宋王应麟《玉海》把嵩阳书院与江西白鹿洞书院、湖南岳麓书院、河南睢阳书院并称为四大书院。

嵩阳书院保存了传统书院的建筑布局,南北长128米,东西宽78米,占地面积9,984平方米,保存清代建筑26座。沿中轴线布置5进院落,由南向北依次为大门、先圣殿、讲堂、道统祠和藏书楼。除道统祠为歇山顶以外,其他建筑均为硬山卷棚布瓦顶,具有河南地方建筑风格。嵩阳书院建筑体量适中,青砖灰瓦,古朴雅致。另外,嵩阳书院还保存有东魏以后石刻15品、古树14株等文物遗存。嵩阳书院格局紧凑,功能完善,作为中国较早的传播儒家理学学说、祭祀儒家圣贤和举行考试的书院,对儒学的发展起过重要作用,对研究我国古代书院建筑、教育制度以及儒家文化具有不可替代的标本意义。

登封"天地之中"历史建筑群之嵩阳书院大唐碑

Tang Dynasty Tablet at the Songyang Academy of Classical Learning as One of the Historic Monuments of Dengfeng at "the Centre of Heaven and Earth"

7. The Songyang Academy of Classical Learning

The Songyang Academy of Classical Learning is located at the foot of Peak Junji of Mount Taishi. Located in the north while facing the south, it nestles among hills and streams on its east, west and north. 165 meters away from the Shuangxi River, it is open and flat in the south. The academy was formerly known as the Songyang Temple built in the Eighth Year (484 A.D.) of the Taihe period of the Northern Wei Dynasty. And it is between the Five Dynasties and the Tang Dynasty that the temple was transformed into an academy. Wang Yinglin, a scholar of the Southern Song Dynasty named in his book *Yuhai:An Encyclopedia* the Songyang Academy of Classical Learning, the White Deer Grotto Academy of Classical Learning of Jiangxi Province, the Yuelu Academy of Classical Learning of Hunan Province, and the Henan Suiyang Academy of Classical Learning the Four Great Academies.

The Songyang Academy of Classical Learning preserves the architectural layout of the traditional academy. It is 128 meters long from the north to the south and 78 meters wide from the east to the west, covering an area of 9,984 square meters, and retains 26 buildings of the Qing Dynasty. Arranged along the central axis from the south to the north are the five courtyards which are respectively the Main Gate, the Sage's Hall, the Lecture Hall, the Daotong Temple and the Library Pavilion. Except for the gable and hip roofs of the Daotong Temple, the other buildings have gabbled paraboloid roof typical of Henan local architectural style. The Songyang Academy of Classical Learning, with its blue bricks and gray tiles, is moderate in size, making itself simple and elegant. In addition, the Songyang Academy of Classical Learning has preserved cultural relics after the Eastern Wei Dynasty, such as the 15 stone engravings and the 14 ancient trees. The Songyang Academy of Classical Learning is compact in structure and fully developed in function. As the earliest Chinese academy in disseminating Confucianism, hosting sacrificial ceremonies to commemorate Confucian sages as well as holding examinations, the Songyang Academy of Classical Learning has played an important role in the development of Confucianism. It is also uniquely significant in studying the architecture of ancient Chinese academies, their educational system and the Confucian culture.

8. 观星台

观星台位于登封市东南15公里告成镇告成村,坐北朝南,创建于元至元十三年至十六年(1276—1279年),形如覆斗,体型高大,灰砖砌筑,细腻挺拔,是保存完好的元代天文观测仪器。

观星台是郭守敬在当时所建的27个观测站的中心天文台。经过郭守敬、王恂等人在观星台的辛勤观测与推算,终于在至元十八年(1281年)颁布了当时世界上最先进的历法——《授时历》。此历法求得的回归年周期为365.242,5日,合365天5时49分12秒,其精确度与现今世界上许多国家使用的《格里高利历》相当,并早了300年。与现代科学推算的回归年周期(365天5时48分46秒)相比,仅相差26秒。在观星台南14.3米,有唐代建立的周公测景台,是唐代在西周测日影、定地中的基础上修建的重要天文遗迹。观星台是中国现存古老的天文台,也是世界上现存最早的观测天象的建筑之一。

登封"天地之中"历史建筑群之历史建筑群之观星台
Astronomical Observatory as One of the Historic Monuments at "the Centre of Heaven and Earth"

8. The Astronomical Observatory

The Dengfeng Astronomical Observatory is located at Gaocheng Village, 15 kilometers southeast of Dengfeng City. Located in the north while facing the south, it is built from the 13th to the 16th year (1276 A.D.—1279 A.D.) of the Zhiyuan Period of the Yuan Dynasty. Huge and tall, with gray bricks, it is shaped like an inverted funnel. Exquisite and straight, it is a well-preserved astronomical observation instrument of the Yuan Dynasty.

The Dengfeng Astronomical Observatory is the central observatory of the 27 observation stations that Guo Shoujing built in his time. After the diligent observations and calculations of Guo Shoujing, Wang Xun and the others in the observatory, the most advanced calendar in the world—*The Shoushi Calender* was finally promulgated in the 18th year of the Zhiyuan Period of the Yuan Dynasty (1281 A.D.). The calendar has a cycle of tropical year of 365.242,5 days (365 days 5 hours 49 minutes 12 seconds). The observatory, though some three hundred years earlier, is comparable in accuracy to *The Gregorian Calendar* used in many countries in the world today. Compared with the modern

登封"天地之中"历史建筑群之周公测景台
Zhougong Sundial Platform as One of the Historic Monuments at "the Centre of Heaven and Earth"

观星台和周公测景台、周公庙等组成一座完整的院落，南北长160米，东西宽37米，占地面积5,920平方米。除测景台和观星台两座天文科技建筑外，中轴线上还保存有照壁、大门、戟门、周公祠、帝尧殿等明、清建筑。位居"天地之中"的观星台、测景台，历来都是中国的天文观测中心。观星台院内现存碑刻12通，还有复制的天文仪器文物。这些文物与观星台、周公测景台有密切关系，也是与天文观测有关的重要历史遗存。

scientific calculation of the tropical year period (365 days 5 hours 48 minutes 46 seconds), there is only a difference of 26 seconds. 14.3 meters to the south of the Observatory, the Zhougong Sundial Platform, established in the Tang Dynasty, is an important astronomical relic built on the basis of how the Western Zhou has measured the shadow cast by the sun to determine the center of the horizon. The Dengfeng Astronomical Observatory is the oldest observatory in China and is one of the earliest astronomical buildings remaining in the world.

  The Dengfeng Astronomical Observatory, the Zhougong Sundial Platform and the Zhougong Temple altogether form a complete courtyard, 160 meters long from the north to the south and 37 meters wide from the east to the west, covering an area of 5,920 square meters. In addition to the Sundial Platform and the Observatory, there are the other Ming and Qing structures along the central axis, such as the Screen Wall, the Main Gate, the Ji Door, the Zhougong Temple and the Hall of Emperor Yao. The Observatory and the Sundial Platform at "the Center of Heaven and Earth" have always been China's astronomical observation center. The 12 steles existing in the Observatory and the reproduced astronomical instruments are the cultural relics that are closely related to the Dengfeng Astronomical Observatory and the Zhougong Sundial Platform. They are also important historical relics related to astronomical observations.

四、丝绸之路（河南段）

丝绸之路是一个交通网络。这个网络从中国汉唐时期的长安和洛阳出发，经过中亚通往西方世界，进行远距离的商贸、宗教信仰、科学知识、技术发明、文化活动和艺术交流。它的起始年代被联合国教科文组织确定为前2世纪时汉武帝派遣张骞出使西域。一直持续到16世纪，这些通道依然在发挥着作用。首批被列入世界文化遗产的文物点分布在中国和哈萨克斯坦、吉尔吉斯斯坦，共计33处，其中，中国境内有22处，哈萨克斯坦境内有8处，吉尔吉斯斯坦境内有3处。这些遗产点类型有商业遗存、佛教石窟和寺庙、古代道路和关隘、佛塔、陵墓、宗教建筑等。

中国遗产点中，河南省有4处，分别是汉魏洛阳城遗址、隋唐洛阳城定鼎门遗址、新安汉函谷关遗址和崤函古道石壕段遗址。

Ⅳ.The Silk Road (Henan Section)

  As a transportation network, the Silk Road starts from the two capitals of Chang'an and Luoyang in the Han and Tang dynasties of China and stretches across Central Asia to the West, carrying out long-distance exchanges in trade, religious beliefs, scientific knowledge, technological inventions as well as cultural and artistic activities. Its date of commencement as determined by UNESCO is the second century B.C. when Emperor Wu of the Han Dynasty sent Zhang Qian to the Western Regions. These passages continued to function until the 16th century. The first cultural relics listed as the World Cultural Heritage are distributed in China, Kazakhstan and Kyrgyzstan, with a total of 33 sites, among which 22 are in China, 8 in Kazakhstan and 3 in Kyrgyzstan. These heritage sites include commercial relics, Buddhist grottoes and temples, ancient roads and passes, Buddhist pagodas, mausoleums and religious edifices.

  Among the Chinese heritage sites, Henan Province has four, which are situated in Luoyang City from the Eastern Han to the Northern Wei Dynasty, the site of Dingding Gate of Luoyang City in the Sui and the Tang dynasties, the site of Han'gu Pass in Xin'an County and the site of the Shihao Section, Xiaohan Ancient Route in the Han Dynasty.

1. 汉魏洛阳城遗址

汉魏洛阳城遗址位于河南省洛阳市东部，是东汉的都城所在，西晋和北魏孝文帝迁都后也以此为都城。该遗址代表了东汉至北魏历代中原王朝的文明与文化特征，见证了北魏时期游牧民族与农耕民族大融合所促生的独特城市文化，展现了城市形制的跨区域、跨时间交流，以及佛教在中原地区的传播和本土化过程。

汉魏洛阳城建于伊、洛河冲积平原上，城址北依邙山，南临洛河。遗址所在的洛阳盆地是黄河中游地区的重要农业区，交通和战略地位突出，历代中原王朝多建都于此。遗址现存格局及遗迹以北魏时期为主，同时分布或叠压有西晋、曹魏、东汉以及更早时期的遗存。东汉时期城市面积约10平方公里，北魏时期扩展为3重城，面积近80平方公里。

东汉时期的城址呈南北纵长方形，城四周共12座城门，城内分布南、北2座宫城，占据大部分城内空间。曹魏及西晋时期原址沿用东汉城址。曹魏时期，南宫已逐渐衰落甚至消失，仅存北宫，城内西北隅新建金墉城。

汉魏洛阳城城墙
City Walls of the Han and Wei Capital Site of Luoyang City

1. The Han and Wei Capital Site of Luoyang City

The Han and Wei Capital Site of Luoyang City is located in the eastern part of Luoyang City, Henan Province. Luoyang City is the capital of not only the Eastern Han Dynasty, but also the Western Jin Dynasty and the Northern Wei Dynasty. The site represents the civilization and cultural characteristics of the Central Plains from the Eastern Han Dynasty to the Northern Wei Dynasty and witnesses the unique urban culture produced jointly by the nomadic culture and the farming culture in the Northern Wei Dynasty. It also shows the cross-regional and inter-temporal exchanges of urban forms and displays the dissemination and localization of Buddhism on the Central Plains.

The Han and Wei Capital Site of Luoyang City is built on the alluvial plains of the Yihe River and the Luohe River, with Mang Mountain on its north and River Luohe on its south. The Luoyang Basin where the site is located is an important agricultural area in the middle section of the Yellow River. With both transportation and strategic importance, it was taken as the capital by a great many dynasties of the Central Plains. The existing patterns and relics of the site are mainly representative of the Northern Wei Dynasty. What can also be found are the remains of the Western Jin Dynasty, the reign of Emperor Cao Pi, the Eastern Han Dynasty and the earlier historical periods. During the Eastern Han Dynasty, the city covered about 10 square kilometers, which was enlarged into 80 square kilometers in the Northern Wei Dynasty when a triple-city layout came into existence.

The capital site of the Eastern Han Dynasty is rectangular from the north to the south. Around the city are 12 gates and inside are two palaces in the south and the north, occupying the greatest proportion of the city's space. During the reign of Emperor Cao Pi and the Western Jin Dynasty, the city site stayed the same with that of the Eastern Han Dynasty. When it came to the reign of Emperor Cao Pi, the southern palace became gradually dilapidated, and only the northern one remained. Jinyong City was newly built in the northwest corner of the city.

The capital site of the Northern Wei Dynasty has inherited the urban forms explored since the reign of Emperor Cao Pi, including the north-south city axis, the single imperial palace, the outer city layout and the Lifang design (the enclosed residential area). With its initiation of influential city pattern, the capital

洛阳出土的北魏镶嵌蓝宝石金戒指
Gold Ring with Sapphire Inlay of the Northern Wei Dynasty, Unearthed in Luoyang City

北魏洛阳城继承并确立了曹魏以来不断探索的南北向城市轴线、单一宫制、外郭城制度、里坊制等城市形制,发展创新出具有重要影响力的城市形态,成为中国古代都城制度变革期的重要城址。北魏洛阳城包括宫城、内城、外郭城3重城。宫城位于内城中部偏北,现存阊阖门遗址、2号门址、3号门址、太极殿遗址等建筑遗址。阊阖门外有作为城市主干道的铜驼街,干道两侧布设官署、太庙、太社、皇家寺院永宁寺等重要建筑。内城还有布局规整的东西向、南北向的城市道路构成城市的路网格局,主路网与内城城门连接并延伸出城外。内城西北角有军事设施金墉城。内城及外郭城内其他区域广设里坊,主要为居住区、手工业区和市场等。

曹魏正始石经
Engraved Confucian Classics during the Reign of Emperor Cao Pi

汉魏洛阳城宫殿遗址发掘出的地面和壁画遗迹
Unearthed Murals and Ground Remains of the Imperial Palace at the Han and Wei Capital Site of Luoyang City

of Luoyang has become an important site which has witnessed the evolution of capital construction. The Northern Wei capital site of Luoyang City consists of three rings of cities, that is, the imperial palace, the inner city and the outer city. The imperial palace is situated in the mid-northern part of the inner city. Remains from the imperial palace include the Changhe Gate, Gate 2, Gate 3 and Taiji Hall. The Tongtuo Avenue, a major road of the city outside the Changhe Gate, has on both its sides a number of important edifices, such as the administration buildings, the Imperial Ancestral Temple, the Temple for Imperial Worship and the royal Yongning Temple. Inside the city is also the neat grid pattern of roads in either east-west direction or north-south one. The main roads are connected with the gate to the inner city and stretch further out of the city. In the northwest corner of the inner city is Jinyong city, a military installation. Lifang is in both the inner and the outer city, further divided into residential areas, handicraft zones and markets.

偃师寇店出土的汉代鎏金铜麒麟
Gold-plated Bronze Qilin Sculpture of the Han Dynasty, Unearthed in Koudian, Yanshi

汉魏洛阳城遗址现存代表性遗存主要包括东汉至北魏时期的城址（北魏内城）及宫城城墙、城门、城濠、道路、水系、建筑遗址（包括宫殿、衙署、寺院、仓库等）和手工业遗址等。

偃师寇店出土的汉代鎏金铜象
Gold-plated Bronze Elephant Sculpture of the Han Dynasty, Unearthed in Koudian, Yanshi

Representative remains of the Han and Wei Capital Site of Luoyang City are mainly from the inner city, including the walls of the imperial palace, the city gates, the city moats, roads, the drainage system, the architectural sites (comprising the sites of palaces, administration buildings, temples, warehouses, etc.) and handicraft workshop sites.

2. 隋唐洛阳城定鼎门遗址

隋唐洛阳城定鼎门遗址位于河南省洛阳市，是中国隋唐时期（7—10世纪）东都洛阳城的城门和街区遗址，主要遗存包括定鼎门门址、城墙遗址、天街遗址、里坊遗址、水系遗址。该遗址是丝绸之路鼎盛时期东方起点城市洛阳城的代表性遗存，见证了东方农耕文明发展鼎盛时期帝国的文明水平，展现了唐代都城城市文化的礼制特征及其影响力，与丝绸之路上繁盛的商贸往来具有密切关联。

定鼎门是隋唐洛阳城外郭城正南门，位于隋唐洛阳城城市中轴线的最南端，南对伊阙（龙门山）。定鼎门始建于隋代（7世纪），称"建国门"，唐代改称"定鼎门"，并一直沿用至北宋，其间多有重修。唐代定鼎门遗址的主体墩台东西长44.5米，南北宽21.04米。墩台内以两道隔墙分隔成3个门道，墩台四周包砖。此外还有飞廊、阙台、马道和涵洞等遗存。

隋唐洛阳城天堂建筑基址
Foundation Site of the Tiantang Palace at Luoyang City in the Sui and Tang Dynasties

2. Site of the Dingding Gate, Luoyang City, in the Sui and Tang Dynasties

Located in Luoyang City, Henan Province, the site of the Dingding Gate is what has remained of Luoyang City's gate and the blocks in the Sui and Tang dynasties (7th-10th century). The main relics include the remains of the Dingding Gate, the city wall, Lifang, the axis street and the drainage system. Representative of the remains of Luoyang City, the Gate is at the eastern end of the then-prosperous Silk Road. It witnesses the civilization of an oriental empire when its agricultural civilization reached its pinnacle. The Dingding Gate has reflected not only the rituals and influences of the urban culture of Tang's capital city but also its close relations with the thriving trade along the Silk Road.

Dingding Gate is the south gate of the outer city of Luoyang. In the Sui and Tang dynasties, it's located at the southern end of the city axis and faces Yique Gate (Mount Longmen). The Dingding Gate was built in the Sui Dynasty (7th century) by the name of "Jianguo Gate" and was renamed "Dingding Gate" in the Tang Dynasty which was used till the Northern Song Dynasty. A number of renovations were conducted in between different dynasties. The main abutment of the site is 44.5 meters long from the east to the west and 21.04 meters wide from the north to the south. Two partition walls divide the gate into three gateways. The abutment is covered all over with bricks. In addition, there are remains of the corridor, Que (a freestanding, ceremonial gate tower in traditional Chinese architecture), bridleways and culverts.

隋唐洛阳城出土的罗马玻璃瓶
Roman Glass Bottle Unearthed in Luoyang City in the Sui and Tang Dynasties

隋唐洛阳城出土的彩绘胡人俑
Painted Tomb Figures of the Northern Barbarian Tribes, Unearthed in Luoyang City in the Sui and Tang Dynasties

门址东西两侧与洛阳城外郭城城墙遗址相接。门址以北为唐代洛阳城的城市中轴线干道——天街，宽约109米。天街东、西两侧分布有洛阳城市中2处里坊遗址——明教坊和宁人坊。里坊南北长约530米，东西宽约460米，坊墙宽1.5米—2米，四面开有坊门，坊内发现有建筑遗址。里坊之间及坊内有坊间道路、坊内十字街、通津渠河道、排水渠等遗迹。定鼎门门址南侧发现有唐代路面，存有人的脚印、动物蹄印和车辙等遗迹。

隋唐洛阳城出土的三彩武士俑
Warrior Tomb Figures Glazed in Three Colors, Unearthed in Luoyang City in the Sui and Tang Dynasties

The east and west of the Gate are connected with the outer wall of Luoyang City. To the north of the Gate is Tianjie Avenue, the axis of the city, about 109 meters wide. To the east and west of the avenue are the remains of Mingjiao Lifang and Ningren Lifang. They are about 530 meters from the north to the south and 460 meters from the east to the west. The wall of Lifang is 1.5 to 2 meters wide, with gates on four sides. Architectural remains have been discovered in Lifang, including roads, crossings, Tongjin Channel and the drainage system. Pavement of the Tang Dynasty has been discovered in the south of the Dingding Gate, together with human footprints, animal hoof prints and ruts.

3.新安汉函谷关遗址

新安汉函谷关遗址主要包括东西向坐落的关楼、南北两侧的夯土关墙和阙台遗迹,以及关墙外向南北两侧延伸的长墙遗迹。该遗址见证了汉帝国大型交通保障体系中的交通管理制度、防御制度及其对丝绸之路长距离交通和交流的保障。

新安汉函谷关遗址位于河南省洛阳市新安县城关镇,北距黄河60公里,西邻镇区,东距洛阳市区23公里。新安汉函谷关始建于西汉元鼎三年(前114年),沿用原设于河南省灵宝市的秦函谷关关名。新安汉函谷关在西汉时期是防卫都城长安所在关中地区的东部重要的军事关隘,至东汉时期都城东移至洛阳盆地,汉函谷关成为洛阳周边八关之首。史料记载,东汉时期汉函谷关具有交通纽带作用,并曾有过"会万国之玉帛,徕百蛮之贡琛。盖纷其云合,车马动而雷奔"(东汉·李尤《函谷关赋》)的盛况。

新安汉函谷关关楼遗址
Gate Tower of the Han'gu Pass in Xin'an County

3. Site of the Han'gu Pass of the Han Dynasty in Xin'an County

Remains of the Han'gu Pass consist of east-west gate towers, rammed earth walls on each of the north and south sides, Que gates as well as the northern and southern extensions of the pass walls. It witnessed the transport management system and the defense system of the Han Dynasty and in the meantime how they had guaranteed the long-distance transportation and communication along the Silk Roads.

The site of the Han'gu Pass is located in Chengguan Town of Xin'an County, Luoyang City of Henan Province. Close to the town on its west, the Pass is 60 kilometers to the south of the Yellow River and 23 to the west of Luoyang City. The Han'gu Pass was built in 114 B.C. and followed the name of the Qin Dynasty pass in Lingbao City of Henan Province. The Han'gu Pass was one of the most important eastern fortresses to guarantee the safety of the Guanzhong Basin where the capital of Chang'an was located. In the Eastern Han Dynasty when the capital was moved eastward to the Luoyang Basin, the Han'gu Pass became the first important one of all the eight passes around Luoyang. According to historical records, the Han'gu Pass was a key transportation hub in the Eastern Han Dynasty, as described in "Ode to Han'gu Pass" by Li You in the Eastern Han Dynasty, "Jade, silk and other tributes from the neighboring countries and tribes were brought to the Empire via this pass, with constant streams of various carriages and in great noises and excitement".

新安汉函谷关考古发掘出土的唐代石柱础
Stone Pillar Base of the Tang Dynasty Excavated at the Site of the Han'gu Pass in Xin'an County

新安汉函谷关考古发掘出土的汉代防御设施
Defense Installations of the Han Dynasty Excavated at the Site of the Han'gu Pass in Xin'an County

关楼遗址东西两侧发现有总长约400米的古代道路遗迹，东侧发现1处建筑基址。关楼遗址与南北两侧的夯土关墙遗迹呈"H"形连接，整体东西长约270米，南北宽约80米，2座阙台建筑基址在其东侧南北对峙，两者之间为通关古道路。南北两侧汉代长墙遗迹分别与两阙台遗址相连，南侧墙体遗迹残长150米，残宽2米—7米；北侧墙体遗迹残长270米，残宽6米—13米。

新安汉函谷关考古发掘出土的"关"字款瓦当
Eave Tile with Chinese Character "关(Pass)" Excavated at the Site of the Han'gu Pass in Xin'an County

To the east and west of the remains of the pass are discovered ancient road remains with a total length of 400 meters and to the east a building foundation. The layout of the pass site with its northern and southern rammed earth walls is in the shape of "H", with about 270 meters from the east to the west and about 80 meters from the north to the south. The foundations of the two Que gates are on the east side of the pass, with the south one in opposition to the north one and the ancient road stretching right through the pass. The remains of the long walls on the north and the south side are connected respectively with the remains of the two Que gates, the south one 150 meters in length and 2 to 7 meters in width while the north one 270 meters in length and 5 to 13 meters in width.

4. 崤函古道石壕段遗址

崤函古道石壕段遗址位于河南省三门峡市，遗址主要包括石灰岩质古道路面、路旁蓄水设施。崤函古道是汉唐时期沟通长安、洛阳两大都城交通要道的组成部分，是丝绸之路长期、长距离交通保障系统的珍贵物证。

崤函古道是对古代中国自洛阳至潼关这段道路的统称，道路穿行于中原地区黄河三门峡河段南岸崤山之中，沟通了华夏文明两大核心地区——关中盆地和洛阳盆地，汉唐时期作为沟通长安、洛阳两大都城的交通要道而兴盛，近现代仍在沿用。其东端分别始于古都洛阳西出道口的新安县和宜阳县，西至关中盆地东侧门户的陕西潼关。因其沿线主要穿行于崤山之中，并曾设有号称天险的秦函谷关，故名崤函古道。崤山以北或是以南，河流纵横，重山叠嶂，行旅都极为困难，由此绕道南北联系长安、洛阳两大古都，都是比较困难的，只有这条濒黄河南岸、穿越崤山的通道才是东西往来捷近易行的道路。

崤函古道
Xiaohan Ancient Route

4. Site of the Shihao Section, Xiaohan Ancient Route

The Shihao Section of Xiaohan Ancient Route is located in Sanmenxia City of Henan Province. Its remains mainly include limestone road pavements and roadside water tanks. Xiaohan ancient route, by connecting the two capitals of Luoyang and Chang'an in the Han and Tang dynasties, has provided rare historical evidence for the sustained long-distance transportation along the Silk Road.

Xiaohan Ancient Route refers to the ancient road from Luoyang to Tongguan. It traverses Mountain Xiaoshan on the south bank of the Sanmenxia section of the Yellow River in Central China, linking the two central regions of Chinese civilization, namely, the Guanzhong Basin and the Luoyang Basin. The route thrived from the Han to the Tang Dynasty as a major road connecting the two capitals of Chang'an and Luoyang and remained in use till modern and contemporarg times. The east of the route started in Xin'an and Yiyang counties on the west of the ancient Luoyang City and reached Tongguan, a fort at the east of the Guanzhong Basin. The name Xiaohan Ancient Route comes from both Mount Xiaoshan which the route went through and the impregnable Hangu Pass which had been built along the way. On either the south or the north of Mount Xiaoshan are rolling hills and crisscrossing waterways, which are hostile to travelers. Meanwhile, it is also highly demanding to take circuitous routes to connect the two capitals of Chang'an and Lucyang, thus leaving Xiaohan Ancient Route the best choice between the east and the west.

The 200-kilometer-long Xiaohan Ancient Route is divided by ancient Shanzhou Prefecture (the present-day ShanXian County) into the eastern and the western sections, namely, the Hangu section and the Xiaoshan section. Each section had a south route and a north one. Shihao section, on the World Heritage List, is on the north route of Xiaoshan section, between Xiashi Town and Shihao Village, 36 kilometers east of Sanmenxia City.

崤函古道遗址中出土的古代铁马掌
Unearthed Ancient Horseshoes at the Site of Xiaohan Ancient Route

崤函古道东西全程200多公里，以古陕州（今陕县）城为枢纽，分为东、西两段，即"函谷道"和"崤山道"，两段道路各分南北两线。列入世界文化遗产的石壕段遗址就处在崤山道北路上三门峡市东约36公里的硖石乡至石壕村之间。

石壕段遗址经考古探明的古道全长1,317米，其中经考古发掘揭露的中部路段位于三门峡市陕县硖石乡车壕村东南，为西北、东南走向，全长230米，宽窄不等，最宽处达8.8米，最窄处5.2米。主要遗迹包括石灰岩质古道路面、路旁3处蓄水设施。自然岩石道路遗存中部两侧各有一处对自然地形略加修整的人工刻凿痕迹，其有3个不同时期刻凿的台级形断壁，每个台级高0.5米。蓄水设施是在自然形成的坑凹地形的基础上略加整修而成，供来往行人以及驾车、驮货的牲畜饮水之用。

崤函古道遗址出土的残铁铃

Unearthed Iron Bell Remains at the Site of Xiachan Ancient Route

    The archaeological work has proved that the Shihao section of the ancient route has a total length of 1,317 meters. The central part of this section that has been unearthed in archaeological excavation is located at the southeast of Chehao Village of Xiashi Town in Shanxian County, Sanmenxia City. The road stretches in a northwest-southeast direction, with a length of 230 meters and a width varying from 5.2 meters to 8.8 meters. Major remains include limestone road pavement and three roadside water tanks. In the middle of the natural rock road remains exist traces of deliberate cutting and chipping, apparently manual improvements to the natural land form, including three stone steps cut in three different periods, each with a height of 0.5 meter. To provide travelers and their horses and other cattle with drinking water, the water tanks were made through adjusting the naturally formed uneven surfaces.

五、大运河（河南段）

大运河是沟通中国南北方的水运交通系统。其营建始于前5世纪的春秋战国时期，到了7世纪的隋炀帝时期则成为具有全国意义的统一的交通网络。隋炀帝营建的隋唐大运河被认为是人类工业革命之前最大规模的建设工程之一，这个工程完成之后，成为隋帝国内陆交通运输的动脉，北方的谷物、南方的稻米等具有战略意义的物资的供应乃至于军队的调遣，大多通过这条黄金水道，延续至宋、元时期。大运河为确保国家经济的繁荣和稳定扮演了重要角色。一直到今天，大运河依然是一条重要的水运要道。

大运河河南段遗存主要包括隋唐大运河的通济渠和永济渠。隋唐大运河是中国大运河的重要组成部分。隋炀帝即位后，为巩固国家统一，有效控制江南地区，特别是掌控调配江南富庶物资，下令开凿大运河。大运河以洛阳为中心，以通济渠、永济渠向南北延伸，沟通了海河、黄河、淮河、长江、钱塘江5大水系，北通涿郡(今北京)，南达余杭(今杭州)，全长2700多公里，成为中国古代南北交通的大动脉。

隋炀帝下江都图
Emperor Yang of the Sui Dynasty Going Down to Jiangdu (Yangzhou)

V. The Grand Canal (Henan Section)

The Grand Canal is the waterway system that links the north and the south of China. Its construction began in the 5th century B.C. during the Spring and Autumn and Warring States Period. When it came to the 7th century A.D. during the reign of Emperor Yang of the Sui Dynasty, the Grand Canal had developed into a nationwide transportation network. The Grand Canal constructed under orders from Emperor Yang of the Sui Dynasty was conceived to be the largest civil engineering project before the Industrial Revolution. Once accomplished, it became the artery of the Empire's inland communication system, transporting not only strategic raw materials such as grains in north China and rice in the south but also military troops. By the Song and Yuan dynasties, the Grand Canal had played an important role in guaranteeing the prosperity and stability of national economy, and remains in use to this day as an important shipping route.

What has remained of the Grand Canal in Henan Province mainly include the Tongji Canal and the Yongji Canal. Constructed in the Sui Dynasty, the Sui and Tang Canal is essential to the Grand Canal. Having acceded to the throne, Emperor Yang of the Sui Dynasty ordered the Grand Canal to be built in order to guarantee the national unity, to keep the south of the Changjiang River under control, and in particular to supervise the use of the abundant resources there. The Grand Canal takes Luoyang as its center and extends to the north and south via the Tongji Canal and the Yongji Canal, linking five of the most important waterways in China, including the Haihe River, the Yellow River, the Huaihe River, the Changjiang River and the Qiantangjiang River. It is 2700 kilometers in length, with Beijing in the north and Hangzhou in the south, hence the artery of ancient China's transportation system from the north to the south.

The seven sites of the world cultural heritage in Henan Province are in Zhengzhou City, Luoyang City, Anyang City, Hebi City, Shangqiu City, Huaxian County and the other counties and cities, covering almost all heritage types, such as waterways, docks, river banks, bridges, silos and hydraulic facilities. They have witnessed the changes of the Grand Canal, from its initial construction, development, prosperity to its decline, hence of great historical value. In particular,

河南省入选世界文化遗产的7项遗产点，涉及郑州市、洛阳市、安阳市、鹤壁市、商丘市和滑县等市县，涵盖了河道、码头、河堤、桥梁、仓窖、水工设施等完整的遗产类型，见证了大运河从开凿、发展到繁荣、没落的历史进程，具有重要的突出普遍价值。特别是发现的3座大型皇家粮仓遗址，排列有序，规模宏大，有力印证了隋唐大运河保障重大军事行动和经济开拓的重要功能。这里我们重点介绍通济渠郑州段/通济渠商丘南关段、浚县黎阳仓遗址以及洛阳含嘉仓遗址。

the three imperial granary sites are found to be in strict arrangement and on a massive scale, which strongly confirms the Canal's function in safeguarding major military operations and economic development. Highlighted as follows are Zhengzhou and Shangqiu section of the Tongji Canal, the site of the Liyang Granary in Xunxian County as well as the site of the Hanjia Granany in Louyang.

1. 通济渠郑州段

通济渠郑州段的前身为战国时期的鸿沟（前5—前3世纪），现存河段包括索须河运河故道和一段汴河遗址。通济渠郑州段反映了通济渠河道的线路、走向以及与黄河的关系等。目前索须河全长约16公里，部分河段面宽达40余米，两岸设有堤防，是郑州市西北部的主要泄洪、排涝、景观河道，河道规整，道路便达，水质较清。

汴河遗址北起黄河南岸流经惠济桥注入通济渠后东折。目前引黄河水入渠的这段河道已经深埋于地下。虽然历史上黄河多次变道，数次湮没汴河故道，但此段河道在元末之前仍作为区域航运水道历经疏浚，直到明、清时代此段运河逐渐废弃不用。考古调查确定，此段古河道宽150至220米。河道两侧残存有断断续续的河堤，堤上有路，宽6米—7米。

通济渠郑州段荥阳惠济桥立面
Profile of the Huiji Bridge of Zhengzhou Section of the Tongji Canal at Xingyang

1. Zhengzhou Section of the Tongji Canal

The precursor of the Zhengzhou section of the Tongji Canal is the Honggou Canal in the Warring States Period (5th to 3rd century B.C.). What is left of the Canal includes the ancient course of the Suoxu Canal and a section of the Bianhe Canal. The waterway reflects the route and direction of the Tongji Canal as well as its relationship with the Yellow River. Today's Suoxu Canal is about 15 kilometers in length, with some sections reaching over 40 meters in width. The canal has dikes on both banks and, with regular waterways, convenient roads and clear water, functions currently as the main watercourse for sightseeing and flood discharge in the northwest of Zhengzhou City.

The northern end of the site of the Bianhe Canal is at the south bank of the Yellow River. The Bianhe Canal went past the Huiji Bridge and turned eastwards after flowing into the Tongji Canal. Now the section of the watercourse for diverting water from the Yellow River to the canal has been buried deep underground. Though the Yellow River has changed its course several times in history and inundated the ancient watercourse of the Bianhe Canal many times, this section has remained as a regional shipping route till the end of the late Yuan Dynasty. It was not until the Ming and Qing dynasties that this canal was gradually abandoned. According to archaeological excavations, dikes remained here and there along the canal, with the watercourse about 150 to 220 meters

通济渠郑州段荥阳大运河西岸河堤平面车辙痕

Tracks of Wheels on the West Bank of the Xingyang Canal of Zhengzhou Section of the Tongji Canal

河堤上还发现有晚期路土堆积。分析认为，在原始的运河古道的河堤上当时有路，在河道和河堤被黄河泛滥淤埋后，这段河堤仍被人们在老路的基础上继续沿用，形成了早晚两期路土相互叠压的现象。下层路土形成的年代不晚于元代。故道中发掘出隋、唐、宋、元、明、清时期堆积层及大量文化遗物，从而证明惠济桥一段河道至迟在隋代已经形成。

wide. On both sides of the watercourse remain discontinuous dikes on which are roads whose width is about 6 to 7 meters.

Road earth deposits in later times have also been discovered on the dikes. Analysis shows that there were roads on the dikes of the ancient canal. Having been covered by silt brought by the floods of the Yellow River, the watercourse and dikes were still in use, which led to the overlay of two adjacent layers of road earth in both early and late times. The bottom layer of road earth came into being no later than the Yuan Dynasty. Deposit layers of the dynasties of Sui, Tang, Song, Yuan, Ming and Qing, together with quantities of cultural relics were unearthed from the ancient watercourse, proving that the Huiji Bridge section took shape no later than the Sui Dynasty.

2. 通济渠商丘南关段

通济渠商丘南关段位于商丘古城南约2.5公里处，是通济渠沿线重要的河道与水工遗存，展现了唐宋时期通济渠夯土驳岸的形制与工艺，以及通济渠巨大的河道规模，反映了河道历史的线路与走向。考古发现的商丘南关遗址段河道长约1公里，宽约120米，河深16米，呈东西走向，是目前通济渠沿线发现规模较大的一处河道、驳岸遗址。

遗址核心内容包括一段长约60米的河岸及大面积伸向河道内的突堤遗存面，距地表深4.2米—5.2米，遗存面上车辙和行人的足迹清晰可见，已清理出的河岸高度约5米，均为夯土筑建，这为真实了解隋、唐至北宋时期通济渠的使用时间、河道变迁、疏浚历史，以及河岸的筑建方法、加固方式、加高过程、用料选择等提供了考古实物资料。

商丘南关遗迹和遗物因有厚达4米—10米的淤沙覆盖，保存完整，考古清理出土遗物丰富，且较为罕见。发掘所见的夯筑河岸地层中，包含了大量砖、瓦、陶器瓷器等遗物，特别是碎瓦块数量众多，可见当

通济渠商丘南关段南关码头遗址
Wharf Site of the Shangqiu Nanguan Section of the Tongji Canal

2. Shangqiu Nanguan Section of the Tongji Canal

The Shangqiu Nanguan section of the Tongji Canal is situated approximately 2.5 kilometers south of the ancient city of Shangqiu. As important remains of the watercourse and of the hydraulic facilities along the Tongji Canal, this section displays the structure and techniques of the rammed earth revetment in the Tang and Song dynasties. The large-scale watercourse of the Tongji Canal reflects the route and direction of the watercourse in history. The excavated watercourse of the Shangqiu Nanguan section is about 1 kilometer long, 120 meters wide and 16 meters deep. Running from the east to the west, it is a massive watercourse and revetment site discovered along the Tongji Canal.

The core of the site includes both a 60-meter-long dike and the remains of a jetty most of which have extended into the watercourse so that they are 4.2 to 5.2 meters from the ground surface. Wheel tracks and footprints of the pedestrians on the surface of the remains are clearly visible. The dikes that have been cleaned up are about five meters high, all built with rammed earth; they have provided archaeological evidence for the knowledge of the Tongji Canal in the Sui, Tang and the Northern Song dynasties, covering the time when the Canal was in use, the changes of the watercourse, the history of canal dredging, the bank construction method, the consolidation mode, the heightening process and the selection of materials.

Covered with the silt 4 to 10 meters thick, the Shangqiu Nanguan site and relics are finely preserved. A great many rare relics have been excavated and cleaned up from this site. The unearthed layer of the rammed earth banks contains a lot of relics such as bricks, tiles, potteries and ceramics, among which broken tiles are of great quantities. It can be inferred that the number of houses and inhabitants in history is great on the banks of the canal. The unearthed bank deposits show that this section of the canal has been used for a long time in history. Judged from the various kinds of relics unearthed in these two excavations, the banks that have been cleaned up should have been built around the Tang and Song dynasties, no later than the Jin Dynasty, which is consistent with the records about the history of the Southern Canal in Shangqiu. The vertical surface which was steep when last used and the various relics on the revetment surface are also completely preserved. They have provided, for the first time, physical evidence

时运河沿岸历史上房屋建筑很多，生活居住的人也较多。从清理出的河岸堆积看，此段运河沿用历史较长。从两次发掘出土的各类遗物综合情况判断，目前经清理揭露的河岸的时代大致属于唐、宋时期，最晚不会晚于金代，这与文献中关于商丘南运河历史的记载相吻合。河岸保存的最后使用时陡峭的立面及驳岸面上的各类遗迹也保存完整，为真实了解隋、唐至北宋时期通济渠的使用时间、河道变迁、疏浚历史；驳岸的筑建方法、加固方式、加高过程、用料选择；驳岸的构建形态、道路分布、功能分区等首次提供了经科学发掘的实物证据。

for people to truly learn about the Tongji Canal in the Sui, Tang and Northern Song dynasties, covering the time when the Canal was in use, the changes of the watercourse, the dredging history as well as the construction method, the consolidation mode, the heightening process, and the selected materials of the revetment, its structure and form, the layout of roads and the division of functional areas.

3. 浚县黎阳仓遗址

浚县黎阳仓是隋唐时期（6-9世纪）重要的官仓之一，是大运河沿线的大型转运漕仓之一。遗址位于黄河与永济渠之间，战略位置十分重要。

浚县黎阳仓始建于隋（581-618年），沿用至北宋（960-1127年）。其中地下储粮方式的仓窖始建于隋代废弃于唐代中期，是隋唐时期国家粮食转运基地，也是隋唐时期平定东北边境的后方物资供应基地，具有重要的战略地位。晚期的地面大型仓库建筑始建于北宋初期，废弃于北宋晚期，同样是国家物资集存基地，也是北宋用兵北方边境的后方物资供给基地。

直到北宋末年（12世纪初）废弃前，黎阳仓都是规模庞大、战略地位显赫的重要粮仓。当时的黎阳城东临黄河，西濒永济渠，水运极为便利。隋唐时期，黄河以北各州征收的粮食，都先集中在黎阳仓，然后经黄河或者永济渠运往洛阳。北宋时期，永济渠更名为御河。由于黄河与

浚县黎阳仓遗址1号建筑基址局部

Part of the Construction Foundation of No. 1 Site of the Liyang Granary in Xunxian County

3. Site of the Liyang Granary in Xunxian County

The Liyang Granary is one of the most important official granaries in the Sui and Tang dynasties (from the 6th century A.D. to the 9th century A.D.). Located between the Yellow River and the Yongji Canal, it is a large granary of great strategic importance along the Grand Canal for the transshipment of grains.

The Liyang Granary was first built in the Sui Dynasty (581-618 A.D.) and continued to be used in the Northern Song Dynasty (960-1127 A.D.). The underground cellar for grain storage was built in the Sui Dynasty and abandoned in the mid Tang Dynasty. As the national grain transshipment base and the material supply base for pacifying the northeastern border in the Sui and Tang dynasties, the Liyang Granary is of great strategic importance. The large aboveground warehouse was first built in the Northern Song Dynasty and abandoned towards the end of the Northern Song Dynasty. It was also a national base for material gathering and storage as well as for material supply for the troops stationed at the northern border in the Northern Song Dynasty.

Before being abandoned in the Northern Song Dynasty (early 12th century), the Liyang Granary remained one of the largest and the most important granaries in China. Liyang City at that time was close to both the Yellow River in the east and the Yongji Canal in the west, enjoying convenient water transportation. In the Sui and Tang dynasties, grains collected from the prefectures north of the Yellow River were all gathered in the Liyang Granary before they were shipped to Luoyang via the Yellow River or the Yongji Canal. In the Northern Song Dynasty, the Yongji Canal was renamed the Yuhe Canal. Since there was no navigation channel between the Yellow River and the Yuhe Canal, grain-transporting ships—after passing the Yellow River—needed to be unloaded first before they headed by land for the Liyang Granary, where the grains were loaded onto ships and transported via the Yuhe Canal to border areas in the North of China.

According to archeological excavations, the main historic sites related to the Liyang Granary are the walls of the granary, the moat, the cellars, the large building foundations and the roads. Furthermore, in the mid-north part of the granary, an 8-meter-deep watercourse joins the granary, the Yellow River and the Yongji Canal into an uninterrupted shipping route for grain transportation. The Liyang Granary is built along the hillside. Its layout is somewhat square,

御河之间并不通航,从黄河来的漕船过黄河后卸船,需经过陆运转运至黎阳仓,再装船入御河,向北运往华北的边境地区。

考古发现与黎阳仓有关的主要遗迹有仓城的城墙、护城河、仓窖、大型建筑基址、路等,并在黎阳仓的中北部有一条深8米河道,形成一个完整的粮仓与黄河、永济渠相互贯通的漕运水系。黎阳仓仓城依山而建,平面布局近正方形,东西宽260米,南北长约280米。城墙整体土筑而成,护城河位于仓城城东墙外。目前,已探明粮仓中心区仓窖84个,占仓城面积的4/5,西北角1/5是仓窖的空白区,疑似码头和管理区。总体上看仓窖排列基本规整有序。仓窖大小不一,小的口径8米左右,大的14米左右,最常见的在10米左右,距现地表最浅4.5米左右,最深的7米以上。

浚县黎阳仓遗址C18号仓窖剖面
Cross-section of C18 Site of the Liyang Granary in Xunxian County

with a width of about 260 meters from the east to the west. The length of the granary remains is about 280 meters from the north to the south. The walls are fundamentally made of earth, with the moat outside along the east wall of the granary. So far, 84 cellars have been discovered in the central area of the granary, occupying four fifths of the granary's total area. One fifth of the northwest corner is an empty area, which is likely to be used as the dock and the administrative spot. Generally speaking, the cellars are arranged neatly. The diameters of the cellars vary from about 8 meters to 14 meters, with the average about 10 meters. Their distances from the ground range from about 4.5 meters to over 7 meters.

4. 洛阳含嘉仓遗址

洛阳含嘉仓160号仓窖位于隋唐洛阳城皇城内，是含嘉仓迄今发现的最完整、储量最大的仓窖遗存。含嘉仓建于隋大业元年（605年），与通济渠开凿于同一时间，唐以后正式作为东都洛阳的大型粮仓沿用。文献记载，唐天宝年间，全国储粮约1,200万石，而仅整个含嘉仓的粮食储量就达到580万石。160号仓窖位于仓城中部，1972年经发掘清理，仓窖口呈圆形，直径11.1米，窖底有2层，上层为平底，下层为圆底，上层窖底是在下层窖底废弃后的面上填土筑成，窖总深6.2米。窖内堆积着大半窖的炭化谷物，按160号仓窖内出土的谷物量推算，它们在当年储藏时的体量约有250吨。发掘工作表明，160号仓窖的窖底防潮措施从下至上依次为：首先夯实窖底、壁，其次烘干窖底、壁，再次铺设防潮材料，最后在窖上层底部用草来防潮。从仓窖内出土的刻铭砖上记载的内容看，含嘉仓的储粮来源主要是河北、山东、河南、江苏、安徽等地。

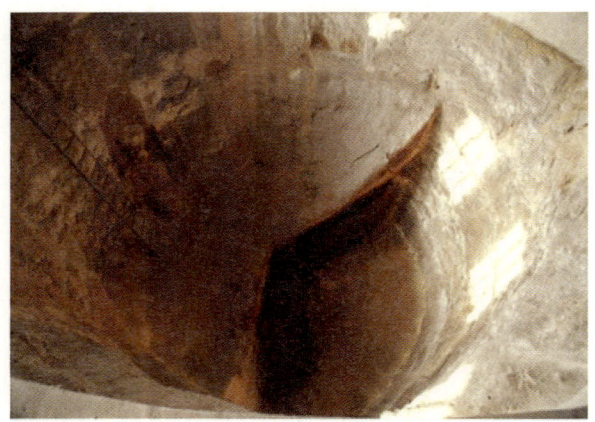

含嘉仓仓窖
Cellar of the Hanjia Granary

4. The Hanjia Granary in Luoyang

Located in the imperial palace of Luoyang in the Sui and Tang dynasties, the No. 160 site is the best preserved cellar with the largest storage capacity ever discovered in the Hanjia Granary. The Hanjia Granary was built in the first year of the Daye period of the Sui Dynasty (605 A.D.), the same time when the Tongji Canal was excavated. It began to be officially used as the major granary at the eastern capital of Luoyang after the Tang Dynasty. According to historical records, in the Tianbao period of the Tang Dynasty, around 12 million dan of grain was stored in the entire country, among which 5.8 million was in the single site of Hanjia Granary. Located in the middle section of the granary, the No. 160 site of the Hanjia Granary was unearthed in 1972. The round opening of the cellar is 11.1 meters in diameter. Two layers are found at the bottom of the cellar: the upper has a flat bottom, while the lower has a round one. The upper is built by filling earth onto the abandoned lower one. The total depth of the cellar is 6.2 meters. Carbonized grains occupy more than half of the cellar. According to the amount of grains unearthed from the No. 160 site, the weight of the original storage is about 250 tons. The excavation work shows that the damp-proof measures for the bottom of the site are in a bottom-up order. Firstly, the bottom and the walls of the cellar are tamped and dried; secondly, damp-proof materials are laid; finally, grass is laid on the upper bottom of the site to resist damp. According to the inscribed bricks excavated from the cellar, the grains stored in the Hanjia Granary mainly come from the provinces of Hebei, Shandong, Henan, Jiangsu, Anhui, etc.

含嘉仓遗址出土的砖铭
Brick Inscriptions Unearthed at the Site of the Hanjia Granary